SO-AFE-206

How To Farm $uccessfully — By Mail

Deborah Johnson, Ph.D.
and
Steve Kennedy

Argyle Press, Inc.

Carson City, Nevada 89701

Also Available from Argyle Press, Inc:

2,001 Winning Ads For Real Estate
Real Estate Advertising That Works!
How To Farm $uccessfully — By Phone

Copyright © 1995 by Argyle Press, Inc.
All rights reserved. Reproduction or translation of any part of this work (except the printed forms and sample letters), beyond that permitted by Section 107 or 108 of the 1976 United States Copyright Act, without the permission of the copyright owner, is unlawful.
Requests for permission should be addressed to the Publications Department, Argyle Press, Inc., Carson City, Nevada 89701.

This publication is designed to provide accurate and authoritative information in regard to the subject matter covered. It is sold with the understanding that the publisher is not engaged in rendering legal, accounting, or other professional services. If legal advice or other expert assistance is required, the services of a competent professional should be sought.

10 9 8 7 6 5 4 3 2

Book design and typesetting by Joel Friedlander, San Rafael, California.
Cover design by Steve Kennedy & Mary-Ellen Shields, Carson City, Nevada.
Cover Graphics by Diana Elkins, Carson City, Nevada

Library of Congress Cataloging-in-Publication Data

Johnson, Deborah, 1952-
    How to farm successfully—by mail / by Deborah Johnson and Steve Kennedy.
      p. cm.
      Includes bibliographical references and index.
      ISBN 1-887145-02-8
      1. Real estate listings.   2. Direct marketing.   I.
Kennedy, Steve.   II. Title.
HD1382.6.J646   1995
333.33—dc20 95-9244 CIP

Printed in the United States of America.

Introduction

What makes this book different from other books on real estate letters? Simple, these are farming letters — not letters that cover all aspects of your business. Other real estate books may have a few letters on farming, but none is devoted exclusively to what is arguably the largest challenge facing any real estate professional.

Our letters are not gimmicky or short notes — they are lenghty, well-reasoned letters based on proven direct marketing principles. Together, we have more than 40 years of direct marketing experience and we know what works.

Other real estate books are full of letters for obscure situations. This one isn't.

But this book is more than sample real estate letters. It takes you step-by-step through choosing a farm, setting up a regular marketing schedule, what to include in your pieces, and even money saving suggestions on printing and mailing.

How To Farm $uccessfully — By Mail has one purpose — to help you get listings from a group of people you cultivate over time. "Time" means longer than six months. That's how long the marketing program outlined in this book should be in place before you see results. You can expect consistent results. Just stick to a regular marketing schedule.

Start now by taking your first step — reading this book.

Dedications

To those with the courage to question and to care — D. J.

To "Chief," thanks for making this happen — S.K.

Acknowledgements

From Deborah Johnson, Ph.D., a special thanks to

Mark Brady, Ph.D., for his guidance, support and helpful suggestions
Porfirio Ramos, for his insights into real estate farming
Betty Hannis, a true "farmer"
Bethany Ramos, for her editorial critiques
Marion Wilson, for the support that freed me to write
The Menlo Park Library reference staff
Ruth Watt at the Peninsula Conservation Library in Palo Alto, Ca.

From Steve Kennedy, a special thanks to

Alyce McCracken, Coldwell Banker-First Western Real Estate, Carson City, Nevada for her knowledgeable insights into real estate
Mary Weber, U.S.P.S., Reno, Nevada, for her time and information on postal regulations
Barbara Shields, Consultant, Carson City, Nevada for her editorial critiques and insights and her unfailing support
Zeke Kniffen-Herceg, for keeping this all in perspective
F.S.K., for keeping me company while I was burning the midnight oil!

Table of Contents

SECTION ONE

How to Choose and Organize Your Farm

CHAPTER 1

FARMING — WHAT IS IT?

It's mid-afternoon on Monday. Behind your desk crumpled and torn boxes tumble together in a ragged heap. Bubble wrap and white peanuts stick to long strips of strapping tape. In front of you, your new oak desk set gleams. You pick up the letter opener and smile a little at its weight.

It's your first day in a new broker's office.

You have a stack of books to tell you what to do.
A broker who believes in you.
Friends who'll give you tips.
Maybe a few years of solid sales behind you.

But now you're starting something different.
You've decided on a different approach.
Something that takes a little more strategizing.
A little more planning.
Maybe a little more thinking.

The pencils are sharpened...
The phone hooked up...
The letter pads stacked high for note-taking...

Are you ready?

FARMING — WHAT IS IT?

Real estate farmers focus on a select and manageable market-place segment. It's called, not surprisingly, a "listing farm" or, simply, a "farm."

You can think of farming as similar to audience targeting in commerical advertising, where advertisements aim at specific groups of people. These groups are based on common characteristics such as income, buying patterns or lifestyles. Using these characteristics, advertisers position products in ways to which the group would respond positively. The basic premise is the same as in real estate farming:

You find out what your prospects want and need, then you concentrate on satisfying them.

In *Direct Marketing Success: What Works and Why*, Freeman Gosden describes an experience he had as a young advertising agency executive. After a year of working on the Rexall Drug Store account, one of the largest in the United States, Gosden felt that he wasn't getting anywhere.

He decided to moonlight at a Rexall retail store. When he got to know Rexall customers face-to-face, he found that his image of the "typical" Rexall customer was all wrong. He discovered what they really liked and disliked. Colleagues at the advertising agency began listening to him. Two years later, Rexall put him in charge of corporate advertising/public relations.

Knowing prospects' needs and meeting them is the key to any sales success.

Farming works because it separates out a group of people that you get to know and take care of. When the time comes to sell a home, you're the first person they think of. Why is farming so effective?

Ernie Blood and Bernie Torrence give four reasons in *The Pocket Prospecting Guide for Real Estate Professionals:*

1. Farming provides a consistent and reliable source of income in the form of listings.

2. Farming allows you do to mass advertising.

3. Farming gives you the opportunity to become a real estate specialist in a particular area.

4. The value of everything you do multiplies when you specialize in a farm.

Despite the fact that farming is behind most top agents' success, many real estate professionals resist it. Why? Because farming takes time and patience. And the rewards are not immediate.

Joyce Caughman in *Real Estate Prospecting* notes that it takes six months before the average real estate farm begins producing satisfactorily. A farmer should expect to get 20% of the farm's total listings by the end of the second year, 50% in the third year and up to 75% after that.

In this book, we discuss three types of farms: (1) a geographic farm, (2) a social farm and (3) a client farm. Geographic and social farms involve making contacts and building relationships with people who have not used your real estate services. A client farm, on the other hand, means maintaining contacts with people who have previously turned to you for real estate assistance. Because geographic and social farms take more strategizing and work than client farms, we'll concentrate on them. However, you will find sample mailings for a client farm in Chapter 11.

GEOGRAPHIC FARMS

According to Michael Abelson, president of Abelson & Company and an associate professor at Texas A & M University, two-thirds of all top performers use a geographic farm.

Realtor® Klaus Huckfeldt of Palm Springs, California defined a geographic farm as "any number or group of homes in a residential neighborhood, subdivision or development that you service on a continued basis." A geographic farm could include two or three small areas at opposite ends of town. What matters is that they have similar housing prices, styles, and residents.

The benefits of a geographic farm are obvious. First, it's easy to manage. You can drive through your farm and count the real estate signs. You also can look at the conditions of homes, locate neighborhood schools, even pinpoint street potholes. When you walk into a local drugstore or McDonald's, you meet potential prospects.

Second, geographic farming creates synergy. That is, as your signs start popping up all over the neighborhood, things will snowball. People will start talking about you and the homes you're selling. The more people talk about you, the better the chance that they'll call you when it's time to sell or buy a home.

Benefits of
Geographic Farm
1. Easy to manage
2. Develops synergy
3. Easy to research
4. Your signs say "Success"

Third, researching a geographic farm is fairly easy. Data kept by the multiple listing service (MLS), U.S. Census Bureau, county tax assessor and other institutions is often by address. Public domain records like these can tell you the average income of people in your farm, average home size, average number of people in the family, average ages, and other important facts. Some of this information is even broken down block by block.

SOCIAL FARMS

While less common than territorial farms, social farms can also be profitable.

A social farm can be formal or informal. Formal social farms are created by "farming" a group of people who belong to the same organization, such as a church, folk dance group, sailing organization, Elks' Club, or volunteer society. Compiling lists for formal social farms is as easy as grabbing a membership directory. Typically the social farmer joins the organization and becomes one of its most visible members.

Informal social farms, on the other hand, are developed by you. You could create an informal social farm of your friends and relatives. Or people who play at the local public golf course. Or people who play the piano. The point is that the people have something in common which gives you a way to access them. Examples of other informal social farms, which also are described as "niche markets," include:

1. ethnic groups,

2. single people,

3. older people,

4. members of the gay and lesbian community,

5. people with disabilities.

According to Julie A. Bleasdale, in the article *"Think Globally, Sell Locally,"* in the June 1992 Real Estate Today®, ethnic groups are a great niche market.

Ethnic groups. According to the Urban Institute and the U.S. Bureau of the Census, at least 20 million Americans speak a first language other than English. Eleven million speak Spanish as their primary language. Three million Asians speak little or no English. *American Demographics* magazine predicts that by the next century one-quarter to one-third of all Americans will belong to racial or minority ethnic groups.

Targeting an ethnic group means designing culturally appropriate marketing materials and learning cross-cultural etiquette. To reach the rapidly growing market of Hispanic buyers, for example, Coast Federal Bank in Los Angeles offers a free Spanish language video to guide them through homebuying. In Danville, California, Coldwell Banker agent Marsha Golangco makes sure to present Japanese clients with her business card in both hands with her name in Japanese facing them. She also has her name printed in English on the other side. When Japanese clients hand her their business cards, she always takes a few seconds to read them as a sign of respect.

The October 1993 Real Estate Today® magazine profiles the following, in *"Specializing An Outlet for Bigger Profits"* by Warren Berger, as examples of Realtors® practicing niche marketing:

Single buyers. Claudia Deprez founded Florida Singles Real Estate in Palm Beach Gardens. She hosts homebuying seminars for singles at hotels and sends direct mail fliers to members of singles organizations and dating services. She also has enjoyed plenty of free media coverage through a local newspaper column. Singles account for 60% of her business.

Older buyers. Linda Brunson of Clements, Realtor® in Dallas markets to senior citizens. While she admits that the effort so far has been only been moderately successful, she has no doubt that it eventually will work. Her primary marketing tools have been seminars and information fairs for seniors. Her company developed a senior-oriented sales training course for its agents and promotes its specialized services in magazines and newspapers directed at seniors.

Members of the gay and lesbian community. In Chicago, RE/MAX saleperson Jim Anderson combines social and geographic farming by targeting the gay community as well as several neighborhood areas. About half his business comes from the gay and lesbian community, which he markets in newspaper ads and through direct mail under the slogan, "Your community real estate professional for the gay and lesbian market."

People with disabilities. In Tucson, Arizona, Craig Runyon of Prudential Aegis Realty considers himself a specialist in helping disabled buyers find homes. He belongs to several organizations that assist disabled people and often speaks at local clubs or business luncheons. He also created a newsletter about housing for the disabled. In his advertisements to the general market, he always includes a wheelchair logo and the line, "If you have special needs, call us." Today half of Runyon's sales come from buyers with disabilities.

In Huntington Beach, California, James C. Anderson was "swamped with business" after less than a year with Century 21-Berg Realty when he tapped the niche market of hearing-impaired buyers and sellers. Hearing impaired himself, Anderson markets hard-to-sell homes within earshot of railroad tracks, freeways, or airport runways to deaf buyers. He distributes fliers to churches and to clubs and organizations serving the hearing-impaired and he uses a Telecommunications Device for the Deaf in his home and business.

Other niche markets include professional women, single parents, families with small children, working mothers, members of religious groups, and members of computer clubs.

Disadvantages of Social Farm

1. Hard to manage
2. Limited marketing appeals
3. Hard to research

Managing a social farm can be more difficult than a geographic farm. First, prospects' homes often are scattered, which makes driving through one area and looking for real estate signs impossible. It also is difficult to create neighborhood-oriented marketing appeals. For example, the potentially powerful appeal that home values have risen 20% in a specific neighborhood over the past year is useless in a social farm. On the other hand, if home values have risen 20% across the city, this appeal could be useful in a social farm.

On the positive side, social farms allow you plenty of opportunities to meet potential prospects in settings that give you the chance to get to know each other. In a recent survey by the National Association of Realtor's®, one out of every five homebuyers used a real estate professional they knew. But even more homesellers — one out of every two — chose a real estate professional on the basis of a personal relationship.

Because members of a social farm usually chat with each other, the same synergy found in a geographic farm can develop. And the more people talk about you, the more likely they are to call you. However, with a social farm, not many prospects will notice all your "sold" signs.

The biggest problem with social farming is research. To farm effectively, you need information about people's homes, incomes, ages, homebuying histories and other factors. Most of that information is only available by address. But you will find a partial solution in the "Survey" letter in Chapter 11. You also can rely on more general, citywide information such as that provided by your local board.

The unseen benefit of a social farm is that you'll probably have some fun cultivating it. After all, there is more to life than sales, listings and board meetings.

THREE WAYS TO CULTIVATE YOUR FARM

You can probably think of hundreds of ways to reach your farm, but the three most common are by: (1) face-to-face contact, (2) phone, and (3) mail. This can be called the "farm marketing mix."

Benefits of
Social Farm
1. More opportunities for personal contact
2. Develops synergy
3. FUN

Reaching the Farm — The three main ways to reach your farm are: in person, by phone, and by mail. Ideally these three work together.

Because every farm — and every farmer — is different, it's good to experiment. For example, prospects in your farm might respond more positively to a mail survey than to one given over the phone. Or maybe it's best to call first, then mail it. The exact mix depends on you and your farm. It's also true that what's most effective one time might not be the next.

In cultivating farms, very few top agents walk door-to-door or initiate contact by telephone. According to Michael Abelson, most rely on direct mail and about half use direct mail exclusively. About 40% of the salespeople earning $15,000 to $70,000 per year and about 30% of those earning $90,000 per year or more combine direct mail, door-to-door canvassing and telephone contact.

FARMING — A COST/BENEFIT ANALYSIS

To figure out how much farming can benefit you, start by looking at how much one lead can be worth.

Let's assume that your average net commission on a listing is $1,875. That's half a gross commission of $3,750, or your net after a 50/50 broker split. If you get only one additional listing a year from your direct mail farming, you "profit" as long as you spend less than $1,875.

How realistic is that?

Well, figure that you mail to your farm every month and each direct mail package costs a total of 35 cents. Divide $1,875 by 35 cents and you get approximately 5,350. Divide 5,350 by 12 — and you can mail to 445 homes a month for an entire year with $1,875.

In other words, you "breakeven" if you get one listing from mailing to 445 homes every month.

If you get four listings, for example, your "breakeven" point moves up to 1,780 homes per month.

The reality is, however, that you'll probably mail to no more than 200 to 300 homes a month. So even if you get only one listing from farming, it's very cost effective.

What's more, if you can persuade your broker to pick up part of the cost, even just the postage, you'll net a higher profit. And the broker benefits, too.

Before starting your direct mail farming program, look at the budget worksheet in Chapter 15.

ABOUT THIS BOOK

This book focuses primarily on the third element of the farm marketing mix — direct mail — and particularly on the sales letter format used to generate prequalified leads.

However, it is important to note that no marketing effort stands alone. Mail, phone, and personal contact all work together to help you reach your goal of increased sales and listings. Throughout this book, you'll see references to our other book, *How To Farm Successfully — By Phone*, which can help you turn cold calls into listings and sales. Together, these books will give you a real head start on successful farming.

If you're relatively new to farming and, in particular, farming by mail, this book should be ideal for you.

If you're already doing a lot of farming by mail, keep reading. Even though you may be familiar with some of the material, you'll find many new tips to save you money and time.

The next two chapters outline an eight-step, two-week plan for choosing and organizing your farm. While two weeks may seem like a lot of time to spend preparing your farm, you'll reap the rewards for years to come.

CHAPTER 2

SIZING UP YOUR FARM

You're excited. The idea of farming sounds great. You'd like to get to know a neighborhood and the people who live there. You'd feel good marketing yourself as a real estate specialist. Maybe you also can develop a social farm out of your bridge club. But don't think about that now. Take it one step at the time. Still... millions of opportunties are waiting for you.

Suddenly you realize that you're stuck. The development where you live has 3,000 homes. Can you farm 3,000 homes effectively? You don't think so. But maybe.

Wait a minute. Work through your problem. Do research. Find the numbers you need. Set a specific goal for yourself. Work from it.

Start working smart.

A TWO-WEEK PLAN FOR ORGANIZING YOUR FARM

In this chapter, we'll show you how to evaluate a potential farm based on your income goal. The statistics you need are simple ones used in everyday real estate matters. By the time you finish, you'll have a realistic farm size based on the average value of homes and turnover in your farm.

Day 1

STEP 1 — LOOK AT YOUR PERSONAL INTERESTS

Whether you choose a geographic or social farm depends on a number of factors. One of the most important is you.

Take five minutes and ask yourself the following questions:

SELF-QUIZ

                        YES NO

1. Do you now belong to any organizations which you could use as a social farm? For example, are you active in the local PTA? Youth soccer? Sierra Club? A hospital volunteer group?
2. Are there organizations you would like to join which you could use as a social farm?
3. Do you enjoy the social atmosphere of these "club" environments?
4. Do you belong to an ethnic group that could serve as your farm?
5. Do you have any special housing needs that you share with others?
6. Would you prefer working with one group of people who have unique needs?
7. Would you prefer working within a more heterogenous neighborhood?
8. Is the neighborhood where you live a potential farm area?
9. Does your neighborhood have good, well-segmented tracts that you could farm?

If you answered "Yes" to questions 1 through 6, start thinking about ways you could effectively manage a social farm. If you answered "Yes" to 7, 8, or 9, consider a geographic farm. But the decision process isn't over yet.

Now think about three potential farm areas. Don't put constraints on your thinking. Start with what you like — areas you find interesting — people you'd enjoy knowing better. Pick three potential farms and write brief descriptions of them on a notepad. Look at the potential farm's approximate size, house value, turnover, and demographics of residents. Is this a group you could feel comfortable with and relate to? If you dislike golf, for example, it would be unwise to choose a golfing club for a social farm. Or if you're into country music, pick-up trucks, and cowboy boots, marketing luxury estates in an exclusive division may not be for you.

Take a drive through the three areas you're considering. Or if you're thinking about a social farm, stop by some of the places where you'd find potential prospects.

After thinking about your needs, narrow your choice to one potential farm. If this is absolutely impossible, then you'll have to perform the next step for each of your alternatives. By the time you finish, however, it's highly likely that one choice will stand out.

DAY 2

STEP 2 — CALCULATE THE FARM SIZE YOU NEED

Most real estate books recommend farming a two to three-year-old area with 200 to 500 homes, depending on the average selling price and turnover. The assumption is that higher priced homes and higher turnover take more work, which means your farm should be smaller.

Rather than basing this important decision on general assumptions, why not run some numbers about the area you're considering farming? What follows works best for geographic farms because it relies on figures available by neighborhood or through your Multiple Listing Service (MLS). But you can also use it to guide your thinking about a social farm. Although you won't have average selling prices and turnover, perhaps you can estimate these figures from city or board figures.

So grab a pencil, some scratch paper, and your calculator.

Before beginning, collect the following statistics:

1. Total number of co-op sales you made last year and total number of own sales. The purpose is to calculate your average commission.

2. Selling prices of all homes sold in your potential farm over the last twelve months.

3. Total number of homes in potential farm.

Remember that it takes six months for a farm to begin producing and then the increases are gradual. This means that you'll need additional revenue from outside your farm, particularly the first year.

The first step in these calculations requires that you set a target goal in farm income from commissions. Be realistic. Everything else builds on this.

INCOME GOAL: $_____

Now figure out your average commission rate. This depends on how many of your listings you expect to sell yourself and how many will be co-op (MLS). Look at your past history. If you sold 20 homes last year, with 15 co-op sales and five on your own, your average commission percentage was:

Your total # sales last year: 20

co-op sales multiplied by commission percentage
     15   x   .03 (3%) =   .45

own sales multiplied by commission percentage
     5   x   .06 (6%) =   <u>.30</u>

                                Add =   .75

$$\frac{\text{Sum}}{\text{\# of sales}} = \frac{.75}{20} = \quad .0375$$

Average Gross Commission Percentage =   3.75%

Now figure it for yourself:

# of sales you get a year: ____
co-op sales: ____
other sales: ____
(# co-op) x .XX (% comm) =   ____
(# other) x .XX (% comm) =   ____
Add above two numbers =   ____
<u>Sum of above numbers</u>   ____
listings you get a year =   ____
AVERAGE COMMISSION PERCENTAGE: ____

Next, we need the average selling price of a home in your farm. Just grab the MLS records for the past year and write down the selling price for every home in your farm. Add the prices so you have a total sales volume, then divide by the number of sales. For example, if 40 homes in your farm sold last year for a total of $4,000,000, the average selling price was $100,000. Now do it yourself:

Selling price: _____

_____

_____

_____

_____

_____

_____

_____

(etc.)

Total sales volume: $_____

Total # homes sold last year: _____

$\dfrac{\text{Total sales volume}}{\text{Total \# homes sold last year}} =$ _____

AVERAGE SELLING PRICE: _____

Next take the average selling price and multiply it by your average commission percentage to figure out what you're likely to get for a listing. If you average commissions of 3.75% and the average home sells for $100,000, you'll make $3,750 on a sale. Do it for your prospective farm:

Average gross commission percentage: _____

Average selling price: _____

Avg. gross commission percentage x

average selling price = _____

AVERAGE INCOME PER LISTING: $_____

Knowing your average income per listing, divide your income goal by it to find out how many listings you need.

For example, if your annual farm income goal is $60,000 and you make an average of $3,750 per listing, you'll need 16 listings.

Do it for your farm:

Income goal: _____

Average income per listing: _____

$\dfrac{\text{Income goal}}{\text{Average income per listing}} =$ _____

 # OF NEEDED LISTINGS: _____

Now you have your:

Income goal _____

Average commission percentage _____

Average home selling price _____

Average income per listing _____

# of needed listings _____

It's time to figure out how large your farm needs to be. First calculate your farm's turnover. Half the work is done, as you've already determined the number of homes sold last year. Just divide that by the total number of homes in your farm. For example, if 88 homes sold in an area with 720 homes, the turnover rate is 12.2%.

Now compute the turnover rate for your farm:

homes sold last year =   _____
Total # homes in farm =   _____
$\dfrac{\text{\# homes sold}}{\text{Total \# homes}} =$ _____
       ANNUAL TURNOVER RATE =   _____

Knowing the turnover rate and the number of listings needed to reach your income goal, you can now figure out the right size for your farm. To get it, just divide the number of needed listings by the turnover rate. If you needed 16 listings in an area with 12% turnover, then you'd have to farm 133 homes.

needed listings =   _____
Turnover rate =   _____
$\dfrac{\text{\# needed listings}}{\text{Turnover rate}} =$ _____
FARM SIZE AT 100% LISTINGS =   _____

The above number assumes you'll get all the listings in your farm. Since it's unlikely that will happen, decide what percentage you can expect. Remember that you can probably count on 20% of the listings your second year of farming, 50% the third year and 75% in future years.

    EXPECTED PERCENTAGE OF LISTINGS = _____

Now take the farm size at 100% listings and divide it by your estimated percentage of listings. This will give you the actual size of the farm you'll need.

Farm size at 100% listings =   _____
Estimated percentage of listings=   _____
$\dfrac{\text{Farm size at 100\% listings}}{\text{Estimated percentage of listings}} =$ _____
ACTUAL FARM SIZE NEEDED =   _____

In the appendix, you'll find a blank worksheet that takes you through the above steps.

DAY 2

STEP 3 — CHECK OUT YOUR COMPETITION

Go back to the multiple listing service records and check who listed homes sold in your farm over the past year. If one company or agent had 75% or more of the listings, think hard about farming that territory. But if four or five agents crop up repeatedly, go for it. Just make a commitment to keep up your efforts for a year.

You also might want to drive around your real estate farm and look for signs. If 10 homes for sale carry the same sign, chances are good that another farmer is firmly planted in that ground. But if the 10 homes have three or four different signs, the neighborhood could be ripe for plucking.

FINAL THOUGHTS ON SIZING UP YOUR FARM

While it's important to let income goals guide you in selecting your farm size, also consider the following:

First, manageability. Will you be able to serve your farm in person, on the phone, and through the mail? If your farm has 1,000 homes, for example, you might be able to handle regular mailings. But if you planned to visit each homeowner twice a year, you'd have to see an average of eight homeowners a day five days a week for 50 weeks a year.

That's quite a bit!

On the other hand, if you mail to your farm, the U.S. Postal Service grants a fairly significant discount if you mail to 200 or more homes. These bulk rates can save you 40% of postage costs. You can find out more about these savings in Chapter 14.

Finally, keep your income goals reasonable. Remember that it will take several years for your farm to become a primary income source.

CHAPTER 3

STAKING OUT YOUR FARM

You've got it. A great little area on the other side of town. Nice houses, winding streets, tall trees, the perfect neighborhood. You've worked out the numbers and they're fine. You'll farm about 400 homes — hope to get 20% of the listings — and make about $15,000 in farm commissions your first year. From there, it'll only go up.

Everything looks good. Now it's time to really get to know the neighborhood. To dig beneath the surface and see what's happening.

It won't take much time...but every minute you spend researching your farm over the next few weeks will pay off for years to come.

DAY 3

STEP 4 — COLLECT REAL ESTATE INFORMATION ON YOUR FARM

Go back to the multiple listing service or county assessor's records on the homes sold in your farm last year. Check back a few more years and see how the total number of homes on the market has changed. Is real estate in the area on an upswing or a downswing?

Now look at average selling prices over the past five years. Calculate the average annual appreciation. Do significant differences exist from year to year?

Also ask these questions: How different are the average listing price and the average selling price? How long do most homes stay on the market? Can you tell whether homes with two or three bedrooms or those with four or more sell better?

From descriptions of the houses, look for special features. Do a lot of homes have views? Screened porches? Three-car garages? Drive around your farm and study it. Do houses along any street stand out?

If appropriate, call or visit the offices of builders and developers of your farm. Ask which house models characterized each construction phase and how, why and if the designs changed over time. Find out which were most popular and why. Note the reputation of builders and developers in your farm.

If brokers in your area don't use MLS, you'll have to take a trip to the county courthouse and examine property records to collect information on your farm.

DAY 4

STEP 5 — COLLECT GENERAL INFORMATION ON YOUR FARM

Visit your local newspaper office or library and ask to see back issues of the paper. Look through the local news section for the past few years and see whether your farm is featured in any stories. If it is, you can probably get an idea of current issues in your farm and who the community leaders are. It's a good idea to make personal contacts with community leaders, as they usually have extensive networks of friends and associates who often turn to them for real estate referrals. You also should stop by the local chamber of commerce.

Other relevant information is available from agencies such as the U.S. Census Bureau. It keeps statistics on monthly housing costs, income, marital status, family size and other demographics. This should be in the reference section of your city library. You also can make specific data requests to the Census Bureau and purchase the information directly on computer tape, CD-ROM or microfiche. For individuals, however, this may be prohibitively expensive.

Your local newspaper office, library and chamber of commerce are good sources of information. You can also use the U.S. Census Bureau and the Department of Labor and Employment Statistics as well as local homeowners' associations and prominent tract builders.

At the library, you should also find statistics compiled by state agencies. In Alaska, the State Dept. of Labor and Employment Statistics issues a report on employment figures and trends by subregional areas that includes housing statistics such as foreclosures, number of new loans, rental housing availability and rates, and average prices for two-, three- and four-bedroom homes. It also outlines cost of living changes in major cities as well as average annual wages and pay scales.

Many local governments have planning departments that track similar changes. You may want to request a meeting with a city manager or local supervisor to ask specifically about issues concerning your farm.

You also can check with local homeowners' associations and promininent tract builders, if your farm is in a development.

DAY 5

STEP 6 — MAP OUT YOUR FARM

Get a big map of your farm. If possible, use subdivision plats or parcel plats of the area from the county courthouse. You want a map that shows each property.

Now mount it on the wall. Use colored push pins to mark all the real estate activity. You might follow this color scheme:

Red — Others' listings

Green — Your listings (keep these handy!)

Yellow — For Sale By Owners

Black — Sold within last year

Do the homes cluster in any particular area? Are a number of homes on the same block for sale? Have recent transactions been in one neighborhood? Where are the FSBOs?

Also mark local schools, shopping areas, parks, recreation facilities, sports arenas, public transportation lines, police and fire stations, government offices, churches, hospitals and anything else of interest in your farm. By the time you finish, you should be able to look at the map and understand how your farm is laid out, how it functions and what's on the market. If you're working with a social farm, mark points of interest to potential clients. For example, you'd note marinas if your farm was a sailing club.

Within the next ten years, most major brokerages will probably have mapping software. Geographic Information Systems (GIS) can give detailed information about any property and its surrounding area. Punch in an address and GIS will identify it on the map while providing a profile of its history including previous sales prices, utility costs and tax information. It also measures distances to points such as shopping centers and schools.

Unfortunately, learning these programs is not easy.

DAYS 6 - 11

STEP 7 — CREATE YOUR FARM FILES

The amount of time it takes to create your farm files depends on whether you use a computer and whether you have access to computerized property records.

For each home in your farm, you'll need the following information:

SAMPLE FARM FILE

SAMPLE FARM FILE

Name:
Address:
Owner-occupant: Renter: Absentee landlord:
Phone number: (h)   (w)
Best time to call/visit:
Home model:
Bedrooms/baths:
Date purchased: Purchase price:
Parcel #:
Land sq. footage: Building sq. footage:
Special features:

Number of adults in home: Number of children:
Schools:
Occupations:
Notes:

Contact Record:

Date	Type	With	Remarks
———	———	———	———————
———	———	———	———————
———	———	———	———————

As you work your farm, you'll want to add prospect and property information to these files. You'll also want to record whenever a resident responds to one of your mailings. You should record each response in two places: the individual farm file and the mailing response record described in Chapter 15.

When you first meet someone who lives in your farm, ask them how long they've lived in the neighborhood, numbers and ages of children, property details, their likes and dislikes. If you can't take notes during the conversation, stop a minute when you leave and write down what you remember. Enter the information in your farm file as soon as you get back to your office.

It's the attention we pay to little things — promotions, births, weddings, even the championship of a child's soccer team — that lead up to big things. Like the commission on selling a house.

You start compiling your farm files by getting names and addresses. Because most information is kept by address, the following applies particularly to geographic farms. With a little work, however, you can also use it for social farms.

In setting up your list, your local title company, Multiple Listing Service (MLS), home-owners' associations, county administrative offices, and/or outside services should be helpful.

Title Insurance Companies — In some areas, title companies and occasionally Boards of Realtor's® will provide complete farm rosters and mailing lists to real estate agents and brokers for no charge or for a nominal fee. They do this, obviously, to promote their own services and develop relationships with the real estate sales community. Some, however, provide only "property profiles" which are useful for establishing comparable housing prices but not for creating farm lists. You can also find valuable information in quarterly reports prepared by some Boards of Realtor's®.

Title company data usually comes from county offices and typically does not contain phone numbers. For these, you'll need a reverse phone directory. To use reverse directories, you look up addresses and find residents' names. Reverse directories are available from local phone companies and the following private companies:

Haines Directories, 216-243-9250.

Stewart Directories, Inc. 410-628-5988.

Cole Directories, 800-228-4571.

Most title company data contains owner rather than occupant information. In creating your farm list, it's important to note who is an owner-occupant, renter, or absentee owner.

You'll know a house is rented when the owners' legal address differs from the parcel address. However, in some cases, this will be only a mailing address or a post office box. To find out if the owner lives at the property, look in a reverse phone directory. Check the home's address and see if the occupant's name matches the owner's. If it does, the owner lives there. If not, someone else does. Write down the renter's name, too.

Because they are often overlooked by other farmers, absentee owners and renters represent potential gold mines for you.

Multiple Listing Services (MLS) — In addition to data provided by title companies, you may be able to get roughly the same information through your local board or MLS. Again, this data will be from county records and therefore will most likely not contain telephone numbers. Before using this information, check with your local board or the MLS to make sure you have the rights to use it for farming.

Homeowners' Associations — Many building projects with some form of cooperative ownership (typically called "common areas") maintain lists of residents. Often this includes phone numbers. Because such information is not public, your access to it is limited. If, however, you're farming an area and come to know association members, you can always ask someone to pass one on to you. Be aware, however, that such directories do not typically break down owner-occupants and nonowner-occupants.

County Administrative Offices — If title company, MLS, or homeowners' association data are not available, you may have to undertake the chore of researching county records yourself. While this may take some time, it should pay off. At the County Assessor's Office, you'll not only find information about property ownership, you'll also find information about all property transactions in the area, including For Sale By Owner and bank foreclosures. These probably wouldn't appear in MLS information.

For farming purposes, the County Assessor's office in our home county in Nevada provides a "Parcel by Street Address List" that gives owners' names. The Assessor's office also sells street address labels for 10 cents each plus 3 cents for special selections.

In our Assessor's Appraisal Record, housing details such as square footage of the land and building, year of construction, outside drawing or photo, number of bedrooms and baths and number of fireplaces are listed.

The third useful item from the Assessor is the Sales Data Bank, which reports on all real estate sales in the area, including For Sale By Owner and private sales.

While not all County Assessors will provide information in the above formats, your Assessor should have owner names, property listings by street address and parcel number, parcel maps and appraisal records. In some areas, you can pay about $1 for field books with this information or spend less than $100 for computer print-outs.

In the Country Clerk-Recorder's Office, you'll find information about deeds, mortgages, liens and foreclosures. This information is often difficult to use, as it's by book and page number instead of owner name.

You also can get addresses from Voters' Registration lists.

Outside Services — Some outside firms compile county owner-ship data. The largest nationwide is TRW REDI (800/345-7334). Covering more than 300 counties in 34 states, it supplies maps, aerial photographs, and ownership information to thousands of real estate offices. Standard available property information includes land use, legal description, mailing address, owner's name, parcel number, property location, assessed value and taxes and exemptions. Depending on the county, TRW REDI also can tell you a property's latest sale date, sale price, year built, zoning, garage type, number of bedrooms, number of bathrooms and other charactertistics.

You could use this service, for example, to ask for all the resi-dental homes valued between $100,000 to $150,000 in a farm area, together with their phone numbers. You also could ask for the names of all veterans or widows/widowers. TRW REDI brings together information from a number of public sources, which makes it easy for you to use.

For an annual fee, TRW REDI will provide you with information on microfiche, in print directories, through on-line services or on CD-ROM.

In addition to real estate-oriented services such as TRW REDI, you can get residential data through outside mailing list services. Your local Yellow Pages will direct you to suppliers in your area. With these brokers, you can specify criteria such as age, income, marital status, years in home, renters, etc.

One problem with these lists is that they're often available only for one-time use. To get the best price from a broker, decide in advance how many times you want to mail the list and rent it for that number up front. List prices vary, but Rocco Erker and Gregory Erker in *The Real Estate Professional* quote the going rate as $65 per thousand names.

When dealing with an outside list rental company, find out its information sources. Often it's telephone directories, which mean the data will describe occupants rather than owners. While this is important, you also will need property owners' names.

Another problem with mailing list services is that they typically have 3,000 to 5,000 name minimums. If you only need 500 names, you'll have to pay a premium.

A final consideration about dealing with an outside list compiler is the time lag between collecting and publishing the information.

Fortunately, updating your list is easy, as you'll see later.

Social Farms

If you work a social farm, creating files will be either greatly simplified or overly cumbersome.

Where you look for names and addresses depends on your social farm. Most of the niche marketers described in the previous chapter joined clubs or organizations that catered to the group they sought to farm. Most clubs and organizations keep mailing lists of members and will make these available in the form of directories. As a member, you should have no problem getting this.

If the club or organization does not maintain a membership list, suggest that they do. In fact, you might even volunteer to create it for them. If possible, try to find out who owns their homes and who rents them.

If you have no access to a membership list, expect a lot of hard work. Typically you'll have to search through local telephone books for members' names and addresses. Before starting this, however, stop by the reference department at your local library. They may direct you to community resources of which you're not aware.

Computerized Farm Files

Personal computers are not required for effective farming — after all, agents have been farming for a lot longer than computers have been affordable.

But they certainly can make your job easier. If you already have a personal computer, farm with it. If you're thinking about buying a computer, do it. Consider a portable or notebook computer which you can take to open houses and on sales calls.

Many general mail lists and data-base management software programs are well-suited to your farming needs. In addition, programs designed specifically for real estate exist. If you're new to computers or not comfortable with them, you probably should look at real estate software first. It may be a little more expensive than more generic data management programs, but it's worth it. Above all, make sure that whatever software you choose is user-friendly. You don't want to spend a lot of time learning it when you could spend the time farming.

The best software programs combine a data base, communications module for making and tracking calls, word processing and automated scheduling. Below is a sampling of available programs. The following list is not a recommendation — just an idea of what's out there:

Howard and Friends
Sanderson Data Systems Compatibles
P.O. Box 527
Suquamish, WA 98392
206/698-6452

On-Line Agent
On-Line Software, Inc.
International Office Center
600 Holiday Plaza Dr.
Matteson, IL 60443
800/996-6547

Power Prospecting
Innovative Software, Inc. Compatibles
3345 Industrial Dr., Ste. 10
Santa Rosa, CA 95403
707/577-0581 or 800/707-5767

REALTY 2000
NDS Software Compatibles
P.O. Box 1328
Gardnerville, NV 89410
800/421-3069

Top Producer
Top Producer Systems, Inc.
10651 Shellbridge Way, Ste. 155
Richmond, BC, Canada V6X 2W8
800/444-8570

Contact Pro
Actoris Software Corp. Macintosh
1100 Centennial Blvd, Suite 248
Richardson, TX 75081
214/231-7588

Real Estate Connections
RealData, Inc.
78 N. Main St.
South Norwalk, CT 06854
203/838-2670

Sales Management Solution
Impact Solution
135 Cumberland Road, Suite 203
Pittsburgh, PA 15237
412/367-8833

Computerizing your list will allow you to divide your farm into a number of groups: owner-occupants, absentee owners, renters, senior citizens, families with small children, former clients, etc. You can also target residents of specific streets or blocks. This allows you to further tailor marketing messages, which makes them much more effective.

It's good to talk to people who already computerize their farm files and ask for software recommendations. You also can call the Real Estate Brokerage Managers Council (312/670-3780) for suggestions.

How to Create Computerized Farm Files

When you start working with these programs, you'll come across two important, and possibly confusing, terms: records and fields.

A record is all the data associated with a single prospect. In the simplest case, this includes the prospect's name, address, city, state, ZIP code and ownership status.

A field is one of the elements in a record such as the name, address, city, state or ZIP code. In short, fields make up records and records are composed of fields.

You'll also read about "sortable" and "nonsortable" fields.

At the very least, you'll want to be able to sort your farm records by owner's last name, ownership status and by ZIP code (for postage). Other "sortable" fields you might want to include are street, city, last and next contact dates and perhaps home size.

When creating fields, always include an extra sortable field or two in case you want to add one later.

As for labels, your local computer store will sell ones that fit into your printer's tractor feed. These typically come one-, two-, three- and four-across. Four-across are usually the cheapest.

Whenever working on a computer, always remember to make a backup of your data and store it in a safe place. You can lose a lot of time and hard work if you don't.

Manual Farm Files

If you can't afford a computer, start with manual records and plan to convert to computer later. Do it as soon as possible, as you'll soon discover how quickly your mailing labels will become obsolete and how often you'll need to update them.

In keeping manual files, you'll need two sets of records:

1. a master index card file,

2. peel-off mailing label sheets.

For the index card file, follow the format on page 28. Keep this file in alphabetical order by prospects' last names. This will make it easy to grab their cards when they call.

Type a master for your mailing labels on blank paper and reproduce it by quick printer onto labels. You won't have to do this if you can obtain label or label-format names directly from your information source (usually title companies and MLS).

Type the labels in ZIP code order. This is required by the post office for bulk mail.

Remember to stick one copy of your labels on the index cards right away. This will save you considerable duplication of effort.

When you're typing, try to minimize spelling errors. If you misspell a prospect's name, you won't make a positive first impression. Since most people find proofing their own work difficult, ask someone whose grammar skills you trust to help you.

Cleaning Your List

Whether you keep a manual or computerized farm list, you have to maintain it. This means checking it with your first mailing. You can do this by noting either "Return Postage Guaranteed" or "Address Correction Requested" on the outer envelope.

With "Forwarding and Return Postage Guaranteed," the post office will return undeliverable letters to you for a fee. With "Address Correction Requested," they'll provide you with the recipient's new address — for an additional fee.

Either way you'll get the new address and can correct your mailing list.

If you don't do either and the post office can't deliver the letter, they'll throw out third class mail and forward first class mail without telling you.

DAY 12
STEP 8 — DEVELOP YOUR MARKETING PLAN

Your Marketing Strategy

To successfully farm, you must develop a marketing strategy. This means positioning yourself. Look at your goals, strengths and weaknesses, competition, target market, their needs, and economic trends.

Jay Conrad Levinson in *Guerrilla Marketing: Secrets for Making Big Profits From Your Small Business* recommends, "Ask yourself basic questions: What business are you in? What is your goal? What benefits do you offer? What competitive advantages? When you know the true nature of your business, your goal, your strengths and weaknesses, your competitors' strengths and weaknesses, and the needs of your target market, your positioning will be that much easier to determine, your strategy easier to plan."

Here's a sample strategy for a real estate farmer:

The purpose of my real estate business is to get and sell a majority of the residential listings in the Castle Pines neighborhood. This will be accomplished by positioning myself as a real estate specialist who can provide excellent service because of my in-depth knowledge of Castle Pines and its real estate market. My target market is Castle Pines residents. Marketing tools will emphasize direct mail contacts supplemented by personal visits and telephone calls. From time to time, I will also organize special events. My niche is that I make Castle Pines my priority and study every aspect of life that affects its real estate values and marketing. My identity is one of expertise, experience, reliability and responsiveness to client needs. Ten percent of my income will be allocated to marketing.

As a farmer, you position yourself as a real estate specialist marketing to a particular group of people. That group has defined needs, desires and values. You take the time to find out what these are. Then you develop skills and language that are responsive to them.

The real farming pro takes the needs and desires of prospective clients seriously. That doesn't mean that you neglect developing expertise. It does mean, however, that when you express that expertise, you do so by showing prospective clients how it will benefit them. Your approach isn't "I am so good," but rather "This is how I can help you."

Now write your seven-sentence strategy:

Name_____

Date_____

MARKETING STRATEGY

_____

_____

_____

_____

_____

_____

_____

_____

_____

_____

_____

_____

_____

_____

_____

_____

_____

_____

Once you have written a marketing strategy, the next step is to create a media plan. That's where the rest of this book becomes important. As we mentioned earlier, a large percentage of top performers rely heavily on direct mail for initial contacts with prospective clients. The following chapters outline a sample direct mail plan for your farm for a year, together with examples of appropriate letters. We're not recommending that you only mail to prospects (we strongly suggest that you also get our book, *How To Farm Successfully — By Phone*). But we recognize that direct mail is often the focal point of a farmer's outreach.

Your Direct Mail Plan

The goal is for you to write a direct mail plan covering one year. Remember that not even the best farming efforts pay off until at least six months.

Based on the 44 letters in Chapter 11, we've created a sample direct mail plan to guide you. Review it carefully and adapt it to meet your own and your farm's needs. In the plan, we assume that you are farming new territory. That's why the first few letters consist of introductions. The next letters establish you as a real estate specialist for a particular area or group. We then move into more specialized offers, all of which are designed to enhance your reputation for caring about your farm and your professionalism.

When you farm, plan to contact prospects by mail every four to six weeks. Six or eight times a year, you may want to supplement this with door-to-door visits or telephone calls. Many of our letters set the groundwork for face-to-face meetings.

SAMPLE DIRECT MAIL PLAN

Month	Direct Mail Package	Page
January	Broker's introduction	126
February	Self-introduction	121
March	Five facts	128 or 132
April	Survey	141 or 143
May	Free home evaluation	164
June	Vacation kit	177
July	Story	156
August	Home fire protection kit	168
September	Seminar	136
October	Home reference booklet	194
November	Annual report	160
December	Home tax record kit	189

Our direct mail plan is only a general guideline. If, for example, your farm area is hit by a rash of burglaries, you may want to offer the "Home crime-stoppers" or "Neighborhood watch" kit instead of the fire protection kit. During the spring, you may think that the "Garage sale" kit would generate more responses than the "Vacation" kit. If you're willing to experiment, you can divide your farm in half and test two letters to see which works best. That way, you'll know which one to use the next year. One of the biggest advantages of direct mail is that it allows you to test different appeals and measure the results.

Now read the next section and the letters in Chapter 11. Then write your own direct mail marketing plan.

Name_____

Date_____

Farm_____

DIRECT MAIL MARKETING PLAN

Month	Direct Mail Package	Page
January		
February		
March		
April		
May		
June		
July		
August		
September		
October		
November		
December		

In summary, here is how you can size up and stake out your farm in two weeks:

TWO-WEEK PLAN FOR ORGANIZING YOUR FARM

DAY 1 Look at your personal interests.

DAY 2 Figure out required farm size based on your income goal. Check out your competition.

DAY 3 Collect real estate information on your farm and its residents.

DAY 4 Collect general information on your farm.

DAY 5 Map out your farm.

DAY 6 to Day 11 Shop for computer software and create farm files.

DAY 12 Develop your marketing strategy and media plan.

SECTION TWO

How to Write Your Own Farm Letters

CHAPTER 4

ELEMENTS OF A DIRECT MAIL FARM PACKAGE

It's Wednesday morning. You've been farming for five months. Calls have yet to come pouring in, but you're seeing good signs. People who call seem friendly; they talk almost as if you know each other. You've met with some of them and gotten listings. Three or four even referred you to friends.

The seminar that you organized for the farm went over really well. You learned a lot, too. Not only when you pulled together facts for the presentation, but as you listened to the audience. They described concerns that you knew very little about. And those concerns affect each one of them as they make real estate decisions. You grin when you remember how they devoured the strawberry shortcakes and chocolate layer cakes.

Now you have an urge to try something different. Something that would be more you. Based on what was said at the seminar, you have some ideas that you're pretty sure would strike responsive chords in farm residents. Shall you try to write a letter on your own? Can you do it?

Sit down and copy a couple of farm letters three times each. Look at the words, the rhythm, the "you" emphasis. Read the following pages.

Then go for it!

THE CLASSIC DIRECT MAIL LETTER

Classic elements of a direct mail package are the outer envelope, letter, response card, response envelope and sometimes, a premium or free gift.

Outer Envelope

The outer envelope is what the prospect sees first. This alone will make him or her decide to open the letter or throw it in the trash. From your standpoint, the most important decision is made in a second or two.

Should you put teaser copy on the outer envelope or not? The right appeal will help get the envelope opened, while the wrong one will hurt.

Be forewarned, however, that at the majority of direct-mail ad agencies (the firms which produce most of the mailings you get) only the most skilled copywriters and creative directors are assigned to write outer envelope copy.

In other words, teaser envelope copy is no job for a novice. It takes considerable thought and can make or break your entire mailing. If you're writing the mailing yourself, a blank outer envelope might be best. This makes it look more like personal mail, which is a plus.

Letter

Many direct mail experts consider the letter the most important element of a successful direct-mail package. Letters can vary from brief notes to 8 to 10 pages. Most are 1 to 4 pages.

Usually the letter is typed (or has the appearance of being typed) and written in a very personal "you-and-me" style.

Most start with a salutation, such as "Dear Neighbor" or "Dear Friend," and immediately move to the single most important benefit of the offer.

From there, the letter expands. It closes with a call for some kind of action — either a sale or follow-up. Other elements in the direct mail package should support the letter's offer.

Joe Jones Realty
123 Main St.
Anytown, USA 12345

Joe Jones Realty
123 Main St.
Anytown, USA 12345

How Much Is Your Home Worth Today?

*...open this
letter—it may be
worth more than
you think!*

*Which envelope would you
be more likely to open?*

Response Card

Generally response cards are pre-addressed, postage-paid cards or cards to be returned in pre-addressed, postage-paid envelopes. Response cards should be simple to fill out and require very little effort. Most important, they should restate the main benefit of the offer in the letter. If you create a generic response card (which we recommend in many of the following samples), you can take a stack

☐ Yes! I'd like to find out how much my home
is worth today. Please set me up for a
Home Market Review!
The best time to reach me is _____

Preprinted label with
respondent's name, etc.

Thank you!

08/96

*A good response card is easy
to complete and clearly
restates the offer in the letter. To track mailing results,
put an inconspicuous key
code on the reply card. See
Chapter 15 for details.*

along with you to open houses and pass them out. Or keep them in your pocket when you head to a community meeting. These postcards are an excellent way to give people you meet — either through the mail or in person — a quick overview of your services and an easy means of reaching you.

Response Envelope

While some direct mail packages have response envelopes that carry out themes expressed in the letter, it's not necessary. To be most cost-efficient, print up a standard postage-paid reply envelope and use it in all your mailings.

Premiums

Premiums, or free gifts, in direct mail farming are a testy subject. Everyone wonders whether they should try them.

Adding a premium can boost a mailing's cost 5 to 10 times, so you want to make sure you select the right one.

You can use either front- or back-end premiums.

FRONT-END PREMIUMS

A front-end premium arrives inside your direct-mail package. Pens, pencils, flower seeds, small writing pads, or greeting cards make good front-end premiums. When selecting one, be sure it can be easily mailed and will not greatly increase your postage cost.

Perhaps the biggest single benefit of front-end premiums is that they make direct-mail packages stand out. If you receive three bulk-mail envelopes in one afternoon — if you can feel something interesting through one envelope — which would you open first?

BACK-END PREMIUMS

Back-end premiums invite the reader to act and then receive a benefit. For example, you might ask the reader to return a reply card to receive a free home evaluation. Or call you for a free "Crime Stoppers" information kit.

Back-end premiums can open doors to hard-to-reach homes in your farm. They give you a non-threatening way to meet prospects and develop relationships. Back-end premiums are more cost efficient than front-end ones, since only a minority of your farm residents will want them.

But back-end premiums also could attract people you'd rather not spend your valuable prospecting time with — people who are always on the look-out for anything free. Learn to spot these people quickly.

When offering a back-end premium, announce it on the envelope. Your outer envelope copy might read something like this: "Get Your Free Home Tax Kit — details inside".

Whether you choose front- or back-end premiums, they're usually worth trying. If you plan to mail your farm 12 times a year, why not plan to offer one of each type at least once?

Other Direct Mail Elements

You can add a brochure, lift note, newspaper article — anything you want to a direct mail package.

Whatever you choose, it should be meaningful and support the offer in your letter. Its purpose is to enhance what is being said, not to say something new or different.

One powerful insert commonly used in direct mail packages is testimonials. For a real estate farmer, this would involve contacting several past clients to see if they will allow you to quote them. Most people agree to these requests. You then draft comments and get their approval (see lift note in "Five Facts" Letter). Put them on a one-page sheet with your picture on top. Remember to use their names and cities.

It's always better to have others say good things about you than to say them yourself.

Self-Mailers

In addition to the classic letter package, another direct mail format is the self-mailer. This doesn't use an outer envelope, but prints the prospect's name and address on the back.

Self-mailers are quick and easy, since you only have to create one element. But the savings in time and money often is lost because self-mailer response rates rarely match those of letter packages.

Many real estate farmers send newsletters as self-mailers.

CHAPTER 5

HOW TO WRITE WINNING SALES COPY

You're pulling your hair out. You've just written the line, "I know the properties here," in your farm letter.

It doesn't feel right.

For one thing, it starts with an I. You have a sneaking suspicion that you shouldn't put so much emphasis on yourself.

You go on anyway.

"I want to ask for your trust and confidence."

Hold on. This approach isn't right. Even you can see that you've given them no reason to trust you. All you've said is, "I know the properties here." So what?

Will you ever get the hang of this?

Yes, you will. If you keep reading.

WHAT IS "COPY"?

"Copy" is the words that you use to convey your message to your farm. Carefully crafted copy is vital to a mailing's success or failure.

In *Tested Advertising Methods*, John Caples, former vice-president of the ad agency Batten, Barton, Durstine & Osborn, describes two identical ads which differed only in copy. One pulled 19.5 times more sales than the other.

FOUR MOTIVATORS

In *Direct Mail Copy That Sells!*, Herschell Gordon Lewis presents what he calls the "four great motivators":

* Fear
* Guilt
* Greed
* Exclusivity

Direct-mail expert Herschell Gordon Lewis says four great motivators — Fear, Greed, Guilt, and Exclusivity — should guide your writing of sales letters.

These motivators, he argues, should guide all your sales writing.

Fear	*Greed*
Guilt	*Exclusivity*

Fear — Fear is the most potent motivator. Fear of failure, fear of not being accepted, and fear of missing an opportunity are the main three.

Here is an example of fear as a motivator:

"You may be missing the best opportunity in the past decade to sell your home for a profit and move into the new home of your dreams."

Greed — The preceding sentence could apply to greed as well. Greed is easy to seek out:

"If you sign up now, we'll waive the normal $25 service charge."

Guilt — It's also easy to apply the guilt appeal. For example:

"If you miss this opportunity, you could regret it the rest of your life."

Exclusivity — Exclusivity makes a prospect feel singled out and special. For example:

"Dear Preferred Client,

Or,

"Frankly, I wouldn't tell just anybody this, but you're important to me."

In *Guerrilla Marketing: Secrets For Making Big Profits From Your Small Business*, Jay Conrad Levinson says that people also respond to one or more of the following:

Achievement	Style
Pride of ownership	Social approval (status)
Convenience	Health and well-being
Comfort	Profit
Love	Savings or economy
Friendship	Peer pressure
Security	Ambition
Self-improvement	Power

As you read through your sales letter copy, check to see that the underlying motivation is based on human needs.

MAKING THE RIGHT OFFER

The offer, or proposition, is the cornerstone of direct mail copy. In *Successful Direct Marketing Methods*, Bob Stone, the "father of modern direct-mail marketing," presented three ways of saying the same thing that got entirely different responses.

His three offers were:

1. Half Price!
2. Buy One — Get One Free!
3. 50% Off!

The second did 40% better than the other two. Why? Because of one word — free. The right offer does make a difference.

The second did 40% better than the other two. Why? Because of one word — free. The right offer does make a difference.

Unique and Personal

A good offer must be unique and personal. In real estate, this is fairly easy because of the nature of our business. After all, what's more personal than someone's home?

Perceived Value

Good offers must have real value in the eyes of your prospective clients. A free pen engraved with your name has limited value, but a report on the effects of a new property tax change might have considerable value to many homeowners.

Kinds of Real Estate Offers

Several offers are commonly used by real estate professionals. They include:

Free Home Evaluation is one of the strongest, since it has both perceived value to a homeowner and allows you to meet prospects personally.

In addition, it tends to appeal to the right kind of prospect (someone concerned about the value of his or her home) without the harshness of a direct listing solicitation.

Furthermore, it is not that uncommon for a Free Home Evaluation to lead to a quick listing.

Home-Seller Kits are also popular, generally as a back-end premium. It's effective since you'll only get responses from people thinking about selling their homes.

Open House Invitations play on neighbors' curiosity. There is not a lot to these offers except to invite neighbors (and their friends) to see a home for which you already have the listing. However, it's a good way of meeting people in your farm and people often do move within the same neighborhood.

A secondary benefit is that it helps develop the synergy that makes your name a household word in your farm.

Free Gifts can be double-edged. While they may increase the number of responses to a mailing, you could find yourself with a bunch of poor prospects. However, as a door-opener, back-end gifts (those not sent with mailing but delivered later) often cannot be beat, especially when you are first farming an area.

FSBO (For Sale by Owner) Conversions can be a gold mine. With their specialized nature, these should not be used in a mass mailing to your farm; but it's good to have one on hand when an FSBO sign pops up in your farm.

Renters are a unique group of prospects. For one thing, since they don't own their homes, they obviously can't list them — which make many farming appeals irrelevant.

On the other hand, renters are open to a variety of other offers, such as financial consultations and information about financing programs designed especially for first time home buyers.

Absentee Owners are the flip side to renters. Since they own properties to produce income, they have decidedly different motivations from other homeowners. For example, a change in tax laws or a sharp hike in property appreciation could be incentive for them to sell. You should treat both absentee owners and renters as special categories within your farm.

Direct Listing Solicitations are tricky and will produce few responses — but any response you do generate will be highly qualified!

The truth is, no one will ever sign up for a listing by mail. It's basically still a two-step process: sales lead, then sale (or in this case, listing). Carefully worded solicitation letters can soften the harshness of a direct appeal and possibly open the door for a listing consultation.

Other popular real estate offers include descriptions of listed homes, property management services, investment property opportunities, and more. Only your imagination limits you.

Write to Individuals, Not the Masses

The most important thing to remember when you sit down to create your direct-mail letter is that you are writing to 300 individual men and women, not a faceless crowd of 300.

To illustrate, here are two sample introductions. The first takes a mass approach; the second speaks to an individual.

Example 1 — Written for the Masses

Dear Neighbor:

Dozens of homes in the neighborhood have been sold in recent months for well above what their owners thought they could possibly get...

(LETTER AMPLIFIES ARGUMENTS AND CLOSES WITH...)

What's more, here at XYZ Realty, we've sold plenty of them...

Example 2 — Written to an Individual

Dear Neighbor,

Your home may well be worth more than you think. Property values in Castle Pines have shot through the roof in the past few months. Even if you're not thinking about selling, now would be a good time to check the current value of your home...

(LETTER AMPLIFIES ARGUMENTS AND CLOSES WITH...)

If you'd like, I'll personally drop by your home, evaluate it with you, and give you a written market comparison based on recent sales of comparable houses nearby. Of course, there's no obligation.

Even though both these letters are mass-produced, the second letter feels warmer and more intimate through its heavy use of "you" copy. (Just try to count the number of "you's" in the first example!)

Personal words give your letters an emotional tone and persuasive appeal that greatly strengthens their impact.

When you write to your farm, think of it as made up of individuals, not one big mass.

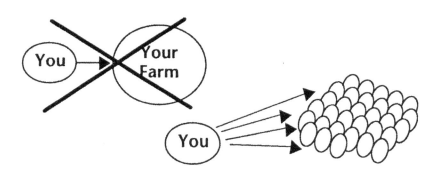

Remember that no matter how large your mailing is, you're always writing to one individual at a time.

You also should notice how the second letter uses "I," instead of the more generic "we" found in the first letter. Like "you," "I" can reinforce the point that you're an individual writing to other individuals.

This is your farm, not your firm's farm. These are your customers. And while you may represent XYZ Realty, only your efforts alone on his or her behalf interest your prospective client.

Write As You Speak

Another rule of thumb in writing direct mail is to write exactly as you speak. Maybe because of what we were taught in school, the minute some of us get behind a typewriter or word processor, we get hung up on format and sentence structure.

Not only does this make writing far more difficult, it becomes awkward and hard to understand. Forget what you learned in school — communicate with simple words and phrases and short, easy-to-read sentences. We personally find that reading what we've written into a tape recorder (and playing it back) helps.

Use Benefits, Not Features

You have probably heard endless advice about selling benefits instead of features. You're going to hear it again.

A "feature" is a tangible, describable part of something. It is an attribute. A "benefit" is what that feature will do for someone. It is the personal advantage that your offer has for someone. Benefits satisfy human needs and are related to motivations and emotions.

A house with a built-in burglar alarm offers the benefit of safety from outside intruders. A house with a swimming pool offers the benefit of pleasurable summer afternoons. A house with an oversized garage offers the benefit of room for a workshop or extra storage.

Before writing to your farm, always take a minute to jump into your prospects' shoes and try to think from their point of view. Turn every feature you can think of into a benefit.

And never overlook the obvious. Sure, your prospects may know that burglar alarms provide safety from outside intruders; but tell them anyway.

The Long and Short of Copy

One of the most often heard sayings in conventional advertising is, "People won't read long copy." Not true!

People will read copy as long as it's interesting. They'll trash a superficial one-page letter long before a well-written four-page letter. It is what you say and how you say it that matters — not how many pages it takes you to do it.

Long copy lets you tell a complete story. That's important, especially when your message involves the complicated world of real estate. If your letter raises questions in the prospect's mind, you're not there to clear them up. If it goes unresolved, you have probably lost a potential client.

That is why you always need to tell the full story in each direct mail package.

And don't assume that your prospects will remember something you wrote in the last mailing, or perhaps something from your full-page ad in last Saturday's newspaper.

Tell them again. Repetition isn't boring — it makes people remember!

Don't Write Above Their Heads

Very few people want to come home from a long day at work, open their mail, and read an essay by William F. Buckley.

According to Evelyn Wood's *Reading Dynamics,* most people read at about a seventh-grade level. While this may be a problem for the education system, you're not responsible for changing it.

Your job as a direct-mail writer — more specifically, as a direct mail farmer — is to communicate your message. And if writing at a seventh-grade level does that — then so be it!

After you have written your mail piece — whether it is the letter, an insert, response card, or anything else — set it aside for awhile. After a day or two, pick it up. Read it aloud. See if you can shorten or simplify the words, sentences and paragraphs.

And if you are looking for some tips on simple grammatical structure, go to your supermarket and pick up *The National Enquirer* or *People.*

Avoid Using Real Estate Jargon

As a real estate professional you become familiar with terms such as "first deed of trust," "wraparound mortgages" and "exclusive right to sell."

Your farm prospects, however, do not. In fact, many of them will not even know what you mean if you use real estate jargon.

A recent mailing from a Pomona, California agent highlighted this point. She offered a free silk flower arrangement "as her way of saying thanks to the first 25 homeowners who take out an 'Exclusive Right to Sell' listing with her for a minimum of six months."

Her letter failed, partly because it was filled with terms such as "lock boxes," "reasonable assessment of value" and "exclusive arrangements with another licensee."

Real estate jargon has no place in your direct mail farm letters. Keep them simple and make your readers comfortable.

Specific Copy Recommendations

What you write in your sales letter will vary tremendously with your message. Here are some general tips on how to keep your copy flowing and interesting.

1. Simple Style

Although mentioned earlier, this bears repeating: Keep your copy simple.

That means simple, short words. Stay away from anything with more than three syllables. One or two are best. Use short sentences. And don't be afraid of one sentence — even one word — paragraphs.

2. Stick with Present Tense

People want to know what is happening now. Not what happened last year, last week, or even yesterday. Use present tense language such as,

"You feel a sense of security knowing your home is well protected."

Double check your letter to make sure that you keep the same tense throughout. It's all too easy to switch from present to future to past without realizing it.

3. Use Specifics

Compare these two sentences:

"Crime is on the rise."

"Last month 11 homes were broken into in our neighborhood."

Or these two:

"Home values are going up."

"The U.S. Dept. of Housing announced last week that home prices increased 13% in the past 12 months — the biggest single-year increase in the last decade. Here in Castle Pines, home prices climbed 15% last year — two percentage points above the national average."

Specifics are much stronger.

4. Avoid Slogans

Ads use slogans all the time. Often they're worthless. A phrase such as, "After all, we're the Realtors® who care," means nothing to your readers — even if it's strewn across your letterhead.

5. Tell Them and Tell Them Again, but Don't Bore Them

Good sales letters give complete sales messages. This often involves repeating benefits. Studies show that repetition helps readers remember what you write. In fact, you really should mention the main benefit several times. Just try to write it a little differently each time. While you want to avoid boring your readers, it usually takes five or more repetitions before you turn them off.

6. Emotional Words Outsell Intellectual Words

Long pretentious words slow down readers and impersonalize your message. Why use "beneficial" when "good" will do the job? Or "omitted" instead of "left out" or "forgotten"? Or "subsequent to" instead of "since"?

Remember to read what you write aloud. If something sounds too jarring to you, look for a simpler word.

7. Use Lots of Connecting Words and Phrases

In school you were taught to write a paragraph with a beginning, middle and end. That formula does not work well for sales letters. You don't want your reader to feel finished until he or she arrives at the very end of your letter.

Short paragraphs help, as do connectors. Some examples are:

And — In addition — Also

And that's not all . . .

What's more,

What this means for you . . .

Most important . . .

In fact — In short — In brief

Why? — The result? — The answer?

If that's not enough . . .

I'm sure you'll agree . . .
And as I said . . .
Even if you don't . . .
Last but not least . . .
You get the idea.

8. Bullets

- Do not be afraid
- To use bullets
- To set off parts of your text.

9. Numbering

1. If you have more than a few unrelated points,
2. Using numbers will help the reader
3. Make transitions for you.

10. One-Sentence Paragraphs

Your high school composition teacher may not like it, but people read one-sentence paragraphs more often than longer ones. The reason is that many of us scan the words first. We only stop to read if something strikes us.

One-sentence paragraphs act like subheads to direct scanning. They're ideal for emphasizing important points:
"Here in Castle Pines..."
"It's yours free — with no obligation!"

11. Visual Aids

In keeping letters flowing, how the letter looks can be almost as important as what it says. Here are some tips on your letter's appearance:

- Use large type face rather than smaller elite type. If you're not having your letter printed at a lettershop, make sure you use a high quality printer. The type should be dark and easy to read.
- Avoid fancy fonts — even with a word processor, letters in "typewriter" style fonts are best.
- Keep margins at least one inch wide — and space between paragraphs.
- Indent paragraphs five spaces rather than starting at the left copy edge. This makes it easier for the eye to follow.
- Sometimes you may want to indent an entire paragraph — make sure it is important. You also can italicize or bold face it.

ABC Realty, Inc.

Here are some tips on protecting your home from outside intruders — and they're FREE!

Making your letter visually appealing is important. The above example has narrow margins, no indented paragraphs, justified text (right-hand margin is squared up), and no continuation at the bottom.

- Use free-flowing punctuation such as ellipses and exclamation points — not just commas and periods!
- If you are using a word processor which can justify text (that is, make both the left and right margins the same), don't bother. The eye prefers ragged right edges.
- Underline important words and phrases.
- Don't be afraid to add brief hand-written notes in the margins, or use checkmarks or exclamation points to highlight your copy. Just make them readable.
- At the bottom of a page, type or handwrite "over, please." Many people will not do it unless you ask them to.

ABC Realty, Inc.

Here are some tips on protecting your home from outside intruders — and they're FREE!

This example is more visually appealing and much more readable. It includes wide margins, indented paragraphs, ragged right edges and broken-up copy blocks.

(over, please)

Though seemingly a minor point, the simple addition of the words "(over, please)" at the bottom tells the reader more is coming. Without it, many will never turn the page.

CAN YOU LEARN TO WRITE DIRECT MAIL?

If you can read this book, you can learn to write direct-mail farm letters.

Most people neither like to write nor believe they're good at it. They cringe when remembering high school composition classes. But actually, this can help you.

Good direct-mail copy, you see, doesn't fit well with so-called "good" grammatical prose. People with degrees in English often can't write effective direct mail because they find themselves locked into more conventional writing styles. The short sentences and simple paragraph structures described throughout this book are despised by most English teachers.

Those who take business courses are often less restricted in their writing and, therefore, communicate more clearly.

In direct mail, being clear is critical.

Helpful Sources

Your library or local bookstore will have many books on direct mail. Over the past few years, in fact, the number of sources has mushroomed. While not specifically on direct mail, the best copywriting book ever written is *Tested Advertising Methods* by John Caples. We've never met a copywriter worth anything who didn't keep a well-worn copy of this classic on a handy bookshelf.

You also can find a trustworthy and easy to reach source right at home — just check your mailbox.

Most of us receive several direct-mail offers a week. Instead of tossing them out, study them. Make a file of the ones that held your interest or those that you just liked a lot. When you sit down to write your own letters, pull out the file and read it. Even if they're not real estate letters, the tone, style and maybe even particular words in these letters should give you valuable pointers.

Don't be afraid to borrow a phrase or two if you need it. Toyota doesn't reinvent the wheel each time it pushes a new Camry off the assembly line.

If you want more samples, respond to a few offers. Once you're targeted as "direct-mail responsive," you'll get more mail than you can handle.

Points to Remember

Make sure your copy is based on human needs. Four great motivators are:

- fear
- guilt
- greed
- exclusivity (status)

Your offer should be:

- unique and personal
- have high perceived value

Examples of real estate offers:

- free home evaluation
- home-seller kits
- open house invitations
- free gifts
- For Sale By Owner conversions
- renters
- absentee owners
- direct listing solicitations

Copy tips:

- write to individuals, not the masses
- write the way you speak
- describe benefits, not features
- long copy is fine, as long as it's interesting
- don't write above readers' heads
- avoid real estate jargon

Specific copy recommendations:

- use simple style
- stay in present tense
- be specific
- repeat main benefits
- choose emotional words
- use connecting words
- use one-sentence paragraphs
- end page with "over, please"

Avoid:

- long words
- slogans and clichés

Make your letters more visually appealing with:

- bullets
- numbers
- large type face
- typewriter style fonts
- wide margins
- indented paragraphs
- free-flowing punctuation
- ragged right edges
- underlining, bold face, italics
- handwritten notes in margins

For more tips on writing effective direct-mail copy, read:
Tested Advertising Methods
John Caples
Reward Books/Prentice Hall, Inc.
Englewood Cliffs, New Jersey

Building a Mail Order Business
William A. Cohen
John Wiley & Sons
New York, New York

Million Dollar Mailing $
Dennis Hatch
Libey Publishing, Inc.
Washington, D.C.

The Greatest Direct Mail Sales Letters of All Time
Richard S. Hodgson
Dartnell Press/The Dartnell Corporation
Chicago, Illinois

Direct Mail Copy That Sells!
Herschell Gordon Lewis
Prentice Hall, Inc.
Englewood Cliffs, New Jersey

Successful Direct Marketing Methods
Bob Stone
Crain Books/Crain Communications, Inc.
Chicago, Illinois

CHAPTER 6

HOW TO WRITE A WINNING SALES LETTER

Over and over, one thought is running through your mind. "Keep it simple," you repeat to yourself. In the past, you always tried to sound smart in your letters. Now you're realizing that smart doesn't mean pretentious. Being simple and clear — that's the best way to reach prospects.

Okay. You understand how you're supposed to write. Now the problem is what you're supposed to write. You've looked ahead over the sample letters, it appears that they have some sort of structure. But what the heck is it?

Turn the page and find out.

STONE'S SEVEN-STEP FORMULA

In *Successful Direct Marketing Methods,* Bob Stone presents a detailed seven-step writing formula perfect for your direct-mail farm letters.

Seven-Step Formula — Specific Example

1. Announce Biggest Benefit to Reader:

"Dear Neighbor,
Your home may well be worth a lot more than you think..."

2. Expand Upon Benefit:

"... with the recent fall in interest rates and improvements in our school system, homes in our neighborhood are showing strong resale values..."

3. Tell the Reader Exactly What He or She Will Get:

"... by returning the enclosed card, you'll get a free Home Market Analysis. With it, you can compare your home with others that have recently sold in our neighborhood..."

4. Prove Value with Past Experience:

"... dozens of your neighbors have already gotten their free Home Market Analyses. And it has helped them make some important decisions..."

5. Tell Them What Happens if They Do Not Respond to Your Offer:

"... for most of us our home is our most valuable asset. And decisions about it without full knowledge of the market can have devastating effects..."

6. Summarize the Major Benefits:

"... your market analysis will not only let you know the current value of your home, but it will also help you answer some serious questions about your future..."

7. Incite Action Now!

"... to take advantage of the opportunity to find out the hidden value of your home, simply fill out the card and return it by mail.

"I urge you to do this right away, since my schedule is filling up as many of your neighbors are returning their cards now ..."

Many of the country's leading direct-mail writers swear by Bob Stone's seven-step formula.

AIDA

Another well known formula taught in many sales training courses is AIDA — Attention, Interest, Desire, and Action.

In short, this simplified approach to direct-mail sales (adapted from fact-to-face sales) calls for you to first gain your prospect's attention. . . then arouse his or her interest in the product or service. . . then create a desire for it. . . and finally call to action, in other words, close the sale.

There is nothing wrong with this formula, although it does not strictly apply to direct mail.

DON'T LET FORMULAS BOG YOU DOWN

While formulas are indeed helpful, don't let them tie you down. They can hinder your creativity and communication.

In fact, many of the most successful sales letters of all time have structures that bear no resemblance to Stone's format.

However, as a beginning direct mail writer, you may find a formula helpful. At least it ensures that you cover everything and follow a logical path.

Remember the bottom line: Direct mail is nothing more than salesmanship in print.

Write It, Read It, and Rewrite It

Just as with any form of writing, rewriting is essential.

Initially you may find it easiest to write as much as possible as fast as possible. Move briskly without slowing down to look up words in a dictionary or to settle on exactly the right word or phrase.

When you finish the first draft, put it down and do something else. Later rewrite and polish it. Do this as many times as necessary. It may help to read it aloud and show it to a friend.

Besides checking for spelling and punctuation, you should ask yourself these nine questions as you read and reread your copy:

- Is the offer clearly presented?
- Have I appealed to the reader in an emotional and personal manner?
- Am I writing from the reader's point of view?
- Are all the important elements covered?
- Is it believable?
- Have I distinguished the benefits from the features?
- Does the copy flow, and is it written in a conversational tone?
- Does it have short words and easy-to-read sentences and paragraphs?
- Is it easy on the eyes?

SUMMARY

If you read enough books on the topic, you are certain to find many formulas for writing direct mail.

The AIDA formula is a simple one, adapted from conventional sales training. First you get attention, then arouse interest, then create desire, and finally call for action — ask for the listing!

A formula more suited for your direct-mail farm letters is Bob Stone's seven-step formula

In a nutshell, you begin the letter by announcing — loudly and clearly — the biggest benefit of your offer to your reader. Then you add details, creating a lovely image of exactly how the benefit will help your reader. You strengthen your arguments with specific examples, carefully chosen so the reader relates easily to them. You then point out what the reader will miss if he or she declines your offer.

Finally, you hit your main benefit one last time — using very strong language as you ask the reader to act now.

While formulas are helpful, do not let them bog you down. And always read and rewrite your direct-mail copy, keeping the nine questions posed at the end of this chapter in mind.

CHAPTER 7

STARTING YOUR SALES LETTER

It's 10 a.m. You've had two cups of coffee. A third sits steaming near your right hand. You shuffle the papers on your desk — and glance back over the previous chapters. You're nervous, but you know you've got a handle on the kinds of words to use and the structure for your letter. You're also excited about your idea.

You flip on the computer and see the familiar glow. A blank page is staring at you.

Your gut tells you to start pouring words in a flood onto the keyboard. Your head tells you to hold back. There's something that needs a lot of care first. Something short and deceptively simple.

OK — let's take that great idea and turn it into a reality.

This chapter takes you step-by-step through the first and most important part of your sales letter. If you don't get readers hooked from the beginning, you'll lose them.

THE HEADLINE

Like the headline on a newspaper or magazine article, the headline of your sales letter calls attention to your offer.

Headlines are not mandatory, but highly recommended.

In Stone's seven-step formula, your first goal is to grab attention by announcing the biggest benefit of your offer. And what better way than through a bold headline?

The headline is the only part of your letter you may want to have in a non-typewritten font or typeset.

Use a headline to gain attention or announce the main benefit of your offer. Typeset headlines (top example) make bolder statements, but typewritten headlines (bottom example) will work, too.

Get This Homeseller's Kit
Absolutely FREE!
Here's How . . .

Guide to Selling Your Home

Dear Neighbor,

Have you thought about selling your home?

If so, then you'll . . .

ABC Realty, Inc.

Get This
Homeseller's Kit
Absolutely Free
-Here's How!

Guide to Selling Your Home

Dear Neighbor,

Have you thought about selling your home?

If so, then you'll . .

When a prospect opens your letter, the headline is the first thing that he or she sees; this is because you fold the letter so the headline faces the reader as he or she pulls it out of the envelope.

And advertising research in direct mail and space advertising has proven its importance time and time again.

In *Tested Advertising Methods,* direct-response ad expert John Caples writes, "The success of an entire advertising campaign may stand or fall on what is said in the headline..."

Keys to Good Headlines

The purpose of a good headline is to make the reader pause and want to read more of your copy. It's the rope that pulls in readers.

Good headlines have emotional appeal, are interesting (or at least arouse the reader's curiosity), and play to the reader's self-interest.

Many good headlines offer news, and are even written in a "newsy" format — such as, Mortgage Rates Slip Twice in Six Months — What can this mean for you?

Questions often work well in headlines because they create immediate involvement. A classic example is the Max Sackheim-created ad for the Sherwin Cody School of English, which ran for over 40 years in various publications. It simply asked: Do You Make These Mistakes in English?

Examples of Winning Headlines

Here are some direct-mail headlines which have proven most successful over the years:

Will There Be BOOM and More INFLATION Ahead? (*The Kiplinger Letter*)

At 60 miles an hour the loudest noise in this new Rolls-Royce comes from the electric clock (Rolls-Royce)

Do you close the bathroom door even when you're the only one home? (*Psychology Today* magazine)

Your Faith Can Move Mountains . . . . . . Start with this one, please (American Bible Society)

How To Win Friends and Influence People (Book of the same title, Simon and Schuster)

If you are a careful driver you can save money on Car Insurance (Liberty Mutual)

You are cordially invited to receive a free Executive Portfolio with your name stamped in gold prepared by the editors of Business Week (*Business Week* magazine)

THE SALUTATION

Salutations may sound simple, but they're not. The most common salutation in direct mail is the generic "Dear Noun" format, such as:

- Dear Friend
- Dear Neighbor
- Dear Professional

Qualifying Salutation

A qualifying salutation, which includes either an adjective before the generic noun or a descriptive noun, is best. Here are some examples:

- Dear Friend of Public Television,
- Dear Castle Pines Neighbor,
- Dear Real Estate Professional,
- Dear Fellow Lodge Brother,

Qualifying salutations tell the reader right off that you either share a relationship or that you're targeting a group to which he or she belongs. If you, as a real estate salesperson, received a letter which began, "Dear Insurance Professional," you'd probably pitch it in the trash right away.

If the letter started "Dear Professional," you'd still be unsure whether it involved real estate.

But if the letter saluted you with "Dear Real Estate Professional," you'd know that it was meant for you.

By helping draw a connection between the reader and writer, the qualifying salutation overcomes a major hurdle in direct mail by enhancing the personal, intimate qualities of the letter.

Open Salutation

Another popular, but not often advised, salutation is the open salutation.

ABC Realty, Inc.

Dear Neighbor,

ABC Realty, Inc.

Dear Castle Pines Neighbor,

Qualifying your salutation lets the reader know the message is for him or her, and adds to your credibility. The top example tells the reader nothing; the middle example at least adds a geographic connection between the writer and the reader; and the bottom example (which would work well for a social farm) draws a strong connection between the reader and the writer.

ABC Realty, Inc.

Dear Fellow Lodge Brother,

There are two other common ways to start letters, neither of which is advised. The Open Salutation (above) and the Shocker (below). Many successful mailings have used the latter approach, but only consider it if you have a dramatic appeal.

ABC Realty, Inc.

Greetings!

ABC Realty, Inc.

Your home may be worth more than you think!

Examples of open salutations are:
- Greetings!
- Hi Neighbor!
- Hello From XYZ Realty!
- Good Day!

There is nothing wrong with "Greetings!" on a handwritten note, but open salutations are formal and impersonal, especially when typed and mass-produced.

Moreover, they are, perhaps even subconsciously, distasteful to the reader.

The Shocker

The famous Kiplinger Letter, which has run essentially unchanged for over 40 years, has no salutation. It starts off boldly with:

Will There Be BOOM and More INFLATION Ahead?

Then it moves directly to dynamic sales copy. Shockers like these, as the name suggests, bypass the salutation altogether — usually with some bold statement or question.

Popular with political fund-raising letters, this format cries for very dramatic subject matter.

Something like this would not do:

Did You Know Your Neighbor Was Moving?

If you have a dramatic event, it might be worth a try. One year, a Coldwell Banker Realtor® sent a letter which started with this shocker.

Will the New Tax Law Hurt You as a Homeowner?

The offer was for a free Price-Waterhouse book on tax revisions, and the sales letter itself was excellent. But remember that this type of offer will only work when tax revisions are big news.

OTHER THINGS ABOUT THE START OF YOUR SALES LETTER

Letterhead

Should you send your letter on your firm's letterhead? Most of the time — but not always.

It depends on what your firm's letterhead looks like. First, you want your name, address, phone numbers and photograph prominently displayed. You also need room for a headline. If the corporate letterhead is too busy or only allows room for your name and a small type headline, don't use it.

And if your firm's letterhead has several colors, it may end up costing you an exorbitant amount to produce your mailings — unless, of course, you can get the blank letterhead and print on it.

However, eliminating the letterhead is not good either. You lose credibility. Moreover, your broker may not like it. If he or she is picking up part of the tab, that becomes especially important. The best solution is probably to create your own letterhead and include the company name and logo. The fact that you work for a well-known real estate company might boost your credibility.

If you do make your own letterhead, keep the type simple, and not too bold. Don't forget to include your address and phone numbers.

ABC Realty, Inc.

Serving all Your Real Estate Needs
in Castle Pines for Over 15 Years

200 Main Street, Castle Pines, AZ 80555

Dear Castle Pines Neighbor,

Letterheads like the top one will compete with and tend to dominate your personal information and headline. Blank paper (middle) is not good either, as you're never identified as a real estate professional. Often it's best to make up your own simple letterhead as in the bottom example. If possible, include your corporate logo.

Dear Castle Pines Neighbor,

ABC Realty, Inc.

From the Desk of Jill Jones

Dear Fellow Club Member,

PHOTOS

The benefits of including your photo on farm mailings have been well-documented. A photo makes you more real to readers and helps them remember you the next time you write. It also may lead to a prospect walking up to you when you're in a local shop and asking, "Aren't you....?" And it could make prospects more comfortable when you drop off information or reference kits at their homes.

ABC Realty, Inc.

From the Desk of Jill Jones

Dear Castle Pines Neighbor,

ABC Realty, Inc.

From the Desk of Jill Jones

Dear Castle Pines Neighbor

ABC Realty, Inc.

From the Desk of Jill Jones

Dear Castle Pines Neighbor

When using a photo on your letterhead, avoid the distraction of having it too large (top) or on the right (middle). Ad research studies have shown that keeping potential distractions to the left limits their ability to compete with your sales message. In addition, formats like the bottom one leave room for a headline on the right-hand side.

However, if you use a photo on your letterhead, keep it small. You don't want it to dominate the page — and your intended message.

Also — put it on the left. Advertising research shows that placing items like photographs on the left helps reduce their distracting from the message, as readers tend to focus on the right side of a page.

Be careful about colors. For example, a blue halftone makes people look bad.

So if you use a photo — keep it small, put it in the upper left and be careful about colors.

DATING YOUR SALES LETTER

When you mail bulk rate, you will probably not want to date your sales letter. Even if you mail locally, it could take up to 14 days for your letter to reach your readers.

While such a lengthy delay is unusual, it could happen.

If you mail First Class, dating the letter is fine. But be aware, especially when you're just starting, that printing and mailing delays are not uncommon.

For example, assume that you planned to mail your letter on Monday, the 15th. A few days before, you dropped your letter at the printer's. Then at an open house over the weekend, you received a solid offer on the property as well as a potential listing. You spent the next few days running back and forth with counteroffers and working out your listing presentation. Pretty soon, it's Thursday and your letters still are sitting at the printers.

Now you have two choices: You can reprint the letters, which will be expensive and delay the mailing another two days, or you can mail them as they are. If you do, you'll show your farm your carelessness when it comes to details, which is not good for a real estate professional.

It is always safer to avoid dates.

This applies to more than the mailing's date. If you include a "limited-time offer" in your mailing, use generic times such as the next 30 days. Or limit it to the first 15 homeowners.

Finally, if you really feel compelled to date your letters, stick with the month and year, such as "May 1997" or "Spring 1998."

PUNCTUATION

Many of us have been taught in school to use a comma (,) for personal mail and a colon (:) for business mail. So we assume that when a letter appears on business letterhead, a colon should be used.

Not true.

Always use a comma after the salutation on personal sales letters to your farm.

ABC Realty, Inc.

Dear Castle Pines Neighbor:

ABC Realty, Inc.

Dear Castle Pines Neighbor,

Using a colon after the salutation (above) makes your letter more formal and less personal. A comma (bottom example) is better. Little things like this add up to make your sales letters more readable — and more powerful!

It may not seem like a big deal, but little things like this add up to make the big things work.

FOLDING AND POSITIONING YOUR LETTER

You were probably taught to fold letters with the text inside. This, however, is exactly opposite of what you do with your sales letters.

You have two or three seconds to persuade readers to open your letter. By folding your headline and copy inside, you force the reader to pull out and unfold the letter to see what it's about. With no incentive, they may not be willing to do that.

After all, they'll see no attention-grabbing headline or offer of a major benefit. Considering that most people open envelopes from the back (the sealed side), doesn't it make sense to have the most important element of your mailing staring them in the face?

Also — don't make your prospects trudge through business cards, reply envelopes, return cards, brochures and the like to reach

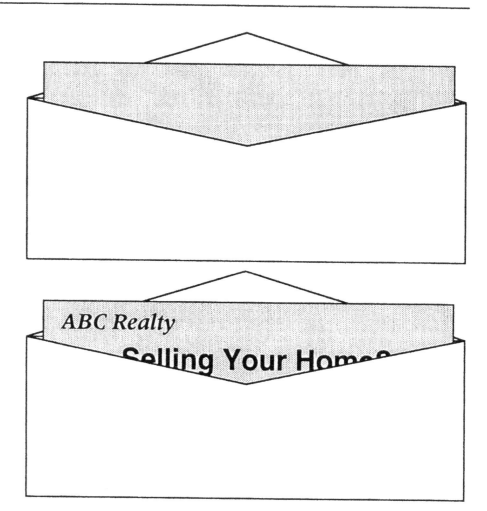

Always fold your sales letter so the copy faces out. Remember the reader will decide within a second or two if he or she is going to read it. Anything you do to help will give you a better chance.

your letter. Most just won't do it. Order the materials from front to back with the most important first, the next most important second and so on. The reply card is usually last.

After spending all that time creating your letter, make it as easy as possible for the reader to get to it.

PERSONALIZED LETTERS

Personalized letters, once a direct mail luxury, have become almost a norm with the advent of the computer. Easy to do with the right software (and the skills to use it!), personalized letters address each prospect by name.

Here are some things you should know about personalized letters.

First, they will usually improve your response. And second, if you do them yourself or have them done by an outside service, they will cost you time and money. It is not at all uncommon to pay up to a dollar a page for word processing on personalized letters. Because the cost increases with each page, most personalized letters are only one or two pages.

While dozens of methods exist for personalization, the two most common for small mailings (less than a few thousand) are conventional mail merge and manual match-fill.

<u>Mail Merge</u> — Most word processing or client contact management software programs facilitate mail merge. Using these systems, the user simply types the letter once and puts in special codes which tell the computer to import data from particular fields in a mail list.

This method is very professional and produces letters rapidly. In most cases, without a hint that they were mass produced.

<u>Manual Match-Fill</u> — This one is a bit tricky since it requires that you type and print the base letter leaving blank areas for the name, address, and salutation. You have the letter mass produced, generally by offset printing. You then manually type in — using a typewriter that matches the print — each name, address, and salutation.

At best this method of personalization is detectable by the human eye, and at worst it looks awful. No matter how carefully you line things up, the type will almost never match. What's more, the process takes a lot of time.

You're probably better off with just a generic ("Dear Neighbor") letter than trying a manual match-fill.

Points to remember:

Your headline can make or break your letter. It should:

- involve the reader

- provide strong emotional appeal

- play to reader self-interest

Use personalized salutations such as, "Dear fellow St. John's member."

Use letterhead that includes your:

- name

- work address

- work, home, pager, fax phone numbers

- company name and logo

- photo

Keep your photo small and in the upper left.

Don't date letters. Month/Year and Season/Year is okay.

Fold your letter so the reader sees the headline first.

Personalize your farm letters whenever possible.

CHAPTER 8

OPENING YOUR SALES LETTER

You finish your coffee. You think about another cup but decide to forget it. Writing this letter feels pretty good. You remember to keep the copy simple. Stone's seven-step formula is lying next to the computer. You're pleased with the letterhead you designed.

You type, "Dear Castle Pines Neighbor," and pause. Now you need to hit the reader right between the eyes with the main benefit of your offer.

But how do you start? What will be punchy and dramatic? Not too dramatic, though. Just enough to "reel" the reader in.

Ugh. This is tough.

Relax. It's really easy.

This chapter will help you with just one thing — your first paragraph.

THE OPENING PARAGRAPH

Used Without a Headline

When you don't have a headline, the first paragraph of your letter becomes your headline. Your second paragraph serves as your opening paragraph.

Used with a Headline

When you do have a headline (which we recommend), the paragraph right after the salutation is the opening paragraph. It's used — to borrow a phrase from the angler — "to set the hook."

Under the headline, the opening paragraph should "hook" the reader and connect him or her with you.

ABC Realty, Inc.

*Now Might Be the Best Time
in Quite Awhile to Sell Your Home!*

Dear Castle Pines Neighbor,

Have you ever thought about selling your home?

ABC Realty, Inc.

Dear Castle Pines Neighbor,

Now might just be the best time in quite awhile to sell your home.

If you've ever thought about it at all, you'll want to hear this important news. . .

Remember, by now the reader has gotten through your outer envelope, past your headline, and past your salutation. But he or she still has not decided to read your entire letter.

It's time to reel them in.

From Stone's seven-step formula, you know you must expand upon the major benefit to hold the reader's interest.

In addition, the opening paragraph should further qualify your readers or connect you to them. And let them know the message is for them.

Example 1 — Consider this opening paragraph from a letter by Omaha Steaks International (a firm that sells mail order steaks):

"I'm writing because I have reason to believe you are a person who appreciates exceptional food. If I'm right, you will be interested in this offer..."

In superb "you-and-me" style, this opening paragraph pulls readers into the copy by subtly yet clearly defining what is in it for them.

Example 2 — A similar example of the same idea appeared several years ago in a mailing by the Franklin Mint:

"If you love and appreciate fine American furniture as I do, then what I'm about to tell you is truly exciting news ..."

Again, the hook is set, and a meaningful qualification presented.

Example 3 — Here is a great opening paragraph from a letter for Conde Nast Traveler:

"We know you...

...You find a few extra dollars in your pocket — a crack in your impossibly busy schedule — and what do you do?

"Take off, that's what!..."

The message is again clear. Interest your readers and pull them into the copy.

Now contrast those opening paragraphs with this one in a letter actually sent by a Realtor® (the names have been changed):

"I'm Doug Simmons, your local XYZ Real Estate agent. We're here to serve all your real estate needs, from selling a home to managing rental properties."

The letter continued for eight more paragraphs, many of which read like Doug Simmons' biography. Unfortunately for Doug Simmons, he gave no one any reason to read on.

No hook was set. No further qualification was made. And the letter failed.

Tips on Opening Paragraphs

Sometimes it's tough to start a letter. Thoughts and ideas buzz around, but you can't pin them down to anything that reads or feels right. Here are some useful tips:

"The reason I'm writing you today..."

Used by thousands of direct-mail writers, this opener, while not exciting, works. In addition, it puts you into the all-important "you-and-me" copy style. This may be reason enough to use it.

Variations include:

"I'm writing you today because..."

"Let me explain why I'm writing you today..."

"Because you are a Castle Pines homeowner, I'm writing you..."

This is a good format to keep in your back pocket, but avoid over-using it.

"If" Starts

The beauty of starting your letter with "if" is that it has a built-in hook:

"If you're a Castle Pines homeowner then..."

"If you're like dozens of your neighbors..."

"If you, like me, think..."

"Whether you're..." (variation)

Negative variations can also work:

"Even if you haven't thought about selling your home..."

> Dear Castle Pines Neighbor,
>
> I'm writing you today to tell you about a special offer only for my neighbors here in Castle Pines.

> Dear Castle Pines Neighbor,
>
> If you're even thinking about selling your home, here are some interesting facts you'll want to consider.

> Dear Castle Pines Neighbor,
>
> As a homeowner in Castle Pines, I'm sure you'll want to hear about . . .

Three of the most popular ways to open a sales letter are with "I'm writing you today," (top), an "If" start (middle), and an "As" start (bottom). All are designed to hook the reader into continuing to read and establish a relationship with you.

Many of the most famous direct-mail letters and ads of all time have begun with the word "if." If you do not try it, you may be missing out.

"As" Starts

Similar in many ways to the "if" start, "as" is not as strong a hook, but serves as a very adequate qualifier.

"As a homeowner in Castle Pines..."

"As dozens of your neighbors have already..."

Two problems with "as" starts are: (1) they often come off a little cold, and (2) they lead you away from "you-and-me" copy, since they put your letter in the third person.

Pose a Question

Questions are automatic hooks. But opening your letter with a question can be dangerous. Why? Because if the reader answers no, he or she has no reason to continue. Take these two questions, for example:

1. "Are you thinking about selling your home?"

2. "Have you ever thought about selling your home?"

Questions are great ways to open sales letters — but be especially cautious with them. Ninety-nine percent of your farm will probably answer "no" to the top question, while 99 percent will most likely answer "yes" to the bottom one.

ABC Realty, Inc.

Now Might Be the Best Time in Quite Awhile to Sell Your Home!

Dear Castle Pines Neighbor,
     Are you thinking about selling your home?

ABC Realty, Inc.

Now Might Be the Best Time in Quite Awhile to Sell Your Home!

Dear Castle Pines Neighbor,
     Have you ever thought about selling your home?

At first glance, the two questions may appear to ask the same thing. But 99% of your prospects will deny that they're thinking about selling their homes. On the other hand, the same 99% will admit that they've thought about it.

Generating a positive response is important if you want prospects to keep reading.

"Have" and "how" are generally safer ways to begin opening questions than "do" and "are" because they're more open-ended.

When writing these questions, take your time. You don't want them to backfire. Which one of the following would work best?

"How can you say no to a free For Sale By Owner Kit?"

"Do you want a free For Sale By Owner Kit?"

The first, of course, because it starts with a "how." The second is too likely to prompt a "no."

Questions also can very easily evoke a big "Who cares?," like this one.

"How much does XYZ Realty care about your home?"

One way to avoid questions sounding abrupt is to preface them:

"Let me ask you..."

"Just between you and me..."

A final word about "no" responses: they are not always bad. If you have a very specialized offer, you could do your reader a favor by allowing him or her to accept or reject it in the opening paragraph. For example, in the case of For Sale By Owner, you'll only send the letter to people already trying to sell their homes. In that case, posing a "killer" question such as, "Are you selling your home?," might just work. However, such specialized offers should not be sent out on a mass basis.

ABC Realty, Inc.

Now Might Be the Best Time in Quite Awhile to Sell Your Home!

Dear Castle Pines Neighbor,

    A few of our neighbors and I got to talking the other day . . .

Do not overlook the story-telling introduction. You need only open and close with it — the rest can be pure sales talk.

Tell a Story

Story-telling in advertising, and in direct-response advertising in particular, has lost some of its luster. Still most people love a good story.

Crafting a story into a meaningful sales message is truly an art. John Caples set the standard in perhaps the most famous story-telling ad of all time, "They Laughed When I Sat Down to Play the Piano...But When I Started to Play!"

Created for a correspondence course in piano playing, the ad takes an entire page to describe how "Jack" learned to play the piano by mail. Then at a party one night with friends who thought he couldn't play a note, he sat down at the keyboard and stunned them into silence. "Jack? Why didn't you tell us you could play like that!"..."Where did you learn?"..."How long did you study?" The ad moved smoothly into a sales pitch for the school.

Only a professional advertising copywriter could make this approach work. Even then, 90% of them would fail.

But as an introductory lead-in, story-telling is not difficult to master. Take a look at three possible introductions for your sales letters:

"Last week a couple of our neighbors and I were talking, and..."

"Times have changed since we were kids..."

"Six months ago nobody thought..."

Good story-telling is the ultimate hook because if done correctly, people will want to read your sales letter just to find out what happens. But you don't have to continue the story throughout. Instead, do as Caples did. Use it to "hook" your readers, then take them right into the sales copy. Of course, a line at the end that refers back to the story is a nice finishing touch.

INVITATIONS

Invitation-type letters score high marks for qualifying readers and connecting them to you, but they fall short of offering major benefits.

Offers that commonly use this format are fund-raising letters, credit card solicitations ("you have been pre-approved to receive a..."), and magazine subscriptions.

ABC Realty, Inc.

There's a "For Sale" Sign up the Street — Come Take a Look!

Dear Castle Pines Neighbor,
    You are cordially invited to view the home of . . .

---

*You Are Cordially Invited
to View the Home*

of

_____

at

_____

this

_____

Traditional invitation formats don't lend themselves to farming letters. The most common in real estate, an invitation to an open house, might be better suited to a card such as the one shown at the bottom.

If you're inviting a prospect to an open house, a traditional invitation format makes sense. But for the bulk of your farming letters, it's inappropriate. Compare the following examples:

Good
    "You are cordially invited to view the home of..."

Bad
    "Here's a special invitation to join dozens of homeowners in your neighborhood who subscribe to my newsletter..."

In situations where you'd like use an invitation, don't try to make it into a letter. Send a simple card.

Points to Remember

Opening your letter:

- Use a headline whenever possible.

- If you don't use a headline, write your first paragraph to "hook" readers in.

Possible starters for opening sentences include:

- "I'm writing you today..."

- "If"

- "As"

- Questions

- Stories

- Invitations

Avoid opening farm letters with invitations.

CHAPTER 9

KEEP YOUR LETTERS FLOWING

Your first paragraph is done. It's short and sweet. Best of all, it's full of "you" and "I" copy and it clearly presents your main benefit. You read it over and smile.

Then you look up. Your fingers start fidgeting with a paper clip. What next?

Somehow you have to make this great benefit more personal. It has to become immediate...real...compelling to every reader.

You sigh. And you turn the page for a handful of words that will take you where you want to go.

THE TRANSITION PARAGRAPH

The second paragraph of your letter is the "transition paragraph." Sometimes, of course, it simply expands on the first paragraph. In that case, it really is considered part of the opener.

The paragraph we're talking about is the one that moves readers from interest in what you're writing about to desire to take a particular action.

Consider the opening and transition paragraphs in a letter you may have received from American Express:

Opening

"Quite frankly, the American Express® Card is not for everyone. And not everyone who applies for Card-membership is approved."

Transition

"However, because you will benefit from Card-membership, I've enclosed a special invitation for you to apply for the..."

Or here's a simpler example from an insurance agent:

Opening

"You need not be rich to need a financial plan."

Transition

"But with a complete financial plan from ABC Mutual, you may just have a better chance of ending up rich."

Like any rule, this "transition" concept can be broken. This is particularly true of story-telling letters, which usually wind a long path before taking the reader into the offer.

Still no matter what format you use, turning the reader from interest to desire is crucial.

COPY TURNERS

A "copy turner" is a phrase or sentence in your transitional paragraph that moves a reader from recognizing a need to desiring your product or service. Here are some examples:

<u>"That's Why"</u>

Perhaps the simplest copy turner, "that's why" works well with most openers.

Opener

"Like many of our neighbors here in Castle Pines, your home has probably gone up in value since you moved in."

Transition

"That's why you'll be interested in the Free Home Evaluation I'm giving this month."

<u>"You, Too"</u>

The phrase, "you, too" is not as popular as "that's why" because it requires more setup.

Opener

"...Dozens of our neighbors have already picked up their Home-Protection Kits from me."

Transition

"You, too, can have the security of knowing your home is protected from outside intruders. And it's free just for the asking."

"You, too" appeals to a sense of belonging — "Well, if others are doing it, then why shouldn't I?"

Other Phrases That Turn Readers

The phrases above are just two examples of the thousands possible. Here are some others to keep handy as you write:

This is your chance to . . .

Here's what I'm offering you . . .

Typically the second paragraph is used to "turn" the reader into your sales message. Transition phrases such as "that's why" and "you, too" help smooth the path.

ABC Realty, Inc.

This Month, Get a FREE Home Evaluation

Dear Castle Pines Neighbor,

Like many of us here in Castle Pines, your home has probably gone up in value since you moved in. Knowing how much might just help you answer some serious financial and personal questions.

That's why you'll be interested in the Free Home Evaluation I'm giving all month long.

It's really quite simple . . .

I'd like to offer you this . . .

Now you can solve this problem with . . .

In short, I've put together a kit . . .

You can have such an evaluation in a few short minutes . . .

Here's how you can eliminate those problems with a single phone call . . .

Here's your chance to find out just how much your home is worth today . . .

My offer is not for everybody . . .

Sales Without a Transition

Many sales letters move into the sales message without a turning transition. Though this can be abrupt, sometimes it works.

Opener

"Last month 11 homes in our neighborhood were broken into."

ABC Realty, Inc.

Here are some tips on protecting your home from outside intruders — and they're FREE!

Dear Castle Pines Neighbor,

Last month, 11 homes in our neighborhood were broken into — 11! I don't know about you, but I think that's scary.

With the help of the local sheriff's office, I've just put together a kit on how to protect your home. And I'd like to give you one.

Though transitions can help smooth the path, sometimes an abrupt paragraph change can add impact, especially if your offer is based on a dramatic preface such as the one above.

No Transition

"So with the help of the local sheriff's office, I've just put together a kit on how to protect your home. And I'd like to give you one."

This works best when your opening paragraph is dramatic and your offer clearly solves the problem presented.

However, these situations are rare.

Points to Remember

Transition paragraphs move readers from interest to desire for what you're offering. Write them with care.

"Copy turners" can help make this transition. Examples include:

- That's why
- You, too
- This is your chance to . . .
- Here's what I'm offering you . . .
- I'd like to offer you this . . .
- Now you can solve this problem with . . .
- In short, I've put together a kit . . .
- You can have such an evaluation in a few short minutes . . .
- Here's how you can eliminate those problems with a single phone call . . .
- Here's your chance to find out just how much your home is worth today . . .
- My offer is not for everybody . . .

Now it's time to move on to closing your letters.

CHAPTER 10

YOUR SALES LETTERS' WINNING CLOSE

Whew!

You've done it. Two nice, tight pages with copy that's colorful, precise and flowing. You've made clear what prospects will get if they take you up on your offer...and you've thrown in facts that apply specifically to your farm. Your letter is both personal and relevant.

You pause for a minute. Just a couple more paragraphs to go. It won't be hard. After all, isn't the toughest part behind you?

Don't kid yourself.

The close of your farm letter is just as important as the opening. This is your last chance to prod your prospects into action. Now you need to insert the final key element — the one that persuades your prospects to act right away. Otherwise they may think that you've made some good suggestions, but they always can do it later. They never will.

Immediacy. Urgency. Deadlines. That's what you need now. You want to move people from their mail boxes to their telephones.

Can you manage it?

No problem.

Just as with personal sales visits, your farm letters need good, strong closes. Before tackling the close, remind yourself of what the letter is trying to accomplish. Are you asking for...

- a face-to-face meeting
- a home evaluation
- a FSBO conversion
- something else?

Whatever your goal is, keep it uppermost in your mind as you turn to the final paragraphs. It's time to close the sale.

IMMEDIATE ACTION

When you farm by mail, the biggest hurdle for you to overcome isn't just "no," it's no answer at all.

With all good intentions, prospects may read your letter, follow it through to the conclusion, and agree 100%.

But you never hear from them.

If you don't have the right kind of close, it's easy for a prospect to tuck your reply card into a drawer — with all intentions of sending it in — and forget it.

For you, this is fatal. But it happens all the time.

How do you overcome it? By compelling prospects to act now!

Offers That Expire

There are two simple ways to add urgency to your offer. One is to limit the time during which it will be available; the other is to limit the quantity.

Here is the close in a letter from a mail order nursery using the limited-number approach.

"But I must caution you. I have only a limited number of these exceptional tulips, and when they're gone I won't have any more for another year. I urge you to send your order in today."

Here's a real estate example:

"I only have a limited number of these For Sale By Owner Kits available, and 'For Sale' signs are popping up all over town."

Now look at a limited-time offer:

"June is Home Protection Month here in Castle Pines, and I am only delivering Home-Protection Kits through the end of the month."

> I only have a limited number of these For Sale By Owner Kits available, and "for sale" signs are popping up all over town.
>
> Don't delay in ordering yours and miss out. Simply return the enclosed card, and I'll drop it by.

An immediate call to action is critical because often the biggest hurdle you have to overcome is not "no," but no answer at all.

Limited-time and limited-quantity offers have an urgency that helps increase your response rate.

"While You're Thinking About It"

Another popular closing technique addresses the problem of people's natural tendency to put things off:

"Order your free Home-Protection Kit now — while you're thinking about it. And know that you're giving your family complete security — and yourself, peace of mind."

This approach is not as strong as expiring offers. But it is much more believable; most readers will relate to it easily.

"While you're thinking about it" is often used with very personal offers, such as fund-raising for charities and insurance. But it also fits well with real estate farm offers such as for a home-protection or a fire-prevention kit.

Conclude Your Story

If you open with a story, your close should refer back to the story, tie it to the sales pitch and move the reader emotionally.

Here is the close to a fund-raising appeal from a children's cancer institute. The letter opened with the story of a little boy stricken with a very rare cancer. The story was especially emotional, since it was told by his parents.

The writer closed with:

"Little Jimmy Miller lost his four-year battle with cancer. But you would have been proud of him up to the end — he never gave up.

"Now it's your turn to carry his strong-willed spirit and put an end to childhood cancer once and for all.

"Your caring gift in his memory will . . ."

Reemphasize Exclusivity

While less strong than expiring offers, reemphasizing the exclusive nature of an offer may help motivate readers. In addition, you can always combine an appeal to exclusivity with other closing techniques:

"This offer is only for Castle Pines homeowners like you and may not be transferred to anyone else.

"I only have a limited number, so don't delay in returning your Reservation Card."

Phrases That Help You Close

Here is a handy reference guide to some words and phrases that may fit well into your closings:

Don't delay — Act now!

Why wait any longer?

Reserve your free Kit now, before they're all gone!

Order now while there's still time!

Do it today — Do it right now!

There's no time like right now to . . .

You need only pick up your phone . . .

I sincerely hope you'll join me . . .

It won't cost you a penny to mail the enclosed card today.

To take advantage of this free, limited-time offer, simply . . .

Go ahead, while you're thinking about it.

Reemphasize a Major Benefit

Just before or, ideally, during your close, you want to reemphasize the major benefit of your offer.

"You'll sleep just a little more soundly, knowing you've done all you can to protect your home. Don't delay — send for your free Crime-Prevention Kit right now."

"I'm sure that knowing the value of your home is important to you. While you're thinking about it, why don't you drop the enclosed card in the mailbox for a Free Home Evaluation?"

Both these examples use emotional language to link the reader to the offer's major benefit and make him or her more willing to act.

This offer is only for homeowners like you here in Castle Pines. It may not be transferred to anyone else.

Don't delay in ordering yours and miss out. Simply return the enclosed card and I'll drop it by.

Reemphasizing the exclusive nature of an offer may not compel the reader to respond, but it may increase the perceived value of the offer as well as pave the way for a stronger, limited-time appeal.

Tell Them How to Respond

What may be obvious to you is not always obvious to your readers. You must tell them step-by-step what they need to do to respond to your offer:

"To get your free Property Tax Update, simply drop the enclosed card in the mailbox. It costs you nothing, since I've already paid the postage."

"Or, if you like, pick up your phone and give me a call weekdays here at the office (555-1234) or evenings and weekends at home (555-9876)."

To get your free Property Tax Update, simply drop the enclosed card in the mailbox. It costs you nothing, since I've already paid the postage.

Or, if you like, pick up your phone and give me a call weekdays here at the office (555-1234) or evenings and weekends at home (555-9876).

However obvious you think it is, always tell readers exactly what they need to do in order to accept your offer.

Do not assume that your readers will know what to do just because you put a reply card in the envelope. If you do, you could spent a lot of time checking an empty mailbox.

SIGNING YOUR LETTER

Readers' eyes will go straight to the signature area of your letter. While debate rages about whether to be cute or colorful in the closing, nothing has been proven. A simple "Sincerely yours" is probably as good and as safe as any other close.

"Sincerely yours" is slightly preferred to plain "Sincerely," just because it gets back to "you-and-me" copy.

"Cordially yours" and "Cordially" are all right, but their common usage is waning.

There's nothing wrong with "Yours truly" if you're comfortable with it.

For some reason, many writers feel that the complimentary close is their last chance to be creative. Unfortunately, they usually end up sounding trite.

"Your partner for all your real estate needs" not only sounds corny, but distracts the reader and dilutes the final sales pitch.

As to the actual signature, try to write legibly. People are suspicious of signatures they can't read.

The complimentary close is your final personal message to the reader. Don't ruin it by being trite or cute. This will take away from your sales message during the most important closing seconds.

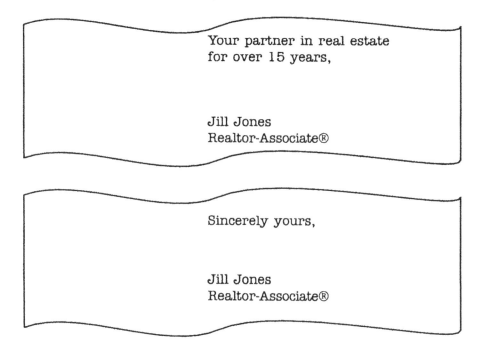

Your partner in real estate
for over 15 years,

Jill Jones
Realtor-Associate®

Sincerely yours,

Jill Jones
Realtor-Associate®

Always remember to type your name and title just beneath your signature.

Usually it's best to leave out the word "sales" (as in "salesperson") and "marketing" (as in "marketing representative").

If you are a member of the National Association of Realtors®, then "Realtor® or "Realtor-Associate® is good. If not, then "Real Estate Agent" or "Real Estate Broker" makes sense.

Traditionally, direct-mail letters are signed with a first and last name. However, if you're fortunate enough to know a majority of your farm on a first-name basis, sign with that.

Brief notes and follow-up correspondence are a different story. On these, only a first name signature is appropriate.

P. S. DON'T FORGET IT!

If your prospects read nothing else on the last page of your letter, they'll read the postscript, or P.S. Advertising studies have proven this for years.

So make your P.S. count.

Many of the same ideas presented for the closing paragraphs apply to your P.S. — if not more so. Urgency, exclusivity, restated benefits, additional benefits and special offers have all been used in good postscripts.

Here are a couple of samples:

"P.S. I urge you to place your reservation soon. We have only a few openings left, and I wouldn't want you to miss out."

"P.S. Don't forget the wealth of information you'll get with your FREE Home-Seller's Kit. Order yours today!"

"P.S. As a bonus gift I'll include a Free Home Tax Record Kit when you call to make an appointment."

Preprinted handwritten postscripts can be effective. But a couple of rules apply: (1) they should be neatly written and (2) they should not be very long (just a sentence or two).

A preprinted handwritten P.S. looks better if you print it in a second color other than black. Blue, for example, has been shown over the years to be the best second color to use on sales letters. This applies to preprinted signatures, too.

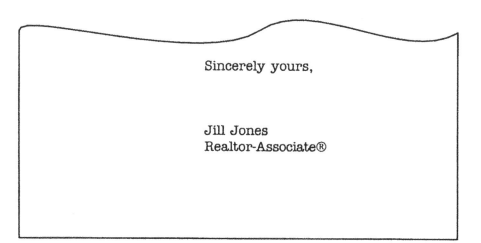

The P.S. is a golden opportunity to add further impact to your closing. You can use it to restate benefits, add urgency, promote exclusivity, show new benefits or do just about anything.

Furthermore, ad research shows that people scan the P.S. before anything else on the page. So you'd better make it strong!

Sincerely yours,

Jill Jones
Realtor-Associate®

Sincerely yours,

Jill Jones
Realtor-Associate®

P.S. There are no hidden strings attached to this FREE offer. Send for yours today before I run out.

You may consider printing some of your letters without postscripts, so you can add special handwritten ones to selected readers.

Whatever you do, never send a sales letter to your farm without including a postscript.

Points to Remember

Your close should motivate readers to act immediately.

Closing techniques:
- offer about to expire
  - limited time
  - limited quantity
- do it now — while you're thinking about it
- refer back to story that started letter
- reemphasize exclusivity

Phrases that help you close:
- Don't delay — Act now!
- Why wait any longer?
- Reserve your free Kit now, before they're all gone!
- Order now while there's still time!
- Do it today — do it right now!
- There's no time like right now to . . .
- You need only pick up your phone . . .
- I sincerely hope you'll join me . . .
- It won't cost you a penny to mail the enclosed card today.
- To take advantage of this free, limited-time offer, simply . . .
- Go ahead, while you're thinking about it . . .

Your close should:
- reemphasize your major benefit
- tell readers exactly what to do to respond
- avoid trite or cute signature closings. "Sincerely yours" is fine.
- have your first and last name
- have your typed name and title below your signature (avoid words like "sales" or "marketing")
- always have a P.S. Make it:
  - neatly written
  - short. No more than a sentence or two.

Consider printing the P.S. and signature in a second color, preferably blue.

SECTION THREE

Sample Direct Mail Letters

CHAPTER 11

FARMING BY MAIL

Now it's time for you to reach out to your farm.

To let them get to know you.

But probably more than a thousand people live in your farm. Meeting them individually would take weeks; maybe even years. And besides, how much chance is there that a handshake at the local little league game would pay off in a listing?

You think, "Not much." Then you shake your head.

Now think about what you can do. Think about something that most people look forward to every day. Something that lets you tell people who you are and what you can do for them. Something that takes your words right into people's living rooms. At a time that's convenient for them. In a gracious way that allows them to listen or not. If they're interested in what you have to say, they can talk about it with family members or friends. Or, you gulp, they can toss your words into the garbage can.

That's OK. You can take it. Not everyone will be interested in what you have to say. You knew that when you entered this business. But if you can reach those who are interested — and those who will be interested in the future — your own future will be taken care of.

You can do it. There's a great system already set up that will carry your message throughout your farm easily —

quickly — inexpensively.

Courtesy of the United States Postal Service, it's called direct mail.

WHAT IS DIRECT MAIL?

Direct marketing differs from other types of marketing in that it aims at an immediate sale. In the sample letters that follow, many of the "sale" offers are for free home evaluations, information kits and reference booklets. These are two-step offers, where you encourage a prospect to respond to one thing and plan to aim for something bigger later. In other letters, the "offer" is information: "call me if you have questions" is an example. Of course, this is weaker than offers of products or free services.

One of the fastest growing areas of direct marketing is direct mail. In *Guerrilla Marketing: Secrets for Making Big Profits From Your Small Business,* Jay Conrad Levinson describes studies showing that 60% of people usually read or scan direct mail; 31% read some of it; only 9% don't read any of it. That means you have a shot at reaching 91% of your audience with direct mail.

Look at the advantages of direct mail.

Targets Your Message	✔
Personal Medium	✔
Uncluttered Medium	✔
Full & Complete Message	✔
Pure Mathematics	✔
Tracked Response	✔

WHY DIRECT MAIL WORKS

Direct mail is unlike any other marketing tool. It has many advantages:

1. You can target your message.

If, for example, you have a listing on a two-bedroom condomimium that would be perfect for retirees, you can write a letter that describes why this would make a good home for older persons. Then you can send it only to people 65 or above who live in large homes in the neighborhood.

2. You can make your message personal.

Direct mail allows you to address prospects by name in the privacy of their own homes. With some software programs, you can even add personal remarks such as, "You've lived in your home for five years now. Are you thinking about moving up?"

3. You don't compete with other messages in the mailbox.

Once prospects open your letter — they read it without distractions.

4. You can present a total message.

Unlike television or radio, direct mail doesn't have time constraints. You can write as much or as little as you like. While costs do increase when you add brochures, lift notes and reply envelopes, these increases are minimal in proportion to a mailing's total cost.

5. You can see whether your message works.

Once a letter goes out, you'll know in a few weeks how well it worked. As long as you included an offer that invites prospects to contact you. If they mail back response cards, you keep track of how many cards you receive. If you use standard reply cards, you can track replies from individual mailings by putting different key codes on the reply cards. This is described further in Chapter 15. If someone calls instead, ask where they heard about you.

No other form of advertising allows you to measure your marketing as well. This is invaluable when you figure your marketing budget, as you can tell which efforts are paying off and allocate funds to continue or expand them.

Response tracking and testing is the cornerstone of traditional direct mail marketing.

6. Direct mail is cost effective.

If you receive just one listing from direct mail farming, your gross commission (let's estimate it at $5,000) would cover the costs of monthly mailings to a 1,000-home farm for an entire year!

ELEMENTS OF SUCCESS IN DIRECT MARKETING

How to Use the Sample Letters

The letters that follow are templates for you to adapt and use. Read them carefully and replace text that doesn't apply to your farm. Some of this text is marked; other text isn't. Be careful to eliminate every wrong reference. Each letter is followed by key points that highlight important aspects. You'll also notice that we've made notes for you, illustrating various parts of the letters.

Letters such as "Five Facts" require that you do research. Others, such as "Seminar," involve you in organizing a special event. Many letters offer information or reference kits.

You'll have to create these kits on your own. But don't worry. Local community groups will probably have many of the brochures and lists you need. You may have to write certain elements yourself, such as a list of local emergency phone numbers. But that won't be hard. Especially if you use a computer. Put a few of the kits together before sending a mailing. You want to make sure that you can deliver what you promise.

You'll find telephone scripts for most of the letters in our other book, *How To Farm Successfully — By Phone*. This gives you the flexibility of using either the mail or phone to make these appeals.

CONTENTS

Introductory Letters

Your farm map stretches across the wall behind you. Colored pins mark houses, stores, schools, hospitals, gas stations, listings. None of the listings are yours. But you know where they are...you know what's on the market...maybe by this time next year, half the green listing pins will be yours.

How?

The people who live in the area don't even know you've claimed them as your farm. Some may have seen your white Buick sedan driving slowly down their streets over the past week. But not one neighborhood homeowner knows who you are or what you do. Not one trusts you.

You pause. That's a sobering thought. Your livelihood...your hopes for the future...depend on people you've never met.

It's time. Time to introduce who you are, what you're about and what you can do for them.

This is how you start.

Introductory letters serve very particular purposes.

In the "Self-introduction" and "Broker's" letters, the goal is not to generate leads, but to pave the way for the next letter. In other words, to begin familiarizing prospects with who you are and what you can do for them. Think of it as the few remarks that accompany a handshake when you meet someone.

"Five Facts" makes a good follow-up, as it demonstrates that you're doing your homework on the farm.

"Survey" is the logical next step — you ask prospects for information about themselves. In other words, you say, "I want to get to know you better."

Finally, "Seminar" gives you the opportunity to meet your prospects face-to-face and discuss matters that highly concern them. For example, the value of their homes. The fact that this occurs in a community setting makes it less threatening for individuals. It also enables you to meet a number of farm residents at once.

If you've just started farming, consider following the above sequence in introducing yourself. If you've been farming for a while but want to revitalize and redirect your efforts, send out the "Survey" letter and follow it up with "Seminar."

With the exception of "Seminar," these direct mail packages have delayed benefits. They probably won't generate a large number of leads now, but they will pay off in the number of leads you get later.

SELF-INTRODUCTION

Type of farm: geographic or social

GREENBRIER REAL ESTATE
Barbara Kozlowski, Realtor-Associate®
90067 Carbondale Road * Campbell, NC 60056
(w) 704/555-8900 (h) 704/555-8897
(fax) 704/555-8901 (pager) 704/555-7703

Photo

IF YOU CARE ABOUT YOUR HOME AND ITS VALUE...please read

Always use a headline

January, 1996

Optional

Dear Castle Pines Neighbor,

How many times have you wondered what your home is worth? What the real estate market is like? How changes in the neighborhood are affecting your home's value?

Be specific. Count the "You's"!

Starting this week, you'll have someone to call for answers. Greenbrier Real Estate has just appointed me its Castle Pines representative. That means that I'll make it my business to know anything and everything related to your home's value. From what a house down the street lists for to the financial impact of the school board changing district boundaries. And I'm going to share it all with you.

Offer

I'm the person to call when...

...you hear rumors about the real estate market and you have questions,

...you see a "For Sale" sign on a property anywhere in town and you're interested,

...you're thinking — even down the road — about selling and would like to know your home's value,

...you're debating whether to remodel or sell and move up into the home of your dreams,

...you need trustworthy referrals for refinancing, property insurance or other home-related matters.

After completing a certified program and passing the state licensing exam, I began working in local real estate two years ago. Since then, my property sales have totaled more than a million dollars.

Support offer with your qualifications

(over, please)

Always use

Personal info.

Satisfied clients have included a number of families, "empty nest" couples, and single professionals. I've handled homes for computer scientists, medical doctors, flight attendants, university professors, retail employees, hair stylists, and retirees.

While I specialize in single family homes, I am very familiar with multi-unit dwellings and property management. Before entering real estate, I taught for six years at Brookhaven Elementary School in nearby Castleton.

Your company cares

I'm affiliated with Greenbrier Real Estate, one of the area's leading real estate companies. If you attend Little League games, you'll see "Greenbrier Real Estate" stitched across the back of the boys' uniforms. At the annual firefighters' breakfast, our agents stand behind the grill and whip up light and fluffy pancakes. All year long, 30 of us participate in fund-raising activities to help children fight disabilities at the local Easter Seals' Society.

Repeat offer and add free gift

Please remember that I'm available to help with all of your real estate needs. I hope that you'll find the enclosed map of Castle Pines useful.

Use of "yours" is good

Sincerely yours,

Barbara Kozlowski
Realtor-Associate®

Always have a P.S.

P.S. During weekdays, you can reach me at the office (555-8900). On evenings and weekends, call me at home (555-8897) or on my pager (555-7703).

KEY POINTS

1. Lists specific situations in which to call
2. Gives professional qualifications
3. Links agent to reputable, caring company
4. Offers front-end premium

OUTER ENVELOPE

Greenbrier Real Estate
90067 Carbondale Road
Campbell, NC 60056

> Bulk Rate
> US Postage
> P A I D
> Campbell, NC
> Permit No 1234

Repeat headline on outer envelope

IF YOU CARE ABOUT YOUR HOME AND ITS VALUE...please open

Mr. Joe Hill
458 Center St.
Castle Pines, NC 60057

REPLY CARD

Standardize your reply card and save $$$!

Photo

BARBARA, I WANT TO KNOW......
( ) what my home is worth
( ) more about the Castle Pines neighborhood
( ) more about your real estate services
( ) other _____

_____

Your Name _____

Your Address_____

_____

Your telephone number

(w)_____ (h)_____

Best time to call _____

BRE REPLY ENVELOPE

> NO POSTAGE
> NECESSARY
> IF MAILED
> IN THE
> UNITED STATES

BUSINESS REPLY MAIL
First Class PERMIT NO.000 Campbell, NC
Postage will be paid by Addressee

Greenbrier Real Estate
90067 Carbondale Road
Campbell, NC 60056

ATTN: Barbara Kozlowski

BROKER'S LETTER

Type of farm: geographic or social

GREENBRIER REAL ESTATE
Edward Reagan, Realtor®
90067 Carbondale Road * Campbell, NC 60056
(w) 704/555-8900 (h) 704/555-7756
(fax) 704/555-8901 (pager) 704/555-7890

FIND OUT ABOUT THE NEW ADDITION TO OUR NEIGHBORHOOD

Dear Castle Pines Neighbor,

I'm pleased to invite you to take advantage of the services offered by Barbara Kozlowski, our newly appointed specialist in Castle Pines homes.

This paragraph is a credibility builder

Over the past two years, Barbara has been a leading member of our real estate team. She can help determine the value of your property, assist you in pre-qualifying for a loan, find you a new home, guide you towards excellent investment opportunities, manage rental units for you, and, most important of all, sell your house quickly. If you have friends or colleagues relocating to this area, she can also help them.

Like all Greenbrier agents, Barbara prides herself on personal service and high quality performance. In her infrequent spare time, she's a great football fan and antiques shopper.

They'll be expecting you

In the next month or so, you'll be hearing more from Barbara. Please welcome her to our neighborhood.

Sincerely yours,

Edward Reagan
Realtor®

Offer is very low key

P.S. If you have immediate real estate needs, call Barbara directly at the office (555-8900) during the day or at home (555-8897) or on her pager (555-7706) evenings and weekends. Thank you!

KEY POINTS

1. Lists variety of real estate services.
2. Contains personal information.
3. Alerts them to expect communications directly from Barbara.
4. You could drop the P.S. and use this as a lift note in the self-introduction package. For an explanation of lift notes, see the "Five Facts" package.
5. Enclose Barbara's business card.

OUTER ENVELOPE

Greenbrier Real Estate
90067 Carbondale Road
Campbell, NC 60056

Bulk Rate
US Postage
P A I D
Campbell, NC
Permit No 1234

*HAVE YOU HEARD ABOUT THE NEW
ADDITION TO OUR NEIGHBORHOOD?*

Mr. Joe Hill
458 Center St.
Castle Pines, NC 60057

REPLY CARD

Photo

BARBARA, I WANT TO KNOW......
( ) what my home is worth
( ) more about the Castle Pines neighborhood
( ) more about your real estate services
( ) other _____
_____

Your Name _____

Your Address_____

_____

Your telephone number

(w)_____ (h)_____

Best time to call _____

BRE REPLY ENVELOPE

NO POSTAGE
NECESSARY
IF MAILED
IN THE
UNITED STATES

BUSINESS REPLY MAIL
First Class PERMIT NO.000 Campbell, NC
Postage will be paid by Addressee

Greenbrier Real Estate
90067 Carbondale Road
Campbell, NC 56

ATTN: Barbara Kozlowski

FIVE FACTS LETTER

Type of farm: geographic

GREENBRIER REAL ESTATE

Barbara Kozlowski, Realtor-Associate®

90067 Carbondale Road * Campbell, NC 60056

(w) 704/555-8900 (h) 704/555-8897

(fax) 704/555-8901 (pager) 704/555-7703

WHAT'S SPECIAL ABOUT WHERE YOU LIVE?

Dear Castle Pines Neighbor,

Notice the use of "you" throughout the letter

For the past few weeks, I've been researching our neighborhood. You might be interested in some facts I've uncovered....

** Castle Pines' first home was built in 1939, on land once known as the Simpson family farm. The Simpsons supplied wheat to bakeries across four counties. Their farm was split for development after Tony Simpson died.

Interesting, diverse facts

** The first Castle Pines' residents were the Taylors. They moved into a three-bedroom, two-bath home at the corner of Pine and Harbor streets. Samuel Taylor owned a small drugstore in nearby Medina.

** Today Castle Pines has 932 houses, 3 schools, 2 gas stations, and 1 hospital.

** Residents like you enjoy one of the lowest tax burdens in the state, as the local area keeps special assessments to a minimum.

** The Castle Pines high school football team has won state championships for 17 of the past 30 years; the girls' swim team won its first state championship last year.

Why am I so interested in Castle Pines? Because I think <u>it's a great place to live and I want to help great people find homes here</u>. People who'd make good neighbors for you and who'd care about our community.

Personalize

Over the next few months, you'll probably see my white Buick driving up and down the streets. I'm just getting to know this area and hopefully, homeowners such as yourself. I'm also keeping in touch with what's happening with the local homeowners' associations, city council, zoning board, school district and new construction. In other words, I'm making it my business to

(over, please)

know anything that affects the value of your home and our neighborhood.

As a professional real estate agent, service is what I do best. I'm always available to answer your questions and to help however I can. The more I know about this neighborhood — the more people I know who live here — the more I can contribute to helping maintain the special qualities of Castle Pines that first attracted you.

Offer

If you have any questions about Castle Pines or would like to talk about your real estate options, call me any time. You can reach me at the office (555-8900) during the day or at home (555-8897) or on my pager (555-7703) evenings and weekends. Thank you.

Repeat offer and make it easy for them

Sincerely yours,

Barbara Kozlowski
Realtor-Associate®

P.S. Please enjoy the enclosed notepad. Keep it by your phone and my number will always be at your fingertips.

Free gift!

KEY POINTS

1. Easy-to-find & interesting facts (history, sports, statistics, $$$$).

2. Immediately positions you as neighborhood expert.

3. "You" in almost every paragraph.

4. If you live in your farm area, tell them. Do it indirectly with something like, "People who'd make good neighbors for you and me..." or directly with "Because I live here — I think it's a great place to live..."

OUTER ENVELOPE

Greenbrier Real Estate
90067 Carbondale Road
Campbell, NC 60056

> Bulk Rate
> US Postage
> P A I D
> Campbell, NC
> Permit No 1234

What's special about where YOU live?

> Mr. Joe Hill
> 458 Center St.
> Castle Pines, NC 60057

LIFT LETTER

Lift letter (could be neat handwritten note or folded over note with teaser — "For Your Information")

Lift letters should be from someone with authority. In this case, preferably a locally well-known, satisfied former client. Other possibilities: mayor, city manager, softball coach, celebrity, bank president, teacher, your real estate broker, construction company owner, mechanic, anyone with local credibility. The key point is that they trust you and will say so in writing. You should draft the letter; let the person whose name will be on it review and sign it.

Dear Neighbor,

It gives me great pleasure to recommend Barbara Kozlowski as a Castle Pines real estate specialist. I've known Barbara for a number of years. In fact, she sold our home on Rocky Drive and helped us find our new home on Point Dickson Road last year.

I encourage you to turn to Barbara with all your real estate questions and concerns. She's not only a pro at her business, she really cares about her clients. From personal experience, I know that you can trust Barbara.

Given her commitment to our quality of life and the value of our neighborhood, you, I, and Castle Pines couldn't do better.

Sincerely,
James Dearborn
President
First National Bank

REPLY CARD

Photo

BARBARA, I WANT TO KNOW......
( ) what my home is worth
( ) more about the Castle Pines neighborhood
( ) more about your real estate services
( ) other _____

_____

Your Name _____

Your Address_____

_____

Your telephone number

(w)_____ (h)_____

Best time to call _____

BRE REPLY ENVELOPE

NO POSTAGE
NECESSARY
IF MAILED
IN THE
UNITED STATES

BUSINESS REPLY MAIL
First Class PERMIT NO.000 Campbell, NC
Postage will be paid by Addressee

Greenbrier Real Estate
90067 Carbondale Road
Campbell, NC 60056

ATTN: Barbara Kozlowski

FIVE FACTS LETTER

Type of farm: social

GREENBRIER REAL ESTATE
Barbara Kozlowski, Realtor-Associate®
90067 Carbondale Road * Campbell, NC 60056
(w) 704/555-8900 (h) 704/555-8897
(fax) 704/555-8901 (pager) 704/555-7703

WHAT'S SPECIAL ABOUT YOUR ST. JOHN'S CHURCH?

Dear fellow St. John's member,

For the past few weeks, I've been researching information about St. John's. As a member of the congregation, you might be interested in some facts I've uncovered...

** St. John's first church was built in 1932, about four blocks from the current building. Three years later, an early morning fire caused by faulty electrical wiring destroyed the structure. Rebuilding at the present site finished in 1936.

** St. John's was organized by a group of factory workers originally from New York. The first minister, Steven Early, arrived fresh out of Union Theological seminary. He stayed for 12 years.

** The Christ statue on the altar was carved by local artist Michael Wellington. He presented it to the church on its 25th anniversary in 1957.

** With 2,000 members, St. John's congregation today is the largest ever.

** The church's soup kitchen feeds lunch to an average of 300 hungry men, women and children five days a week, 52 weeks a year.

You care about St. John's church and so do I. That's why I'm writing. I want you and other St. John's members to have homes that are comfortable and inviting. A home which you can feel proud to open up for a church committee meeting or a youth group party. A home that gives you pleasure and joy. A home in which you can share many special moments with people you love.

(over, please)

Over the next few months, I'll be spending time getting to know you and other St. John members. You'll recognize me by my big brass nameplate. Please don't hesitate to come up and introduce yourself.

Have a name tag

I know what homes are worth, where to look for financing, how much increased value you can expect from remodeling, and who offers the best property insurance. I also am familiar with local homeowner associations, city councils, zoning regulations, school districts and new construction. In other words, I make it my business to know everything that affects your property and neighborhood values.

As a professional real estate agent, I'm always available to answer your questions and to help however I can. You can reach me at the office (555-8900) during the day or at home (555-8897) or on my pager (555-7703) evenings and weekends. Call any time. Thank you.

Low key offer

Sincerely yours,

Barbara Kozlowski
Realtor-Associate®

P.S. Please enjoy the enclosed notepad. Keep it by your phone and my number will always be at your fingertips.

KEY POINTS

1. Warm tone appropriate for readers.

2. Connects home to farm — i.e. can have church committee meeting or youth group party.

3. Describes identifying marker (brass nameplate).

4. Don't expect many calls from this letter — the goal is to build familiarity and prepare the way for the next letter.

OUTER ENVELOPE

Greenbrier Real Estate
90067 Carbondale Road
Campbell, NC 60056

| Bulk Rate |
| US Postage |
| P A I D |
| Campbell, NC |
| Permit No 1234 |

What's special about Your St. John's Church?

Mr. Joe Hill
458 Center St.
Castle Pines, NC 60057

LIFT LETTER

This letter should be from a client associated with St. John's such as a minister, Sunday School teacher, youth minister, or any well-liked and respected member of the congregation. You can draft it, then present it to the person for a signature and approval.

Give personal story

> *Dear St. John's Friend,*
> *It gives me great pleasure to recommend Barbara Kozlowski as a real estate specialist. I've known Barbara for a number of years. In fact, she sold our home on Rocky Drive and helped us find our new home on Point Dickson Road last year.*
> *I encourage you to turn to Barbara with all your real estate questions and concerns. She's not only a pro at her business, she really cares about her clients. From personal experience, I know that you can trust Barbara.*
> *Given her commitment to our quality of life and the values of our community, you and I couldn't do better.*
> *Sincerely,*
> *Kathy Longwell*
> *Teacher*
> *St. John's Sunday School*

REPLY CARD

Photo

BARBARA, I WANT TO KNOW......
( ) what my home is worth
( ) more about my real estate options
( ) more about your real estate services
( ) other _____
_____

Your Name _____

Your Address_____
_____

Your telephone number

(w)_____ (h)_____

Best time to call _____

Note the difference from a geographic farm.

BRE REPLY ENVELOPE

NO POSTAGE
NECESSARY
IF MAILED
IN THE
UNITED STATES

BUSINESS REPLY MAIL
First Class PERMIT NO.000 Campbell, NC
Postage will be paid by Addressee

Greenbrier Real Estate
90067 Carbondale Road
Campbell, NC 60056

ATTN: Barbara Kozlowski

SEMINAR LETTER

Type of farm: geographic or social

GREENBRIER REAL ESTATE
Barbara Kozlowski, Realtor-Associate®
90067 Carbondale Road * Campbell, NC 60056
(w) 704/555-8900 (h) 704/555-8897
(fax) 704/555-8901 (pager) 704/555-7703

IS YOUR HOME WORTH MORE THAN A YEAR AGO?

Here's how to find out...

Dear Castle Pines Neighbor,

Use present tense & active verbs

When you read in the papers about home construction trends and mortgage rate fluctuations, do you ever wonder what the national statistics mean for you personally? If new home sales are up, is it good or bad for you? If mortgage rates rise, is the value of your home affected?

Factors like these do influence your home's selling price. And your home's value is important. You're asked about it every time you fill out a credit application, apply for a loan or open a bank account. It only makes sense to treat your home as you would any other significant investment — by keeping yourself informed and following market trends that matter.

Offer

Underlining helps people read your letter quickly

On Thursday, October 7, I'm sponsoring <u>a seminar that will look specifically at the real estate market for Castle Pines homeowners.</u> I'll show you graphs that describe <u>what has happened to the value of your home over the past five years.</u> I'll explain how the neighborhood in general has been affected by new construction and improvements. We'll talk about changes in the quality of the school system, local services and shopping areas.

More about offer

In this "town hall" meeting, we'll also discuss <u>ways to improve the value of our properties — individually and collectively.</u> You'll have the chance to get feedback on how others have coped with problems similar to yours. That could be anything from keeping insects away from the garden to dealing with noisy neighbors. The point is that we'll have the chance to gather together and discuss issues important for maintaining the value of our most significant asset — our homes.

(over, please)

In one hour, you'll find out more about the value of your home than a year of reading about real estate trends in the newspaper would teach you. I'll also provide a hand-out that you can take home and keep for further reference.

For your convenience, the meeting will be in the Castle Pines Community Center recreation room. It will start at 7 p.m. and free child care will be provided. If you're planning to attend, I'd appreciate it if you'd fill out and return the enclosed R.S.V.P. card. Or you can call me at the office (555-8900) during the day or at home (555-8897) or on my pager (555-7703) evenings and weekends.

Make it easy for them to respond

Please — grab a pencil and pad of paper and join us. Finding out how much your home is really worth could make for a very pleasant evening.

Sincerely yours,

Barbara Kozlowski
Realtor-Associate®

P.S. Skip dessert that night — I'll have assorted cakes and hot coffee ready and waiting!

Added incentive

KEY POINTS

1. Emphasizes uniqueness of Castle Pines' real estate market.

2. Uses "you" and "we" a lot.

3. Offers free food & child care.

4. Depending on your farm's size, you may have to organize several seminars. Figure out how many the room will hold & invite 10 times that number.

5. Don't forget to prepare & distribute a hand-out.

REPLY CARD

Special R.S.V.P. reply card

> **Photo**
>
> *R. S. V. P.*
>
> YES, BARBARA, I plan to attend your October 7th seminar. I'm interested in finding out more about:
> ( ) my home's value ( ) school system
> ( ) property taxes ( ) other_____
> ( ) community improvements _____
> I will need child care: ( ) Yes ( ) No
>
> Your Name _____
> Your Address_____
> _____
> Your telephone number
> (w)_____ (h)_____
> Best time to call _____

BRE REPLY ENVELOPE

> NO POSTAGE
> NECESSARY
> IF MAILED
> IN THE
> UNITED STATES
>
> **BUSINESS REPLY MAIL**
> First Class PERMIT NO.000 Campbell, NC
> Postage will be paid by Addressee
>
> Greenbrier Real Estate
> 90067 Carbondale Road
> Campbell, NC 60056
>
> ATTN: Barbara Kozlowski

THANK YOU NOTE (Handwritten or typed)

March 31, 1996

Les and Mary Brown
8993 Butterfield Drive
Castle Pines, NC 60056

Dear Les and Mary,

Thank you very much for attending the real estate seminar last night.

I hope that you found the seminar informative and worthwhile. If you have any questions about your property specifically, I'd be glad to stop by. Just give me a call at my office (555-8900) during the day or at home (555-8897) or on my pager (555-7703) evenings and weekends.

People like you make working in Castle Pines a real pleasure.

Sincerely,

Barbara Kozlowski
Realtor-Associate®

Only use first names if you're comfortable with them

Get these in the mail the next day

(NOTE: IF POSSIBLE, ADD A COMMENT DIRECTED SPECIFICALLY TO THE PERSON. FOR EXAMPLE, "I thought your questions about property taxes were excellent." or "It was interesting to see how many neighbors agreed with you about road problems.")

TIPS FOR PRESENTATION:

Prepare a 20-minute presentation with lots of colorful figures and tables. For pointers, watch talk shows such as "Oprah" or "Donahue" to see how to get your audience involved in the discussion.

Before you begin, make sure everyone fills out and puts on a name tag. Pass around a sign-up sheet asking for names, addresses, phone numbers and specific areas of concern.

Have pictures, graphs and figures prominently displayed.

1. Create large, easy-to-see tables and graphs that...

    a. trace the value of homes in your farm area over the past five years,

    b. list five factors that have significantly affected property values,

    c. list number of homes on market last year and average selling price compared to number of homes on market this year. Compare upper and lower end selling prices.

2. Have a local real estate finance expert talk briefly about new types of mortgages, refinancing, home equity lines of credit, etc. You also may want a property insurance representative or an investment counselor to make a brief presentation. Select speakers who'd address issues of concern to the community. For example, if a new development is planned nearby, you may want to invite a developer or city official who can discuss its impact on the surrounding area.

3. Project future property value trends for the next few years.

4. Prepare one-page summary sheet that they can take home. Distribute at end of presentation so they're not reading it as you're talking.

5. Allow time for questions and answers at end of presentations.

6. Be sure to provide child care and food.

TIPS FOR ORGANIZING DISCUSSION

1. Prepare 15-20 questions. Avoid yes/no questions; ask open-ended ones.

2. Select three or four people that you know will attend and prepare them with questions to ask you.

3. Allow audience members to raise issues of concern but keep discussion focused on those related to property values. Don't be afraid to step in and change topics.

4. Have a colleague in the audience take extensive notes on the discussion (or if possible, tape record it). This will give you a record of important homeowner concerns towards which you can direct future marketing efforts.

SURVEY LETTER

Type of farm: geographic

Survey

Conducting a mail or telephone survey of residents in your farm offers three big advantages:

1. It positions you as an agent who takes people's needs seriously and is willing to listen to them,

2. It gives you credibility by demonstrating your use of a highly valued, somewhat sophisticated research tool,

3. It gives you information that can help you create effective, targeted marketing materials for months to come.

The biggest problem in a survey is making sure that people fill out and return them. But you can help increase response rates by including BRE envelopes and doing at least one follow-up mailing to those who don't respond. Schedule your follow-up mailing two weeks after the initial mailing. Remember to delete those who responded.

Keep questionnaires short and easy-to-understand, with broad white margins at the top, bottom and sides. Make sure the print is large enough to read easily.

Always include a cover letter that identifies your survey as a legitimate research instrument.

Remember to keep track of your responses.

GREENBRIER REAL ESTATE
Barbara Kozlowski, Realtor-Associate®
90067 Carbondale Road * Campbell, NC 60056
(w) 704/555-8900 (h) 704/555-8897
(fax) 704/555-8901 (pager) 704/555-7703

CASTLE PINES HOMEOWNERS SURVEY

Questions are good openers

Dear Castle Pines Neighbor,

Did you know that you live in a community where the average annual income is $35,000 and the average home costs $156,000?

<u>Would you like to know more?</u>

You're not alone

It's Quick!

It's Private

Rationale

I'm enclosing a survey being mailed to all Castle Pines residents. You'll see that it's very simple. You can finish it in about five minutes. The results are confidential. No one will ever know what you wrote. With the information you and other Castle Pines homeowners provide, a profile will emerge. That's very important in determining what real estate services Castle Pines residents need most. It also will increase our understanding of <u>what attracts people like you to this neighborhood.</u>

Urge immediate action

Please take a few minutes right now to complete the survey. Then mail it back in the envelope provided.

If you have any questions, call me at my office (555-8900) during the day or at home (555-8897) or on my pager (555-7703) evenings and weekends. The kitchen magnet is a small thank you gift for your participation.

Free gift

Sincerely yours,

Barbara Kozlowski
Realtor-Associate®

Your reason to drop by their house

P.S. If you'd like a summary of the results, please check the box at the bottom of the survey. I'll rush them to you as soon as they're ready!

KEY POINTS
1. Short letter.
2. Offers interesting facts to grab attention.
3. Free gift (could instead give a quarter as a premium. Everyone loves $$$$ — J.D. Powers, for example, includes a dollar with its questionnaires).
4. Promises confidentiality.
5. HAND DELIVER SURVEY RESULTS TO THOSE WHO REQUEST THEM.

SURVEY LETTER

Type of farm: social

Photo

GREENBRIER REAL ESTATE
Barbara Kozlowski, Realtor-Associate®
90067 Carbondale Road * Campbell, NC 60056
(w) 704/555-8900 (h) 704/555-8897
(fax) 704/555-8901 (pager) 704/555-7703

SEACOAST SAILING CLUB SURVEY

Dear Seacoast Sailing Club Member,

Did you know that you belong to a club where the average member charters a sailboat once every six months and takes one sailing vacation a year?

<u>Would you like to know more?</u>

I'm enclosing a survey being mailed to all Seacoast Sailing Club members. It concerns your real estate needs. You'll see that it's very simple. You can finish it in about five minutes. The results are confidential. No one will ever know what you wrote. With the information you and other Seacoast Sailing Club members provide, a profile will emerge. That's very important in determining what <u>real estate services club members need most.</u>

Please take a few minutes right now to complete the survey. Then mail it back in the envelope provided.

If you have any questions, call me at my office (555-8900) during the day or at home (555-8897) or on my pager (555-7703) evenings and weekends. The kitchen magnet is a small thank you gift for your participation.

Sincerely yours,

Barbara Kozlowski
Realtor-Associate®

P.S. If you'd like a summary of the results, please check the box at the bottom of the survey. You'll get them as soon as they're ready!

FOLLOW-UP LETTER

Type of farm: geographic

GREENBRIER REAL ESTATE
Barbara Kozlowski, Realtor-Associate®
90067 Carbondale Road * Campbell, NC 60056
(w) 704/555-8900 (h) 704/555-8897
(fax) 704/555-8901 (pager) 704/555-7703

CASTLE PINES HOMEOWNERS SURVEY

Dear Castle Pines Neighbor,

Be direct

Several weeks ago, I sent you a Castle Pines Homeowners Survey. I haven't heard from you and since <u>this survey is very important,</u> I'm sending you another. I hope that you'll take a few minutes to fill it out.

This survey is being mailed to all Castle Pines residents. Your answers are confidential. No one will ever know what you wrote. With the information you and other Castle Pines homeowners provide, a profile will emerge. That's very important in determining what real estate services Castle Pines residents need most. It also will increase our understanding of what attracts people like you to this neighborhood.

Adds urgency

Please while you're thinking of it, complete the survey right now. Then mail it back in the envelope provided. I've already taken care of the postage.

Another free gift

If you have any questions, call me at my office (555-8900) during the day or at home (555-8897) or on my pager (555-7703) evenings and weekends. The quarter is a small thank you gift for your participation.

Sincerely yours,

Barbara Kozlowski
Realtor-Associate®

P.S. If you'd like a summary of the results, please check the box at the bottom of the survey. I'll rush them to you as soon as they're ready!

KEY POINTS

1. Offers new premium.

FOLLOW-UP LETTER

Type of farm: social

Photo

GREENBRIER REAL ESTATE
Barbara Kozlowski, Realtor-Associate®
90067 Carbondale Road * Campbell, NC 60056
(w) 704/555-8900 (h) 704/555-8897
(fax) 704/555-8901 (pager) 704/555-7703

SEACOAST SAILING CLUB SURVEY

Dear Seacoast Sailing Club Member,

Several weeks ago, I sent you a survey being mailed to all Seacoast Sailing Club members. I haven't heard from you and since <u>this survey is very important,</u> I'm sending you another. I hope that you'll take a few minutes to fill it out.

Remember that your answers are confidential. No one will ever know what you wrote. With the information you and other sailing club members provide, a profile will emerge. That's very important in determining what real estate services club members need most.

Please while you're thinking of it, complete the survey right now. Then mail it back in the envelope provided. I've already taken care of the postage.

If you have any questions, call me at my office (555-8900) during the day or at home (555-8897) or on my pager (555-7703) evenings and weekends. The quarter is a small thank you gift for your participation.

Sincerely yours,

Barbara Kozlowski
Realtor-Associate®

P.S. If you'd like a summary of the results, please check the box at the bottom of the survey. I'll rush them to you as soon as they're ready!

KEY POINTS

1. Offers new premium.

CASTLE PINES HOMEOWNERS SURVEY

I'm trying to learn as much as I can from Castle Pines homeowners so I can offer the best possible real estate services. Please take a few minutes to fill out this questionnaire. Your answers will be confidential. Thank you for helping.

1. Year purchased current home: _____

2. Year purchased first home: _____

3. Number of homes owned in lifetime: _____

4. Number of adults living in home: _____

5. Number of children in home: _____

6. Favorite shopping area: _____

7. Favorite restaurant: _____

8. Children's school(s): _____
_____

9. Do you use public recreation areas? ( ) Yes ( ) No

If yes, which ones? _____

10. Do you use public transportation? ( ) Yes ( ) No

11. Biggest neighborhood advantages:

(1) _____

(2) _____

(3) _____

12. Biggest neighborhood drawbacks:

(1) _____

(2) _____

(3) _____

13. What are your favorite features of your home?

(1) _____

(2) _____

(3) _____

14. How much longer do you expect to live in it? _____

15. Your occupation: _____

16. Occupations of other adults in home: _____
_____

17. Street address: _____
_____

( ) YES, I'd like the survey results.

Please return in the envelope provided to Barbara Kozlowski, Realtor-Associate®, Greenbrier Real Estate, 90067 Carbondale Road, Campbell, NC 60056.

KEY POINTS

This survey will give you the following information which you should enter into your file for each farm resident:

1. Home buying habits,

2. How crowded the home is,

3. Neighborhood pluses,

4. Neighborhood drawbacks,

5. Home's special features,

6. When they're thinking about moving.

OUTER ENVELOPE

```
Greenbrier Real Estate                          Bulk Rate
90067 Carbondale Road                          US Postage
Campbell, NC 60056                               P A I D
                                               Campbell, NC
                                              Permit No 1234

                   Your Special Survey Enclosed

          Mr. Joe Hill
          458 Center St.
          Castle Pines, NC 60057
```

BRE REPLY ENVELOPE

```
                                              NO POSTAGE
                                              NECESSARY
                                               IF MAILED
                                                IN THE
                                             UNITED STATES

        BUSINESS REPLY MAIL
   First Class PERMIT NO.000 Campbell, NC
   Postage will be paid by Addressee

                Greenbrier Real Estate
                90067 Carbondale Road
                Campbell, NC 60056

   ATTN: Barbara Kozlowski
```

General Letters

You're sitting in your office on a sunny spring afternoon. You've checked the front desk for messages and found only two. One from a 35-year-old dental hygienist who bought a condo from you a few months ago. She has questions about property insurance. The other was from a "Mr. Mikas" about a property you'd advertised. You call them back. As you introduce yourself to Mr. Mikas, you allow a note of anticipation to creep into your voice. You hide your disappointment when it turns out that he doesn't like the location. You give him your number for future reference and say good-bye.

When you hang up, you take a minute to reflect. What can you do to pick up your business? You're busy all day long...but the activity isn't producing many sales.

What's the answer? Slow down. Focus your energy. Start working smart.

Do only what will pay off for you.

Begin by sending letters like these to your farm.

General letters touch on an area of interest to all homeowners — the local real estate market and its effect on the value of their home. The first two, "Good times" and "Bad times" give local angles to national trends. They provide you with offers whether the market is heading up or going down. What's important in them is their logic. Look at it closely.

"Story" is a heart-tugger. Use it only as an example. In thinking of your own story, don't be content with the "typical." Think of the most dramatic home sale you've been involved in. Think of the people you liked the most. Think of how the sale affected you personally. What really pulled at you emotionally? Chances are that if it made you feel strongly, it'll do the same for your readers.

"Annual Report" is a terrific direct mail package. To minimize your preparation time, update your farm real estate records monthly. You should do this anyway, as it will enhance the professionalism of your listing presentations and face-to-face meetings. You can mail the "Annual Report" any time of the year, although most similar reports are issued in June, September, December or January. Just be sure you cover a 12-month period.

GOOD TIMES LETTER

Type of farm: geographic or social

GREENBRIER REAL ESTATE
Barbara Kozlowski, Realtor-Associate®
90067 Carbondale Road * Campbell, NC 60056
(w) 704/555-8900 (h) 704/555-8897
(fax) 704/555-8901 (pager) 704/555-7703

NOW MAY BE THE BEST TIME EVER TO OWN YOUR DREAM HOUSE

Dear Castle Pines Neighbor,

Personalize

Even if the thought has only briefly crossed your mind, now might be the best time to <u>move up to that home you've always dreamed about.</u> Interest rates are as low as they've been for a while and Castle Pines property values are on the rise.

As a homeowner, this gives you two benefits. First, you'll find it easier to finance your dream house. Second, prospective buyers will find it easier to finance their purchase of your home.

<u>Plus — buyer demand is great right now!</u>

Be truthful. Give your own example.

In fact, we're experiencing such high demand for Castle Pines homes that we've had to turn away several prospective buyers. Just last week an attorney stopped by the office looking for a home like yours — and I couldn't help her.

Quite simply, I can't find enough listings to meet buyer demand.

Good incentive

You and I know that it's unlikely interest rates will stay this favorable for long. In fact, some economists predict an increase by the end of the year.

<u>So why wait — and miss a golden opportunity?</u>

At least consider the possibilities. You have a highly desirable home and the real estate market has seldom been better.

I'd love the chance to sit down with you informally and discuss your options. I could also bring some pic-

(over, please)

tures so you could see what other homes are on the market right now.

If you're interested in getting together — and, of course, there's no obligation whatsoever — simply fill out the enclosed postage-paid card and drop it in the mail. Or give me a call at the office (555-8900) during the day or at my home (555-8897) or pager (555-7706) evenings and weekends.

Medium sell is better than hard sell

It costs you nothing to find out if the home you've always dreamed about lies within your reach. Why not call me today?

Sincerely yours,

Barbara Kozlowski
Realtor-Associate®

P.S. Refinancing is another smart move now. I can put you in touch with local lenders. Give me a call.

Adds a twist

KEY POINTS

1. "You" is emphasized.

2. Personalizes facts.

3. Easy to respond.

OUTER ENVELOPE

Don't miss out!

Greenbrier Real Estate
90067 Carbondale Road
Campbell, NC 60056

Bulk Rate
US Postage
P A I D
Campbell, NC
Permit No 1234

**Now may be the best time ever to own your
dream house**

Mr. Joe Hill
458 Center St.
Castle Pines, NC 60057

REPLY CARD

*Standard reply card saves
you $$$!*

Photo

BARBARA, I WANT TO KNOW......
( ) what my home is worth
( ) more about real estate options
( ) more about your real estate services
( ) other _____

_____

Your Name _____

Your Address_____

_____

Your telephone number

(w)_____ (h)_____

Best time to call _____

BRE REPLY ENVELOPE

NO POSTAGE
NECESSARY
IF MAILED
IN THE
UNITED STATES

BUSINESS REPLY MAIL
First Class PERMIT NO.000 Campbell, NC
Postage will be paid by Addressee

Greenbrier Real Estate
90067 Carbondale Road
Campbell, NC 60056

ATTN: Barbara Kozlowski

BAD TIMES LETTER

Type of farm: geographic or social

GREENBRIER REAL ESTATE
Barbara Kozlowski, Realtor-Associate®
90067 Carbondale Road * Campbell, NC 60056
(w) 704/555-8900 (h) 704/555-8897
(fax) 704/555-8901 (pager) 704/555-7703

IS THE REAL ESTATE MARKET
READY TO COLLAPSE?

June, 1996

Dear Castle Pines Neighbor,

Almost every week you read something about how bad the real estate market is. But quite frankly, <u>you can't always believe what you read.</u> *Arouses interest*

Yes, interest rates are up and home sales have slowed. But the fact is that <u>good, well-marketed homes sell every day.</u> *Truth*

Helping the market is the growth of adjustable rate mortgages (ARMs). Compared to fixed rate mortgages, ARMs offer lower initial interest rates which make monthly payments more affordable. *Support argument 1*

Also helping the market are rent increases driven by higher demand for rental units. Over the past few weeks, rent hikes have brought at least a dozen people into my office. They figure that with the amount they pay in rent, they could easily handle monthly mortgage payments. And they're right. *Support argument 2*

If you consider the market from these viewpoints, today isn't such as bad time to sell a home — as long as circumstances (such as a job transfer) don't force you to move immediately. *Conclusion*

And if you're looking to buy, a number of excellent opportunities have been created by people who do have to sell immediately. These sellers often will be flexible in negotiating and possibly help with financing. *Effect of conclusion*

So the next time you read or hear that times are tough for home sales, remember what I said. *"I'm" telling the truth*

(over, please)

So don't wait!

Offer

Why not do it?

Adds twist

> And if you're thinking about making a move or taking advantage of some of the great buys on today's market, I'd love to sit down and discuss it with you.
>
> To set up an informal meeting — of course, there's no obligation whatsoever — simply fill out the enclosed postage-paid card and drop it in the mail. Or give me a call at the office (555-8900) or at my home (555-8897) or on my pager (555-7706).
>
> It costs you nothing to find out what the market offers you. And it might be worth quite a bit. Why not call me today?
>
> Sincerely yours,
>
> Barbara Kozlowski
> Realtor-Associate®
>
> P.S. I also have references for local contractors, repair services, landscape designers and others that you might find useful. Give me a call today!

KEY POINTS

1. Gets beneath surface of "facts."

2. Presents opportunities.

3. Makes it easy to respond.

OUTER ENVELOPE

Greenbrier Real Estate
90067 Carbondale Road
Campbell, NC 60056

> Bulk Rate
> US Postage
> P A I D
> Campbell, NC
> Permit No 1234

IS THE REAL ESTATE MARKET READY TO COLLAPSE?

> Mr. Joe Hill
> 458 Center St.
> Castle Pines, NC 60057

REPLY CARD

Photo

BARBARA, I WANT TO KNOW......
( ) what my home is worth
( ) more about real estate options
( ) more about your real estate services
( ) other _____

_____

Your Name _____

Your Address_____

_____

Your telephone number

(w)_____ (h)_____

Best time to call _____

BRE REPLY ENVELOPE

> NO POSTAGE
> NECESSARY
> IF MAILED
> IN THE
> UNITED STATES

BUSINESS REPLY MAIL
First Class PERMIT NO.000 Campbell, NC
Postage will be paid by Addressee

Greenbrier Real Estate
90067 Carbondale Road
Campbell, NC 60056

ATTN: Barbara Kozlowski

STORY LETTER

Type of farm: geographic or social

THIS LETTER IS AN EXAMPLE ONLY. RE-WRITE IT WITH YOUR CLIENT'S STORY. BE SURE TO GET CLIENT'S APPROVAL FIRST.

Suggested structure: Description of person.

Description of house.

Personal history.

Problem behind listing.

How you could help resolve that problem.

Specifics of how you helped.

Client's situation today.

How you'd like to help other clients.

GREENBRIER REAL ESTATE

Barbara Kozlowski, Realtor-Associate®

90067 Carbondale Road * Campbell, NC 60056

(w) 704/555-8900 (h) 704/555-8897

(fax) 704/555-8901 (pager) 704/555-7703

Dear Castle Pines Neighbor,

Arturo Rodriquez has thick, dark hair, a stocky build and eyes that crinkle at the corners when he talks. His warm smile tells you he is a gentle man. Not long ago, Arturo was trapped in a situation that's especially difficult for gentle people. It involved the home where he had lived for 43 years. The home his parents had bought in a flush of optimism after World War II. The home in which he knew every ceiling crack, every sticky doorknob, every creaky floorboard.

The well-worn house gleamed with care. In the dining room, the unpainted wood had mellowed to a soft honey. In the kitchen, heavy cabinet doors swung open comfortably on their hinges. Arturo's favorite spot was the stairway landing. In mid-afternoon, sunlight spilled through a high, small stained glass window made by his mother and splintered into a rainbow of purple, blue and green on the fading peach carpet.

Arturo's parents had both died eight years before I met him. In their photographs, they stood tall and dignified. If you looked closely, you could see how much Arturo's eyes resembled his mother's. Thrifty and

(over, please)

Use this only as an example

Think of your own dramatic story

hard-working, they had left Arturo, their only child, several thousand dollars and the home. Arturo didn't worry much about money. He had a middle level management job at a local company and felt secure. But then his roof started leaking...his furnace went out...and a neighborhood kid put a baseball through the floor-to-ceiling living room window. Bills piled up. At the same time, Arturo's company hit a slump. He was laid off.

Arturo called me one hot July afternoon. We sat on the front porch, sipping iced tea and enjoying the roses that his mother had planted 30 years earlier. Although he spoke softly, I could hear desperation behind his words. He had sent out 125 resumes and received no interviews. A few friends had mentioned possibilities, but nothing worked out. He read the classified ads every day. He planned to sign up for a community college computer class, but it didn't start until September. In the meantime, the house needed more and more repairs. Arturo couldn't keep up with it. Selling would break his heart, but he saw no other options.

After we finished talking, Arturo and I walked through the house. He obviously was very unhappy and upset about his decision. In the economic downturn, I had helped other people in similar situations. It always distressed me. But I had also seen how often these people survived the sales of their homes and wound up in better places, both financially and in terms of their living arrangements. Constant financial pressure from a high mortgage or expensive repairs can be extremely stressful. Arturo and I didn't talk yet about what he would do when the home sold...that would come later.

I told Arturo that he could probably get about $135,000 for the house. He signed the papers that evening. I showed the house three times. The third group, a young couple with a small baby, made an acceptable offer. Artruo's hand shook as he agreed to it. Within 90 days, he would have to leave the only home he had known.

I helped Arturo find a condominium about five miles away. With his profit, he took time off to re-educate himself. He started with the computer class and went on to more advanced business classes. Today Arturo is continuing his education while moving quickly ahead on the fast track at a growing high-tech company.

(over, please)

I think Arturo's parents would be very proud of him. The home they loved and cared for gave their son a new lease on life. I know that leaving it was hard for Arturo. But today a new couple — and a new family — are building new memories around the stained glass window...the roses blooming by the front door...the cabinets that hang softly on their hinges.

Offer

Selling a home is a transaction that involves opportunity, emotional risk and lifestyle change. During this stressful process, it helps to have someone by your side who not only understands the financial and marketing aspects, but who can empathize with your personal feelings and struggles.

Goes back to beginning

Please...if you're thinking about buying or selling a home...let me help you as I helped Arturo.

Sincerely yours,

Barbara Kozlowski
Realtor-Associate®

Warm copy

P.S. Call anytime. During business hours, try the office (555-8900) first. On evenings and weekends, you can find me either at home, (555-8897), or on my pager, (555-7703).

OUTER ENVELOPE

Greenbrier Real Estate
90067 Carbondale Road
Campbell, NC 60056

> Bulk Rate
> US Postage
> P A I D
> Campbell, NC
> Permit No 1234

> Mr. Joe Hill
> 458 Center St.
> Castle Pines, NC 60057

REPLY CARD

Photo

BARBARA, I WANT TO KNOW......
( ) what my home is worth
( ) more about my real estate options
( ) more about your real estate services
( ) other _____
_____

Your Name _____

Your Address_____

_____

Your telephone number

(w)_____ (h)_____

Best time to call _____

BRE REPLY ENVELOPE

> NO POSTAGE
> NECESSARY
> IF MAILED
> IN THE
> UNITED STATES

BUSINESS REPLY MAIL

First Class PERMIT NO.000 Campbell, NC
Postage will be paid by Addressee

Greenbrier Real Estate
90067 Carbondale Road
Campbell, NC 60056

ATTN: Barbara Kozlowski

ANNUAL REPORT
Geographic or social farm

GREENBRIER REAL ESTATE
Barbara Kozlowski, Realtor-Associate®
90067 Carbondale Road * Campbell, NC 60056
(w) 704/555-8900 (h) 704/555-8897
(fax) 704/555-8901 (pager) 704/555-7703

CASTLE PINES ANNUAL REAL ESTATE REPORT

Dear Castle Pines Neighbor,

Emphasizes importance

With this letter, you'll find <u>a complete record of real estate listing and sales in our neighborhood over the past year.</u> Please keep it with your important papers, as it can help document recent changes in the value of your home.

Higher interest rates slowed the market last January, but the economic upturn in June had an impact on home sales. From August through December, sales slowly but steadily increased. <u>Throughout the year, 39 Castle Pines homes sold at an average price of $183,000. About half sold either at their full listing price or within $10,000 of it. Homes stayed on the market an average of five weeks.</u> The fact that such a large percentage sold at or near their listed prices and that they sold in a relatively short time indicate that the slump in the Castle Pines real estate market is over.

This information is valuable to your readers

All together, 43 Castle Pines homes were listed during 1996. Only 2 of these homes were taken off the market unsold. Much of the real estate activity centered on the Pine Knoll area of Castle Pines, although listings existed in every neighborhood. <u>Greenbrier Real Estate was involved in 45% of the Castle Pines sales.</u>

Plug your company

Enclosed is a report of Castle Pines homes which sold, came under contract or were put on the market last year. For those homes where the transaction is complete, I've included both the listing price and the actual selling price. For listed homes and those under contract, you'll find the asking price.

Doesn't hurt to ask

If anyone is interested, on the market right now is <u>a charming starter home</u> at 456 Rockaway Drive. With 3 bedrooms, 1 bath and a large yard, it's listed at only $129,500 and perfect for a new family. Also available

(over, please)

is a <u>dramatic English Tudor</u> home at 245 Wind Crest Circle with 4 bedrooms, 2 baths and a fragrant rose garden. Drive by and see how lovely it is. At $295,000, you'd get a real bargain.

As you look through the enclosed list, keep an eye out for homes like yours. The prices will give you a very general approximation of your home's worth. Don't rely on this as anything more than a guideline. How well a home is maintained, its layout, decor and added features can make a huge difference in its value.

Offer

<u>If you want to find out specifically how much your home is worth, give me a call.</u> I'd be happy to stop by, look at it, and present you with an analysis based on the actual selling prices of comparable homes in your area. Because I've seen most, if not all, of the homes on the market this year, I'll know which ones are most similar to yours. You can reach me at 704/555-8900 (office) during the day or at 704/555-8897 (home) or 704/555-7703 (pager) evenings and weekends. Of course, <u>you'd be under no obligation.</u>

Rationale

Over the past year the average selling price of a Castle Pines home has increased by $8,000. That means <u>your home has probably appreciated at least 4% in just 12 months.</u> You and I are fortunate to live in an area where the real estate market is on the upswing.

Sincerely yours,

Barbara Kozlowski
Realtor-Associate®

P.S. Call me if you have questions about the Castle Pines Real Estate market in general, your own home or any of the properties on the list.

KEY POINTS

1. Make this businesslike & detailed.
2. Can change appeal — keep in or delete paragraph with properties now on market/ keep in or delete paragraph offering home evaluation.
3. Double-check your numbers for accuracy.
4. You can send this any time of the year — just make sure that the homes included go back 12 months.
5. To make this easy, keep monthly records on listings, sales, homes taken off market, etc.
6. Adapt for social farm by focusing on entire city or county rather than one neighborhood.

Keep these figures monthly and preparing the report will be a snap!

1995 CASTLE PINES REAL ESTATE REPORT

Photo

Prepared by: GREENBRIER REAL ESTATE
Barbara Kozlowski, Realtor-Associate®
90067 Carbondale Road * Campbell, NC 60056
(w) 704/555-8900 (h) 704/555-8897
(fax) 704/555-8901 (pager) 704/555-7703

REAL ESTATE ACTIVITY IN GENERAL (January, 1995-December, 1995)

Average selling price:

Percentage of homes sold at
full listing price or within 10%:

Number of weeks average home on market:

Total number of listed homes:

Number of listed homes
taken off market unsold:

Number of Greenbrier real estate
listings in Castle Pines:

REAL ESTATE ACTIVITY BY SPECIFIC HOMES

SETTLED

Address	Bedrooms/ Baths	List Price	Actual Days on Market	Mo. Sold	Style

UNDER CONTRACT

Address	Bedrooms/ Baths	List Price	Actual Days on Market	Mo. Sold	Style

LISTED

Address	Bedrooms/ Baths	List Price	Actual Days on Market	Mo. Sold	Style

(Create key for style abbreviations and place at end)

OUTER ENVELOPE

Greenbrier Real Estate
90067 Carbondale Road
Campbell, NC 60056

> Bulk Rate
> US Postage
> P A I D
> Campbell, NC
> Permit No 1234

Castle Pines Annual Real Estate Report

Mr. Joe Hill
458 Center St.
Castle Pines, NC 60057

REPLY CARD

Photo

BARBARA, I WANT TO KNOW......
( ) what my home is worth
( ) more about real estate options
( ) more about your real estate services
( ) other _____
_____

Your Name _____

Your Address_____

_____

Your telephone number

(w)_____ (h)_____

Best time to call _____

BRE REPLY ENVELOPE

> NO POSTAGE
> NECESSARY
> IF MAILED
> IN THE
> UNITED STATES

BUSINESS REPLY MAIL
First Class PERMIT NO.000 Campbell, NC
Postage will be paid by Addressee

Greenbrier Real Estate
90067 Carbondale Road
Campbell, NC 60056

ATTN: Barbara Kozlowski

HOME EVALUATION OFFER

Type of market: geographic or social

Perhaps the more common direct mail offer in real estate is for a free home evaluation. While a type of back-end premium, this really is a very directed appeal. It stops just short of asking for a listing.

Many real estate agents say they have the most success with this kind of letter. The reason is simple: it's a great way to pre-qualify prospects. While you can expect a high rejection rate, those who do respond will be excellent prospects. After all, anyone interested in a free home evaluation is at least considering selling.

Questions are good

Count the "you" words

Mystery

Use personal story

Photo

GREENBRIER REAL ESTATE
Barbara Kozlowski, Realtor-Associate®
90067 Carbondale Road * Campbell, NC 60056
(w) 704/555-8900 (h) 704/555-8897
(fax) 704/555-8901 (pager) 704/555-7703

DOES YOUR HOME HAVE HIDDEN VALUE?

Dear Castle Pines Neighbor,

Right now, you may have a golden opportunity. An opportunity to seek out your home's hidden value and use it to move up to the home of your dreams.

If your home is worth a lot more than you imagine, just think what you could do...

Five months ago, Tom and Becky Brewer were sitting around their kitchen table and talking about selling their home. Their children were entering high school; they wanted a less practical, more stylish home. Tom thought they could get about $145,000 for their Century Drive house. Then I visited. I found their immaculate three-bedroom, two-bath ranch radiant with charm. Three weeks later, it sold for $180,000. As I'm writing this, the Brewers are celebrating their second month in their French country dream house.

<u>Having a house you love is not an impossible dream.</u> With current interest rates and recent neighborhood improvements, your home, too, has probably appreciated more than you realize.

(over, please)

It's easy to find out. Just pick up the phone. All this month I'm scheduling FREE home evaluations for Castle Pines neighbors.

Offer

With the evaluation, you'll receive a complete written analysis of your home's value based on recent sales of comparable area homes.

Premium

Five years ago — during a similar market — <u>many homeowners were caught off guard. They missed an ideal opportunity because they didn't realize their homes had appreciated so much.</u> You, too, may be missing out if you don't at least take the time to find out your home's worth on today's market.

Fear appeal

It will only take about a half hour. And there is absolutely no obligation. I hand you the evaluation, then I say good-bye. You decide on your own whether to act on the information.

To take me up on this offer, just return the enclosed reply card in the envelope provided. Or, better yet, give me a call. You can reach me at the office (555-8900) during the day or at home (555-7703) or on my pager (555-7703) any other time. But please don't wait. I'm scheduling regular evaluations only through the end of the month.

Limited time appeal

This is a chance to find out <u>how easy it is for your dream to come true.</u>

Sincerely yours,

Barbara Kozlowski
Realtor-Associate®

P.S. If your home is worth even 20% more than you think, you may easily move up into a home with an extra bedroom, bath or acreage. I have some great listings. Call right now!

Don't miss out!

KEY POINTS

1. Personal story adds interest.

2. Mystery angle — home's hidden value.

3. Deadline — scheduling regular evaluations only through the end of the month.

4. Be sure to get your clients' permission to use their story.

OUTER ENVELOPE

Greenbrier Real Estate
90067 Carbondale Road
Campbell, NC 60056

> Bulk Rate
> US Postage
> P A I D
> Campbell, NC
> Permit No 1234

DOES YOUR HOME HAVE HIDDEN VALUE?

Mr. Joe Hill
458 Center St.
Castle Pines, NC 60057

REPLY CARD

Photo

BARBARA, I WANT TO KNOW......
( ) what my home is worth
( ) more about the real estate options
( ) more about your real estate services
( ) other _____

_____

Your Name _____

Your Address_____

_____

Your telephone number

(w)_____ (h)_____

Best time to call _____

BRE REPLY ENVELOPE

> NO POSTAGE
> NECESSARY
> IF MAILED
> IN THE
> UNITED STATES

BUSINESS REPLY MAIL
First Class PERMIT NO.000 Campbell, NC
Postage will be paid by Addressee

Greenbrier Real Estate
90067 Carbondale Road
Campbell, NC 60056

ATTN: Barbara Kozlowski

Information Kits

These letters offer back-end premiums which, hopefully, will attract hard-to-reach prospects. In the letters, you ask prospects if they'd like one of your special "kits." If they do, drop off the kits at their homes. Call first to make sure they'll be there. These kits are a great way to meet people in your farm and they present you in a very positive light. After all, you're distributing free gifts of perceived value.

But creating the kits does take a little work. Most have five or six elements. Because you list these in the letter, you'd better be certain that you can get them. You'll have to spend about a day contacting local community organizations to see what they have available. For many of the kits, you can work out "cooperative" arrangements with the local police department, fire station, hardware stores and others. Under a cooperative arrangement, you'd include, for example, a discount coupon from the hardware store or a brochure produced by an insurance company. Look for these opportunities, as they'll strengthen your community ties and increase your letter's credibility.

In some cases, you'll have to prepare the element yourself. For example, you may have to type up a list of emergency local phone numbers. With a computer, this should be easy. Most of the information for the elements you'll have to create is available in the yellow pages of your phone directory or from the reference department at your city library.

When you finish, package the kits attractively and inexpensively. Be sure to display your business card or name, address and phone numbers prominently.

HOME FIRE-PROTECTION KIT

Type of farm: geographic or social

GREENBRIER REAL ESTATE
Barbara Kozlowski, Realtor-Associate®
90067 Carbondale Road * Campbell, NC 60056
(w) 704/555-8900 (h) 704/555-8897
(fax) 704/555-8901 (pager) 704/555-7703

FIRE SEASON IS HERE —
IS YOUR HOME FULLY PROTECTED?

July, 1996

Dear Castle Pines Neighbor,

Story open

Like most of us, Brad Taylor thought his home was safe. Then, on a chilly November night last year, a towel dangling over a bathroom space heater caught fire. Fist-sized flames exploded into a fiery blaze that ripped through the bedroom, kitchen and living room. Three hours later, only smoldering ashes and a blackened foundation remained.

Brad was fortunate. He ran through a wall of fire and escaped with minor burns on his back. No one was hurt, but his small home was completely destroyed.

"The fire could have been prevented," Brad says today, "if I had only taken a few simple steps..."

<u>How safe is your home?</u>

If you're like me, fire prevention is one of the last things you think about.

But it shouldn't be.

Co-op opportunity

Fires damage 360,000 homes in the United States each year. Most homeowners, I'm sure, never expected it to happen to them. That's why, in cooperation with the Castle Pines Fire Department, I've put together a Home Fire-Protection Kit for you and your Castle Pines neighbors.

Offer

<u>And it's absolutely free for the asking!</u>

Adapt to describe your kit

Your Home Fire-Protection Kit includes...

* the 48-page booklet, "99 Ways To Protect Your Home Against Fire,"

* the 12-page comic-book style booklet, "What Children Should Know About Fires,"

(over, please)

* a handy directory of emergency phone numbers to keep by your phone, and

* a 25% discount coupon from Fred's True-Value Hardware for a home fire extinguisher and smoke alarm.

Co-op opportunity

I know that prevention is easy to put off. Few of us like to think about tragedy striking. But don't let what happened to Brad Taylor — or something even worse — happen to you.

Tie back to story

Right now, while you're thinking about it, take the return postcard and drop it in the mail. To get your free Home Fire-Protection Kit even faster, call me at 555-8900 during the day or at 555-8897 (home) or 555-7703 (pager). As soon as I hear from you, I'll make sure you get your Kit promptly.

Adds urgency

Remember...better safe than sorry.

Sincerely yours,

Barbara Kozlowski
Realtor-Associate®

P.S. Because my supply is limited, I can only guarantee delivery of your FREE kit through the end of this month. Please order yours today!

Limited quantity appeal

KEY POINTS

1. Personal story at beginning grabs attention.

2. Statistics on fires add credibility.

3. Limited supply adds urgency.

4. Cooperative opportunity with local fire dept., insurance company, alarm company or hardware store.

OUTER ENVELOPE

Greenbrier Real Estate
90067 Carbondale Road
Campbell, NC 60056

> Bulk Rate
> US Postage
> P A I D
> Campbell, NC
> Permit No 1234

HOW TO GET YOUR FREE HOME
FIRE-PROTECTION KIT

Mr. Joe Hill
458 Center St.
Castle Pines, NC 60057

REPLY CARD

Photo

YES, BARBARA, I WANT MY HOME TO BE SAFE FROM FIRE.

( ) PLEASE RUSH ME A FREE HOME FIRE-PROTECTION KIT.

Your Name _____

Your Address_____

_____

Your telephone number

(w)_____ (h)_____

Best time to call _____

BRE REPLY ENVELOPE

> NO POSTAGE
> NECESSARY
> IF MAILED
> IN THE
> UNITED STATES

BUSINESS REPLY MAIL
First Class PERMIT NO.000 Campbell, NC
Postage will be paid by Addressee

Greenbrier Real Estate
90067 Carbondale Road
Campbell, NC 60056

ATTN: Barbara Kozlowski

HOME CRIME-STOPPERS KIT

Type of farm: geographic or social

GREENBRIER REAL ESTATE
Barbara Kozlowski, Realtor-Associate®
90067 Carbondale Road * Campbell, NC 60056
(w) 704/555-8900 (h) 704/555-8897
(fax) 704/555-8901 (pager) 704/555-7703

FREE TIPS ON HOW TO PROTECT YOUR HOME FROM INTRUDERS

Dear Castle Pines Neighbor,

It's no secret that crime is on the rise. No neighborhood — not even ours — is really safe. Over the past year, at least five homes in Castle Pines have been burglarized. Don't you find that pretty scary?

Use your farm's statistics

If you're concerned about your home's safety, please keep reading. With the help of the local police, I've put together a kit of how to "crime-proof" your home. And I'd like to give you one FREE.

Offer

Each "Home Crime-stoppers Kit" includes:

* a booklet on how to "burglar-proof" your home,

* a booklet on how to inventory and protect your possessions,

Tailor to describe your kit

* identification labels for your valuable personal and household articles,

* identification labels to post at or near the doors of your home,

* emergency stickers for your telephones,

* handy directory of emergency phone numbers, procedures, and more.

I know that it's easy to put things like this off. None of us ever dreams that tragedy will strike our home. But when it's so easy to take steps to protect yourself — doesn't getting this Kit make sense?

Right now, while you're thinking about it, fill out the enclosed card and drop it in the mail. To get your free Home Crime-stoppers Kit even faster, call me at 555-8900 during the day or at 555-8897 (home) or 555-7703 (pager) evenings and weekends. As soon as I

Adds urgency

(over, please)

Repetition is good

hear from you, I'll see that you get your Kit right away.

Don't you have the right to live in a home where you feel safe...where you don't have to worry about intruders, theft, or worse?

Local police officers tell me that taking the few simple steps described in the Kit can protect you. Please call me today.

Sincerely yours,

Barbara Kozlowski
Realtor-Associate®

P.S. This Kit tells you the best type of "burglar-proof" locks, where to put lamps on timers, and other detailed information you need to protect yourself. Get it right away!

KEY POINTS

1. Local statistics add credibility. Use break-ins per month or year, whatever is most impressive.

2. If possible, give details of local police involvement in kit.

3. Could change P.S. to read that supplies are limited.

4. Cooperative opportunities with local police, alarm or insurance companies.

OUTER ENVELOPE

Greenbrier Real Estate
90067 Carbondale Road
Campbell, NC 60056

Bulk Rate
US Postage
P A I D
Campbell, NC
Permit No 1234

HOW SAFE IS YOUR HOME
FROM INTRUDERS?

Mr. Joe Hill
458 Center St.
Castle Pines, NC 60057

REPLY CARD

Photo

YES, BARBARA, I WANT A CRIME PROOF HOME.

( ) PLEASE RUSH MY FREE "HOME CRIME-STOPPERS" KIT

Your Name _____

Your Address_____

_____

Your telephone number

(w)_____ (h)_____

Best time to call _____

BRE REPLY ENVELOPE

NO POSTAGE
NECESSARY
IF MAILED
IN THE
UNITED STATES

BUSINESS REPLY MAIL
First Class PERMIT NO.000 Campbell, NC
Postage will be paid by Addressee

Greenbrier Real Estate
90067 Carbondale Road
Campbell, NC 60056

ATTN: Barbara Kozlowski

NEIGHBORHOOD WATCH KIT LETTER

Type of farm: geographic

GREENBRIER REAL ESTATE

Barbara Kozlowski, Realtor-Associate®

90067 Carbondale Road * Campbell, NC 60056

(w) 704/555-8900 (h) 704/555-8897

(fax) 704/555-8901 (pager) 704/555-7703

WOULD YOU LIKE A SAFER HOME AND NEIGHBORHOOD?

Dear Castle Pines Neighbor,

Story open

Like you, my friend thought that she lived in a relatively safe neighborhood. <u>But no one — not anywhere — is 100% safe.</u>

One afternoon she left the house for about a half hour. She had to stop by the grocery store and pick up the kids at school. When she got back, the kids ran out of the car and into the house. One headed straight for the pantry, looking for a snack. The pantry was next to the back door. Her daughter came out to the kitchen, asking, "Mommy, what happened to the window on the back door? It's broken." My friend rushed to the door, saw a pile of broken glass and then ran through the house. The upstairs bedrooms were a mess. Drawers had been opened; jewelry stolen; all the children's piggy banks were gone.

She found out later that a teenage boy in the neighborhood, a family friend, had seen another boy walking away from the house with loaded arms. But <u>the teenager just watched. It never crossed his mind to call the police.</u>

When it comes to keeping your house safe, your neighbors are important. They know when you usually turn on your lights. Where you park your car. Even what time you come out in the morning to pick up your paper. Often they're there when you're not. That's why neighborhood watch groups are so effective. <u>But if your neighbors don't know what to do, they probably won't do anything.</u>

Offer

Please consider getting my <u>"Neighborhood Watch Kit."</u> With the help of local police sergeant Tim Brown, I put it together just for Castle Pines residents like you.

(over, please)

It's yours for the asking and it's absolutely free. In it, you'll find:

* a 10-page booklet on how to prevent crime in your neighborhood,

* window stickers for your home,

* a handy card with emergency numbers to put by your phone,

* information from the local police department on how to set up your own neighborhood watch group.

Describe your kit

I know that it's not pleasant to think about crime, especially not right in your own neighborhood. But a "Neighborhood Watch" group could really make a difference. It tells people what to do — gives them a plan of action — and protects you from the tragedy that struck my friend.

Right now, while you're thinking about it, fill out the enclosed card and drop it in the mail. For a faster response, call me at 555-8900 (office) during the day or at 555-8897 (home) or 555-7703 (pager) any other time. As soon I hear from you, I'll get the "Neighborhood Watch Kit" to you right away. I'll also help arrange a meeting with the local police department to organize your Neighborhood Watch.

Through a Neighborhood Watch, you look out for your neighbors; they look out for you. The idea may be old-fashioned; but it's as powerful as ever. People caring for people works. Please...call or write for your FREE "Neighborhood Watch Kit" today.

Sincerely yours,

Barbara Kozlowski
Realtor-Associate®

P.S. My friend never felt safe in that home again. She moved soon after the robbery. Don't live in fear — get your Neighborhood Watch Kit today.

Fear appeal

KEY POINTS

1. Personal story attracts audience interest.

2. Emphasizes old-fashioned American values.

3. Make sure no Neighborhood Watch already operating in the area.

4. Cooperative opportunity with local police dept.

5. Can re-write letter as invitation to attend meeting to organize Neighborhood Watch group. See "Seminar."

OUTER ENVELOPE

Greenbrier Real Estate
90067 Carbondale Road
Campbell, NC 60056

> Bulk Rate
> US Postage
> P A I D
> Campbell, NC
> Permit No 1234

WOULD YOU LIKE A SAFER HOME & NEIGHBORHOOD?

Mr. Joe Hill
458 Center St.
Castle Pines, NC 60057

REPLY CARD

Photo

YES, BARBARA, I'M INTERESTED IN A SAFER HOME AND NEIGHBORHOOD.

( )PLEASE RUSH MY FREE NEIGHBORHOOD WATCH KIT TODAY.

Your Name _____

Your Address_____

_____

Your telephone number

(w)_____ (h)_____

Best time to call _____

BRE REPLY ENVELOPE

> NO POSTAGE
> NECESSARY
> IF MAILED
> IN THE
> UNITED STATES

BUSINESS REPLY MAIL
First Class PERMIT NO.000 Campbell, NC
Postage will be paid by Addressee

Greenbrier Real Estate
90067 Carbondale Road
Campbell, NC 56

ATTN: Barbara Kozlowski

VACATION KIT

Type of farm: geographic

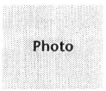

GREENBRIER REAL ESTATE
Barbara Kozlowski, Realtor-Associate®
90067 Carbondale Road * Campbell, NC 60056
(w) 704/555-8900 (h) 704/555-8897
(fax) 704/555-8901 (pager) 704/555-7703

HERE'S HOW TO GET YOUR FREE VACATION KIT

June, 1996

Dear Castle Pines Neighbor,

If you're like me, you know what it's like to <u>start a vacation dashing out the front door at the last minute.</u> In the car on the way to the airport, I've realized that I forgot to cancel my newspaper...make arrangements for a neighbor to water my plants...or re-fill a prescription that will run out the next day. That's not a good way to begin a week or two of fun and relaxation.

Build rapport

To help you avoid this kind of frustration, I've prepared a special <u>VACATION KIT.</u> It includes:

Offer

* "To Do" checklist similar to airplane pilot's checklist before take off. Covers everything from turning off the air conditioning to pulling the drapes before you walk out the front door,

* tip sheet on how to keep your home safe during your absence,

Tailor to fit your kit

* telephone numbers and addresses of local kennels and other pet care services,

* vacation hold form to drop off at the post office,

* list of all relevant telephone numbers, including police, newspapers, & airport shuttles,

* a small personal gift for your trip.

With the help of this VACATION KIT, <u>you can leave for your vacation relaxed and with peace of mind.</u> Everything you need to do is covered on the checklist, together with the numbers you'll need to call. You won't have to worry about forgetting a thing.

Benefit of offer

To get this FREE VACATION KIT, just fill out and return the enclosed card. For faster delivery, call me at 555-8900 (office) during the day or at 555-8897 (home) or 555-7703 (pager) any other time. As soon

How to get it

(over, please)

Ask for immediate action

as I hear from you, I'll rush the VACATION KIT right to your door.

With so many of us having such busy schedules, it's hard to keep everything organized. This VACATION KIT will help start your trip off right. Call or write for it today.

Sincerely yours,

Barbara Kozlowski
Realtor-Associate®

Limited quantity

P.S. I'm expecting a flood of orders as vacation time approaches. Please order your FREE Kit today, before I run out.

KEY POINTS

1. For the personal gift, pick up a supply of inexpensive travel toothbrushes, small bottles of suntan lotion or other inexpensive items.

2. Builds on similarity between agent and reader.

3. Keeps positive tone: pitches "peace of mind."

4. Cooperative opportunity: local police department, travel agencies, airport shuttle or limousine services.

5. Recommended mailing time: early summer.

OUTER ENVELOPE

Greenbrier Real Estate
90067 Carbondale Road
Campbell, NC 60056

> Bulk Rate
> US Postage
> P A I D
> Campbell, NC
> Permit No 1234

INSIDE: HOW TO GET YOUR
FREE VACATION KIT

Mr. Joe Hill
458 Center St.
Castle Pines, NC 60057

REPLY CARD

Photo

YES, BARBARA, I WANT HELP GETTING READY
FOR MY VACATION

( ) PLEASE RUSH MY FREE VACATION KIT TODAY.

Your Name _____

Your Address_____

_____

Your telephone number

(w)_____ (h)_____

Best time to call _____

BRE REPLY ENVELOPE

> NO POSTAGE
> NECESSARY
> IF MAILED
> IN THE
> UNITED STATES

BUSINESS REPLY MAIL

First Class PERMIT NO.000 Campbell, NC
Postage will be paid by Addressee

Greenbrier Real Estate
90067 Carbondale Road
Campbell, NC 60056

ATTN: Barbara Kozlowski

HOME SAFETY KIT

Type of farm: geographic or social

Photo

GREENBRIER REAL ESTATE
Barbara Kozlowski, Realtor-Associate®
90067 Carbondale Road * Campbell, NC 60056
(w) 704/555-8900 (h) 704/555-8897
(fax) 704/555-8901 (pager) 704/555-7703

HOW SAFE IS YOUR HOME?

Dear Castle Pines Neighbor,

Hook

It's hard to believe, but <u>you face more danger in your own home than in most other places.</u> That's right. Home is where accidents kill 20,000 Americans every year and disable more than 10 times that number.

Questions

Think about it. How many times have you heard about a toddler tumbling through a loose window screen? A homeowner slipping and falling off the roof? A young child grabbing and drinking a highly toxic chemical from an unsecured cabinet beneath a sink? And remember the recent tragic death of Swedish tennis star Vitas Gerulaitis when carbon monoxide silently leaked from a faulty furnace as he slept?

The question!

<u>Now think about your home. Is it as safe as it could be?</u>

Offer

To help make your home safer, I've created the <u>"Home Safety Kit"</u> for you and your Castle Pines neighbors.

<u>And it's absolutely free!</u>

Your Home Safety Kit includes:

Details of offer

* a checklist to determine how safe your home is,
* a detailed booklet describing how to "accident-proof" your home,
* a brochure on important safety measures to take when small children are in the home,
* a guide to basic First Aid,
* a handy card with emergency numbers and services to put next to your telephone,
* "tamper-proof" plastic locks for your cabinets and inserts for your electrical plugs.

(over, please)

I know that none of us likes to think about accidents happening in our homes. But the fact is that they do. And when prevention is so easy, taking the simple steps described in the Kit makes sense.

Why you need this

Right now, while you're thinking about it, fill out the enclosed postage-paid card and drop it in the mail. To get your free Home Safety Kit even faster, call me at 555-8900 during the day or at 555-8897 (home) or 555-7703 (pager) any other time. As soon as I hear from you, I'll make sure you get one right away.

What to do

Remember...a safe home is no accident!

Sincerely yours,

Barbara Kozlowski
Realtor-Associate®

Limited supply

P.S. I have only a limited supply of plastic plugs and locks — call me before they run out!

KEY POINTS

1. You should be able to find a home safety brochure already prepared. Ask at your local library.

2. For First Aid tips and emergency numbers, look at your local phone directory.

3. Instead of providing the plugs & locks yourself, contact a local hardware store and see if they're interested in having a coupon in this package. If so, change copy.

OUTER ENVELOPE

Greenbrier Real Estate
90067 Carbondale Road
Campbell, NC 60056

Bulk Rate
US Postage
P A I D
Campbell, NC
Permit No 1234

HOW SAFE IS YOUR HOME?

Mr. Joe Hill
458 Center St.
Castle Pines, NC 60057

REPLY CARD

Photo

YES, BARBARA, I WANT A SAFE HOME.

( ) PLEASE RUSH MY FREE "HOME SAFETY KIT."

Your Name _____

Your Address_____

_____

Your telephone number

(w)_____ (h)_____

Best time to call _____

BRE REPLY ENVELOPE

NO POSTAGE
NECESSARY
IF MAILED
IN THE
UNITED STATES

BUSINESS REPLY MAIL
First Class PERMIT NO.000 Campbell, NC
Postage will be paid by Addressee

Greenbrier Real Estate
90067 Carbondale Road
Campbell, NC 60056

ATTN: Barbara Kozlowski

GARAGE SALE KIT

Type of farm: geographic or social

GREENBRIER REAL ESTATE
Barbara Kozlowski, Realtor-Associate®
90067 Carbondale Road * Campbell, NC 60056
(w) 704/555-8900 (h) 704/555-8897
(fax) 704/555-8901 (pager) 704/555-7703

LIKE SOME EXTRA MONEY?
TRY A GARAGE SALE!

Spring, 1996

Dear Castle Pines Neighbor,

If your closets are crammed with clothes you never wear...and your cabinets are stacked with things you never touch...why not <u>turn your little used possessions into pure profit?</u> It's easy. Find out just how easy with your own FREE Garage Sale Kit.

Lots of "you's"

I've prepared this Kit for busy homeowners who don't have the time to do the research or preparation themselves. In this <u>handy Garage Sale Kit,</u> you'll find:

Offer

* large, attention-grabbing signs with room for directions to post around your neighborhood,

* colorful flags for the end of your driveway,

* price stickers,

Describe your kit

* thick black magic marker,

* sample classified ads,

* tip sheet on how organize and manage your garage sale most efficiently.

One friend collected a tidy <u>$300 in four hours</u> one Saturday. Another took <u>in $500 over a weekend.</u> People snapped up outgrown children's clothing, unmatched dishes, odd-shaped vases, old radios, and little-used golf clubs. One woman laughed when she described a couple's excitement over a mahogany end table that had belonged to her grandmother. They called it an antique; she had thought of it only as old and slightly warped. After seeing their excitement, she was tempted to raise the price. But she didn't.

Benefits of offer

Garage sales are a great way to <u>clean out your closets, make some money, and have fun.</u> In just eight hours, you can meet more people than you would in eight months. It's fun, too, to see people smile and get

(over, please)

Act now

Repeat benefit

Limited quantity

excited over things that lost their thrill for you long ago.

So if you're looking forward to pocketing some extra money through a garage sale, don't wait. Fill out and return the enclosed card today. For an even quicker response, call me at 555-8900 (office) during the day or at 555-8897 (home) or 555-7703 (pager) any other time. You can call evenings — weekends — whenever it's convenient.

Right now, get your free Garage Sale Kit. And start dreaming about what you'll do with your extra dollars.

Sincerely yours,

Barbara Kozlowski
Realtor-Associate®

P.S. I ordered only 50 Kits — they'll go quickly so get in touch with me today!

KEY POINTS

1. Emphasizes garage sales as way to earn extra money.

2. Offers lots of freebies.

3. For already prepared Kits, check with office supply stores or ads in real estate magazines. Garage Sale Promotions has a product, The Garage Sale Book, which you could use as a premium (1-800-663-7054).

4. Cooperative opportunity with local newspaper's classified department or weekly publication such as "Penny-Saver"...office supply store...sign and banner shop.

OUTER ENVELOPE

Greenbrier Real Estate
90067 Carbondale Road
Campbell, NC 60056

> Bulk Rate
> US Postage
> P A I D
> Campbell, NC
> Permit No 1234

LIKE TO MAKE SOME EXTRA MONEY?
IT'S EASY—LOOK INSIDE

Mr. Joe Hill
458 Center St.
Castle Pines, NC 60057

REPLY CARD

Photo

YES, BARBARA, I'M INTERESTED IN HAVING A
GARAGE SALE.

( ) PLEASE RUSH MY FREE GARAGE SALE
KIT TODAY.

Your Name _____

Your Address_____

_____

Your telephone number

(w)_____ (h)_____

Best time to call _____

BRE REPLY ENVELOPE

> NO POSTAGE
> NECESSARY
> IF MAILED
> IN THE
> UNITED STATES

BUSINESS REPLY MAIL
First Class PERMIT NO.000 Campbell, NC
Postage will be paid by Addressee

Greenbrier Real Estate
90067 Carbondale Road
Campbell, NC 60056

ATTN: Barbara Kozlowski

ENVIRONMENTAL ACTION KIT

Type of farm: geographic

GREENBRIER REAL ESTATE
Barbara Kozlowski, Realtor-Associate®
90067 Carbondale Road * Campbell, NC 60056
(w) 704/555-8900 (h) 704/555-8897
(fax) 704/555-8901 (pager) 704/555-7703

WOULD YOU LIKE TO HELP SAVE THE ENVIRONMENT?

Dear Castle Pines Neighbor,

Offer

If you're concerned about the environment, I've put together a FREE "Environmental Action" Kit to help. Created especially for Castle Pines residents, it focuses on the place where your contribution to <u>saving the environment begins — right in your own home.</u>

For example, did you know that —

* burning a wood fire on high pollution days is the equivalent of smoking 4 to 16 cigarettes?

Rationale

* dumping soap from washing your car down a convenient drain can kill fish miles away?

* used plastic bottles, glass jars, and metal cans creates a crisis at local landfills?

In this Environmental Action Kit, you'll find facts like these and many more. Your Kit includes:

* a colorful booklet with easy tips on how to protect the environment in your everyday life,

* information on how to prepare your old newspapers, plastics and glass materials for pick-up, together with the local pick-up schedule,

Details of offer

* a list of convenient recycling centers and landfills, along with their hours and acceptance policies,

* tips on how to dispose safely of things such as paint, toxic household cleaners, insect pesticides, and motor oil,

* names and telephone numbers of agencies to contact with more specific questions such as the county household hazardous waste hotline.

I created this Kit because during my conversations with Castle Park neighbors, it has been clear that many

(over, please)

of you want to do your part for the environment but you're not sure how. This Kit makes it easy.

<u>Everything you need — from basic information on things to do around the home to people to call when you have specific questions — is right here.</u>

To receive your FREE Environmental Action Kit, just fill out and return the enclosed card. Or save a piece of paper and call me at 555-8900 (office), 555-8897 (home) or 555-7703 (pager) anytime. As soon as I hear from you, I'll get the "Environmental Action Kit" to you right away.

Act now

Please...start doing your part at the place where it counts the most.

Sincerely yours,

Barbara Kozlowski
Realtor-Associate®

Guilt appeal

P.S. This Kit is unique in that it focuses exclusively on services available to Castle Pines' residents. You may want an extra one to pass along to a friend or neighbor. Just mention it when you reach me.

Uniqueness of offer

KEY POINTS

1. Valuable Kit that pulls together hard-to-find information.

2. Positions you as environmental advocate, which could be good or bad depending on your farm's demographics.

3. If possible, print this letter and everything in the Kit on recycled paper and mention in small type at bottom.

4. For writing booklet on things to do in everyday life, see *50 Things You Can Do to Save the Earth* by the Earth Works Group, Earthworks Press, Berkeley, CA.

5. Cooperative opportunities with utility companies, recycling centers, waste disposal companies, water companies.

OUTER ENVELOPE

Greenbrier Real Estate
90067 Carbondale Road
Campbell, NC 60056

Bulk Rate
US Postage
P A I D
Campbell, NC
Permit No 1234

HOW TO GET YOUR HOME
"ENVIRONMENTAL ACTION KIT"

Mr. Joe Hill
458 Center St.
Castle Pines, NC 60057

REPLY CARD

Photo

YES, BARBARA, I WANT TO DO MY PART TO
HELP SAVE THE ENVIRONMENT.

( ) PLEASE RUSH MY FREE ENVIRONMENTAL
ACTION KIT TODAY.

Your Name _____

Your Address_____

_____

Your telephone number

(w)_____ (h)_____

Best time to call _____

BRE REPLY ENVELOPE

NO POSTAGE
NECESSARY
IF MAILED
IN THE
UNITED STATES

BUSINESS REPLY MAIL
First Class PERMIT NO.000 Campbell, NC
Postage will be paid by Addressee

Greenbrier Real Estate
90067 Carbondale Road
Campbell, NC 60056

ATTN: Barbara Kozlowski

TAX RECORD KIT

Type of farm: geographic or social

Photo

GREENBRIER REAL ESTATE
Barbara Kozlowski, Realtor-Associate®
90067 Carbondale Road * Campbell, NC 60056
(w) 704/555-8900 (h) 704/555-8897
(fax) 704/555-8901 (pager) 704/555-7703

GET YOUR FREE HOME TAX RECORD KIT

Dear Castle Pines Neighbor,

Every year around tax time, I vow that I'm going to do it differently. I'll work hard to keep up my records and by the end of the year, everything will be in order. Despite these good intentions, however, it never happens. Each year I face the same ugly mess as the last. I wind up frustrated, angry and confused. *Story open*

About two weeks ago, a friend dropped by my office with a stack of what she called "Home Tax Record Kits." Inside the kit were compartments for pay stubs, mortgage receipts, loan payments, miscellaneous expenses, stock and bond records, and a whole lot more.

I was pretty impressed. Keeping track of receipts has always been a problem. After just a few minutes, I asked, "How many of these do you have in your car?"

"About 75," she replied.

Without missing a beat, I said, "Give me all of them."

On the way home that night, I stopped to show them off to my accountant. He grabbed a couple. As I carried them into the house, a curious neighbor lifted one off the top of the pile. I never saw it again. Later that night, Mom told me that she wanted one. That leaves me with 71, including one for myself. *Highly desirable*

I'd like for you to have one, too. You're very important to me. And I think you would find this useful. *Offer*

Best of all, it's FREE...but you'd better get to me before your neighbors do. Once the 71 are gone, that's it. *Limited quantity*

To receive your FREE Home Tax Record Kit, fill out the enclosed postcard today and drop it in the mail. *Act now*

(over, please)

For faster delivery, call me at 555-8900 (office) or at 555-8897 (home) or 555-7703 (pager) any other time. You can call evenings — weekends — whenever it's convenient.

I hope you enjoy your Kit. Good luck with your taxes.

Sincerely yours,

Barbara Kozlowski
Realtor-Associate®

Quantity going down!

P.S. My boss just grabbed one of the Kits, so I'm down to 70. Better call for yours today!

KEY POINTS

1. Running story adds urgency. So does limited quantity.

2. Accountant's response increases credibility.

3. Check with local office supply store for kits. Or look for ads in real estate magazines.

4. Best to mail in spring (leading up to 4/15) or at year-end.

5. Cooperative opportunities with — CPA or tax preparer — local office supply store — financial institutions (banks or S&Ls) for IRAs.

OUTER ENVELOPE

Greenbrier Real Estate
90067 Carbondale Road
Campbell, NC 60056

Bulk Rate
US Postage
P A I D
Campbell, NC
Permit No 1234

GET YOUR FREE
HOME TAX RECORD KIT

Mr. Joe Hill
458 Center St.
Castle Pines, NC 60057

REPLY CARD

Photo

YES, BARBARA, I WANT MY FREE HOME TAX
RECORDS KIT.

( )PLEASE RUSH IT TO ME TODAY

Your Name _____

Your Address_____

_____

Your telephone number

(w)_____ (h)_____

Best time to call _____

BRE REPLY ENVELOPE

NO POSTAGE
NECESSARY
IF MAILED
IN THE
UNITED STATES

BUSINESS REPLY MAIL
First Class PERMIT NO.000 Campbell, NC
Postage will be paid by Addressee

Greenbrier Real Estate
90067 Carbondale Road
Campbell, NC 60056

ATTN: Barbara Kozlowski

Booklet Offers

Like information kit offers, booklet offers are back-end premiums. These, however, take a little more work to pull together. But once you've finished them, all you need to do is update them every six or twelve months. They're also great gifts for new owners moving into your farm neighborhood.

The "Home Reference Booklet" contains the names and numbers for every home-related service in your farm area. Put in as many as you can think of — the more you have, the better you'll look. Try as best you can to eliminate anyone with a questionable reputation. To find this out, run the names by a few long-time farm residents (this will give you an excellent excuse to call them!). If they can't help, ask them to recommend a friend or neighbor who could advise you.

The "Home Investment Services Booklet" lists other service representatives working with local real estate. It includes insurance agents, bank officers, appraisers, attorneys — again, check with people who have lived in your farm a long time for recommendations. While there will be some overlap with those interested in the first booklet, the two premiums may well appeal to different audiences. You could test this by mailing one offer to half your farm and the second offer to the other half of your farm.

As with other premiums featured in this book, the most time-consuming part is pulling the information together. Once you've done that, you have a great premium to send out year after year.

HOME REFERENCE BOOKLET
Type of farm: geographic

GREENBRIER REAL ESTATE
Barbara Kozlowski, Realtor-Associate®
90067 Carbondale Road * Campbell, NC 60056
(w) 704/555-8900 (h) 704/555-8897
(fax) 704/555-8901 (pager) 704/555-7703

SAVE TIME WITH YOUR
HANDY HOME REFERENCE BOOKLET

Spring, 1997

Dear Castle Pines Neighbor,

Question open

Have you ever had a water pipe break in the middle of the night and not known who to call? Had your automatic garage door get stuck in the middle and needed someone to fix it right away? Watched your sink stop up and overflow five minutes before dinner guests arrived?

In the best of all possible worlds, you'd have one number to call for any household problem.

Unfortunately, life isn't that easy. Whether it's repairing the plumbing or finding a gardener, <u>keeping up your home takes work</u> and lots of time on the telephone.

Offer

Taking care of your home can now be a lot simpler. To help you, I've put together a small <u>booklet of handy reference numbers especially for Castle Pines residents.</u>

Details of offer

It <u>covers every type of home-related service</u> in the area — regular house cleaning, handyman help, appliance repairs, closet organizers, garbage pick-up, heating and plumbing, chimney sweeps, gardeners, tree trimming, pool cleaning and maintenance, landscapers, architects, painters, carpenters, contractors, propane suppliers, firewood suppliers, utility companies, brick layers, concrete specialists, roofing repairs, and window companies. It even includes teenagers willing to do odd jobs and baby-sit. Every referral was made by someone familiar with the service; I marked my favorite services with a "*."

Benefits of offer

<u>Having this booklet will save you time.</u> When searching through the Yellow Pages, you often don't know whether a service covers your neighborhood or

(over, please)

what kind of reputation it has. This booklet takes care of both. It eliminates any service that either doesn't cover Castle Pines or has a poor reputation.

Getting your "Handy Home Reference List" is easy. Just fill out and return the enclosed card. For faster delivery, call me at 555-8900 (office) or 555-7703 (pager). You can call anytime. As soon as I hear from you, I'll send your "Handy Home Reference Booklet" right away.

Act now

After you look at the booklet, I'd be glad for any suggestions. It's possible I left out someone that you use frequently and would like to recommend to your friends. Or perhaps I've included someone with whom you had a bad experience. Either way, your feedback would be welcome.

Build rapport

Right now, save time for the things you really want to do. Please...give me a call or write today.

Repeat benefit and ask for action again

Sincerely yours,

Barbara Kozlowski
Realtor-Associate®

P.S. Keeping up your home is like putting money in your pocket. I just listed a house at 456 Windy Rock Way for $195,000 — because of its mint condition, the home will probably sell for $7,500 more than the average home of this size. Get your handy home reference booklet today!

Another benefit of the offer

KEY POINTS

1. Emphasizes "you."

2. Selling point is a big benefit — the booklet will save time.

3. Booklet is specialized & unique to Castle Pines area.

4. Once it's done, you can easily update it every 6 months. It also gives you something to ask people about in your farm when you meet them in person.

5. VERY IMPORTANT that you make this booklet as comprehensive as possible. Otherwise it will not be useful and people will throw it out.

6. Make sure the "*" referrals really are good ones — otherwise this could backfire for you.

7. Could use making this booklet as a reason to telephone people in your farm (see our other book, *How To Farm Successfully — By Phone*)

8. Great gift for new homeowners moving into area.

9. Cooperative opportunities are obvious!!!

OUTER ENVELOPE

Greenbrier Real Estate
90067 Carbondale Road
Campbell, NC 60056

Bulk Rate
US Postage
P A I D
Campbell, NC
Permit No 1234

*SAVE TIME WITH YOUR HANDY
HOME REFERENCE LIST*

Mr. Joe Hill
458 Center St.
Castle Pines, NC 60057

REPLY CARD

Photo

YES, BARBARA, I WANT TO SAVE TIME FOR THE THINGS I CARE ABOUT.

( ) PLEASE RUSH MY FREE HANDY HOME REFERENCE LIST TODAY.

Your Name _____

Your Address_____

_____

Your telephone number

(w)_____ (h)_____

Best time to call _____

BRE REPLY ENVELOPE

NO POSTAGE
NECESSARY
IF MAILED
IN THE
UNITED STATES

BUSINESS REPLY MAIL
First Class PERMIT NO.000 Campbell, NC
Postage will be paid by Addressee

Greenbrier Real Estate
90067 Carbondale Road
Campbell, NC 60056

ATTN: Barbara Kozlowski

HOME INVESTMENT BOOKLET

Type of farm: geographic

GREENBRIER REAL ESTATE
Barbara Kozlowski, Realtor-Associate®
90067 Carbondale Road * Campbell, NC 60056
(w) 704/555-8900 (h) 704/555-8897
(fax) 704/555-8901 (pager) 704/555-7703

BE SMART ABOUT YOUR INVESTMENT IN YOUR HOME

Dear Castle Pines Neighbor,

Story open

I was sitting at my desk the other afternoon when the phone rang. A schoolteacher who had bought a home from me the year before was on the line. She wanted a referral for an insurance agent. She had just been notified of a sharp hike in her homeowner's coverage and thought she could get a better deal someplace else. She probably could. I gave her two names and hung up.

Then I began wondering how many other Castle Pines residents could use referrals to reputable insurance agents or mortgage brokers or home equity representatives or others who handle home-related legal and financial matters. I bet that quite a few of you could.

Offer

So I put together the "Home Investment Services Booklet". Designed especially for Castle Pines' residents, it lists agents, brokers, property lawyers and other representatives with whom I've worked. These are people you can trust. People who will take the time to answer your questions and pay attention to your concerns. I've also included local title companies and relevant county offices, such as the tax assessor's.

Details of offer

I know what it's like. Mortgage rates go up and down. You need a magnifying glass to read your insurance policy. Your annual property tax assessment seems unchangeable and sometimes, unfair. If you're like me, often it's simpler just to write out a check than ask questions.

Benefits of offer

But when it comes to insurance or re-financing, it makes sense to shop around. Unhappy with ever-increasing insurance rates on my own home, I recently got bids from four other carriers. I switched and am saving $200 a year. I didn't realize until I started call-

(over, please)

ing that I could change carriers in the middle of the policy...which saved me $100 the first year alone.

Act now

To get your FREE "Home Investment Services Booklet," just fill out and return the enclosed card. To get your booklet even faster, call me at 555-8900 (office) during the day or at 555-8897 (home) or 555-7703 (pager) during evenings and weekends. You can call anytime. As soon as I hear from you, your booklet will be on its way.

Build rapport

After you look at it, please make suggestions. Maybe you think I should add someone you've worked with and would recommend to your friends. Or I may have included someone with whom you had a bad experience. Either way, I'd love your feedback.

Again—act now

With your home your most significant financial asset, it only makes sense to treat your investment in it with care. Please...call or write me today.

Sincerely yours,

Barbara Kozlowski
Realtor-Associate®

Limited quantity

P.S. I've only made about 40 booklets. To make sure I've got one for you, call or write right away.

KEY POINTS

1. Opens with personal story that flows into "you."

2. Limited supply adds urgency.

3. Great opportunity for establishing networks with non-competing salespeople in your area, e.g. mortgage brokers and insurance agents. Make this a cooperative effort.

OUTER ENVELOPE

Greenbrier Real Estate
90067 Carbondale Road
Campbell, NC 60056

Bulk Rate
US Postage
P A I D
Campbell, NC
Permit No 1234

*BE SMART ABOUT YOUR INVESTMENT
IN YOUR HOME*

Mr. Joe Hill
458 Center St.
Castle Pines, NC 60057

REPLY CARD

Photo

YES, BARBARA, I WANT TO BE SMART ABOUT MY
HOME INVESTMENT.

( ) PLEASE RUSH MY HOME INVESTMENT
SERVICE KIT TODAY.

Your Name _____

Your Address_____

_____

Your telephone number

(w)_____ (h)_____

Best time to call _____

BRE REPLY ENVELOPE

NO POSTAGE
NECESSARY
IF MAILED
IN THE
UNITED STATES

BUSINESS REPLY MAIL
First Class PERMIT NO.000 Campbell, NC
Postage will be paid by Addressee

Greenbrier Real Estate
90067 Carbondale Road
Campbell, NC 60056

ATTN: Barbara Kozlowski

Announcement Letters

Announcement letters are for specific circumstances and for mailing only to selected individuals. So instead of sending them to "Dear Castle Pine Neighbor," you may prefer to write, for example, "Dear Mr. and Mrs. Sithan."

Announcing a listing not only helps you promote a property, it also enhances your professional credibility. The more listings you have, the more successful people in your farm will think you are. And everybody likes to be associated with a success. Especially when they decide to list their own houses.

You reinforce this positive impression with the follow-up letter describing your success in selling the house.

In these letters, beware of falling into the trap of tooting your horn too loudly. Matter-of-factly announcing what you've done is enough.

NEW LISTING - LONG LETTER

Type of farm: geographic or social

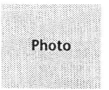

GREENBRIER REAL ESTATE
Barbara Kozlowski, Realtor-Associate®
90067 Carbondale Road * Campbell, NC 60056
(w) 704/555-8900 (h) 704/555-8897
(fax) 704/555-8901 (pager) 704/555-7703

ATTENTION!!! ATTENTION!!! ATTENTION!!!

Dear Castle Pines Neighbor,

I'm happy to tell you that Don and Betty Cherry have just asked me to help them sell their lovely home at 3220 Oakwood Drive.

Their home was a top-of-the-line model in the first phase of Broadcourt Development's 1981 award-winning Cambridge Group. Its 2100 square feet include three bedrooms, three baths and many added features such as a screened porch, walk-in closets, skylights, and brand-new appliances.

Betty's talent as a graphics designer is obvious in the home's tasteful, comfortable and interesting interior. It's also in exquisite shape. Don, an engineer, spends a lot of time in the backyard, which has a large pool and complete playground.

Because Don recently was promoted and has to relocate, the Cherrys need to sell their home quickly. At $197,500, it's priced well below what comparable — even less than comparable — homes have been selling for.

I've been involved in Castle Pines real estate for more than six years. I truly believe this is <u>one of the most outstanding values to hit the market.</u>

In neighborhoods as nice as yours, quite often friends or family members are looking to move in. You may even know someone yourself. If so, Don and Betty's home could be ideal.

If you or someone you know would like to see the Cherry's home, please give me a call at my office (555-8900) during the day or at home (555-8897) or on my pager (555-7703) anytime.

(over, please)

Use your own client's story (Get their permission!)

Adds urgency

More urgency

Act now

Even more urgency

I honestly don't think this home will be on the market for long. So if you have anyone in mind, I urge you to give them — and me — a call right away. Thanks.

Sincerely yours,

Barbara Kozlowski
Realtor-Associate®

P.S. Keep a look-out for "Open House" signs around Don and Betty's during the next few weekends. If you have a moment, please stop by and say hello.

KEY POINTS

1. Lots of details bring the house (& owners) to life.

2. Nice low-key sales pitch.

3. Can easily adapt for social farm (revise "your neighborhood" references).

4. Follow up with invitation to open houses.

5. Low price is big selling point.

6. Send or fax this letter to other Realtors® in the area. Change the P.S. to give the MLS number.

OUTER ENVELOPE

Greenbrier Real Estate
90067 Carbondale Road
Campbell, NC 60056

Bulk Rate
US Postage
P A I D
Campbell, NC
Permit No 1234

NEIGHBORHOOD NEWS

Mr. Joe Hill
458 Center St.
Castle Pines, NC 60057

NEW LISTING - SHORT LETTER
Type of farm: geographic or social

 **GREENBRIER REAL ESTATE**
Barbara Kozlowski, Realtor-Associate®
90067 Carbondale Road * Campbell, NC 60056
(w) 704/555-8900 (h) 704/555-8897
(fax) 704/555-8901 (pager) 704/555-7703

Replace with your clients—ask for permission

Describe property

Adds urgency

Warm and personal

Dear Castle Pines Neighbor,

I thought you'd be interested to know that Than and Trina Pok have asked me to list their home at 775 Window Drive in Castle Pines.

This 3,200-square-foot home offers a master bedroom suite, three smaller bedrooms, four baths, and a lovely wood-paneled family room. It has extensive decking and mature landscaping. The listed price is $305,000.

The home is in great shape and shows beautifully. I'm writing to see if you know anyone who might be interested in it. Do you have a friend or family member who'd like to live in Castle Pines? Is there someone you'd like to have closer to you?

If so, this is a great opportunity. I'm just starting to show the home, so a lot of prospective buyers aren't yet aware that it's on the market. Please — if you or a friend would like to see it — call me at my office (555-8900) during the day or at home (555-8897) or on my pager (555-7703) anytime.

Thank you.

Sincerely yours,

Barbara Kozlowski
Realtor-Associate®

P.S. Watch for "Open House" signs around the Pok home during the next few weekends. If you have a moment, please stop by and say hello.

KEY POINTS

1. To adapt for social farm, change "like to live in Castle Pines" to "friend or family member who is thinking about moving? Is there someone you know who would love a home like this?"

2. Send or fax to other Realtors®, changing P.S. to give MLS number.

3. Big selling point is fact that home is new on market. You can see it before anyone else.

NEW LISTING POSTCARD

Type of farm: geographic or social

<NEWS — NEWS — NEWS>

Dear Neighbor,

    * 453 Brookhaven Terrace is on the market! *

    Do you have any friends or relatives who'd like a 2-bedroom, 2-bath home with a fragrant rose garden and charming sun porch? It's listed at only $134,500. Some owner financing available. To see this lovely home, call me at 555-8900 (office) or at home (555-8897) or on my pager (555-7703) anytime.

                Sincerely yours,

                Barbara Kozlowski
                Greenbrier Real Estate

KEY POINTS

1. For social farm, change "Dear Neighbor".

2. Big selling point — opposite side can be full color picture of house. Some mail order services provide this. Also check with big photo finishers (e.g. K-Mart, Wal-Mart) in your area.

NEW SALE LETTER - IN ESCROW

Type of farm: geographic

GREENBRIER REAL ESTATE
Barbara Kozlowski, Realtor-Associate®
90067 Carbondale Road * Campbell, NC 60056
(w) 704/555-8900 (h) 704/555-8897
(fax) 704/555-8901 (pager) 704/555-7703

NEIGHBORHOOD UPDATE

March, 1996

Dear Castle Pines Neighbor,

I wasn't surprised when Betty and Don Cherry's home at 3220 Oakwood Drive sold quickly. They accepted an offer very close to the listed price of $197,500. As soon as escrow closes next month, the new owners plan to move in.

While working on this, I ran across several people extremely interested in buying homes in our neighborhood. Some made up their minds too late to put in offers for the Cherry's; others wanted something a bit different. But all are eager to live in Castle Pines. Unfortunately, at this moment, I have very little to show them.

If you've ever thought about selling your home — or if you know of a friend or neighbor who's thinking about selling — now is a good time. Resale values in Castle Pines are high and interest rates, particularly on adjustable rate mortgages, are favorable.

In either case, I'd like to hear from you. Especially now, when I have eager buyers. You can reach me at the office, 555-8900, during the day and at home, 555-8897, or on my pager, 555-7703, any other time. Call me if you're at all interested. Thank you.

Sincerely yours,

Barbara Kozlowski
Realtor-Associate®

P.S. While I'm confident this sale will go through, in today's market anything can happen. Remember that this is a 3-bedroom, 3-bath home with an award-winning design. The Cherrys still are accepting back-up offers.

Offer

KEY POINTS

1. Strong logic behind sending letter ("I have eager buyers").
2. Note that back-up offers still being accepted.
3. P.S. saves "face" in case sale falls through.

NEW SALE LETTER - ESCROW CLOSED

Type of farm: geographic

GREENBRIER REAL ESTATE
Barbara Kozlowski, Realtor-Associate®
90067 Carbondale Road * Campbell, NC 60056
(w) 704/555-8900 (h) 704/555-8897
(fax) 704/555-8901 (pager) 704/555-7703

NEIGHBORHOOD UPDATE

Dear Castle Pines Neighbor,

I wasn't surprised when Betty and Don Cherry's home at 3220 Oakwood Drive sold quickly. The new owners, Debbie and David Chen, will move in next month. Debbie is a physician at the local Kaiser Hospital; David owns an architectural firm in Chapel Hill. Please introduce yourself and welcome the Chens to the neighborhood.

Ask clients if okay

While working on this, I ran across several people extremely interested in buying homes in the neighborhood. Some made up their minds too late to put in offers for the Cherry's; others wanted something a bit different. But all are eager to live in Castle Pines. Unfortunately, at this moment, I have very little to show them.

If you've ever thought about selling your home — or if you know of a friend or neighbor who's thinking about selling — now is a good time. Resale values in Castle Pines are high and interest rates, particularly on adjustable rate mortgages, are favorable.

In either case, I'd like to hear from you. Especially now, when I have eager buyers. You can reach me at the office, 555-8900, during the day and at home, 555-8897, or on my pager, 555-7703, any other time. Call me if you're at all interested. Thank you.

Offer

Sincerely yours,

Barbara Kozlowski
Realtor-Associate®

P.S. The Cherry home sold within 97% of its listed price of $197,500. If you'd like to take advantage of a strong and healthy real estate market, do it now!

KEY POINTS

1. Lots of personal details.
2. Gives reasons for asking if interested in selling.
3. Everyone loves to know how much a house sells for.
4. Could give percent of listing price or price itself.

NEW SALE LETTER - ESCROW CLOSED

Type of farm: social

GREENBRIER REAL ESTATE

Barbara Kozlowski, Realtor-Associate®

90067 Carbondale Road * Campbell, NC 60056

(w) 704/555-8900 (h) 704/555-8897

(fax) 704/555-8901 (pager) 704/555-7703

March, 1996

Dear fellow St. Johns member,

I wasn't surprised when Betty and Don Cherry's home at 3220 Oakwood Drive sold quickly. The new owners, Debbie and David Chen, will move in next month. Debbie is a physician at the local Kaiser Hospital; David owns an architectural firm in Chapel Hill. They're very happy about their new home, which gives me a good feeling.

Makes you look good

While working on this, I ran across several people extremely interested in buying homes now. Some made up their minds too late to put in offers for the Cherry's; others wanted something a bit different. But all are very eager to move. Unfortunately, at this moment, I have very little to show them.

If you've ever thought about selling your home — or if you have a friend, relative or neighbor who's thinking about selling — now is a good time. Resale values are high and interest rates, particularly on adjustable rate mortgages, are favorable.

Offer

In either case, I'd like to hear from you. Especially now, when I have eager buyers. You can reach me at the office, 555-8900, during the day and at home, 555-8897, or on my pager, 555-7703, any other time. Call me if you're at all interested. Thank you.

Sincerely yours,

Barbara Kozlowski
Realtor-Associate®

P.S. The Cherry home sold within 97% of its listed price of $197,500. If you'd like to take advantage of a strong and healthy real estate market, do it now!

NEW SALE POSTCARD - ESCROW CLOSED

Type of farm: geographic

<UPDATE — UPDATE — UPDATE>

Please welcome Debbie and David Chen to your neighborhood.

The Chens bought the Cherry's lovely home at 3220 Oakwood Dr. It was on the market only three weeks and sold for 97% of its listed price of $197,500.

Right now, we have other buyers interested in our neighborhood. If you've ever thought about selling, now is a good time. Call me at 555-8900 (office), 555-8897 (home) or 555-7703 (pager).

Please give the Chens a great big Castle Pines "Hello."

Thanks.

Sincerely yours,

Barbara Kozlowski
Greenbrier Real Estate

NEW SALE POSTCARD - ESCROW CLOSED

Type of farm: social

<UPDATE — UPDATE — UPDATE>

* 3220 Oakwood Drive is sold! *

Dear Friend,

Last week we closed escrow on Don and Betty Cherry's lovely 3-bedroom home. The new owners are Debbie and David Chen. The house was listed for $197,500. After only 3 weeks on the market, it sold for $194,000.

While showing the Cherry's home, I ran across a number of other very motivated buyers. If you've ever thought about selling your home, now might be a good time. Call me at 555-8900 (office), 555-8897 (home) or 555-7703 (pager). Thanks.

Barbara Kozlowski
Greenbrier Real Estate

Invitations

Open house invitations play on neighbors' curiosity to draw them into face-to-face meetings with you.

These are warmed up by the highly personal copy and "urgent" notes such as "this is priced well below"...

While you can't expect a flood of responses to these invitations, handle the ones you get well. People may not be interested in moving now, but if they're interested in looking, there's a possibility down the line...

OPEN HOUSE LETTER

Type of farm: geographic or social

GREENBRIER REAL ESTATE
Barbara Kozlowski, Realtor-Associate®
90067 Carbondale Road * Campbell, NC 60056
(w) 704/555-8900 (h) 704/555-8897
(fax) 704/555-8901 (pager) 704/555-7703

You're invited to an Open House...
...hope to see you there.

January, 1997

Dear Castle Pines Neighbor,

A few weeks ago, I wrote you about Don and Betty Cherry selling their lovely 3-bedroom home at 3220 Oakwood Drive. Several of you called and arranged to see it with your friends.

For those of you who didn't and who are interested in a look-see (remember that Betty is a graphics artist — she did a great decorating job!), I'm inviting you to an open house at the Cherry's this Sunday from noon to 5 p.m.

Arouse interest

As I mentioned before, Don received a promotion and has to relocate quickly. As a result, the Cherrys' home is priced well below what comparable — even less than comparable — homes have been selling for.

Adds urgency

There's no doubt that this is one of the nicest homes — and best values — in Castle Pines. I hope to see you and your friends or relatives this Sunday. Thanks.

Sincerely yours,

Barbara Kozlowski
Realtor-Associate®

P.S. For you football fans, I'll have the game on the big-screen TV in the den and lots of snacks.

Personal and warm

KEY POINTS

1. Use the second paragraph to describe the home's biggest selling point. If nothing stands out, use a basic description of the house.

2. Use food as an enticement in the P.S.

OUTER ENVELOPE

Greenbrier Real Estate
90067 Carbondale Road
Campbell, NC 60056

Bulk Rate
US Postage
P A I D
Campbell, NC
Permit No 1234

YOU'RE INVITED TO AN OPEN HOUSE

Mr. Joe Hill
458 Center St.
Castle Pines, NC 60057

OPEN HOUSE POSTCARD

Type of farm: geographic or social

• **YOU'RE INVITED** •

You are cordially invited to an open house at Don and Betty Cherry's home at 3220 Oakwood Drive on

Sunday, June 22, from noon to 5 p.m.

This charming 3-bedroom, 3-bath home features a screened porch, walk-in closets, skylights, a large pool & complete playground. At $197,500, it's priced well below comparable homes in the neighborhood. Hope you can join us Sunday.

Barbara Kozlowski
Greenbrier Real Estate
(w) 555-8900
(pager) 555-7703

Adds urgency

Special Circumstances

Go to any real estate office in the country and one of the hottest conversation topics is how to handle for sale by owners. Often when a new agent comes on board, the broker hands over the classified ads and tells him or her to start calling all the private party real estate ads in it.

As any FSBO will tell you, more agents than prospects call on a for sale by owner sign. Obviously we all have our own approach, but I think using the mail to pave the way for a phone call can be many times more effective than only using the phone. More than anything else, it allows you to stand above the crowd of Realtors® and gives you a softer entrance into the prospect's home.

Many professionals have found the FSBO Kit to be an effective introduction, as it provides a valuable free gift. It is, however, a double-edge sword — if your Kit doesn't do the job, then how well can you do it?

For this reason, it's best to keep FSBO materials as generic as possible — reprints out of magazines and newspapers, listings and directories, and how-to material from third party sources. Make sure that the prospect knows this material is designed for FSBOs and is not what you would use to sell the home.

According to a recent survey by the National Association of Realtors®, 54% of the FSBOs in the hot market of 1993 would go it alone again. In the slow housing markets of 1989 and 1991, only 36% and 41%, respectively, said they would try it again. That means if the market in your area has been dragging, FSBOs might be an excellent source to tap for listings.

Expired listings can also be a gold mine — just keep your ethics on the up and up. Sending a letter before calling can help clarify the situation.

Relocations are a growing source of revenue for real estate professionals, especially corporate ones. We've designed one letter for individuals; a second for corporate human resource personnel. Both feature extensive information about the area.

With renters as prospects, of course, you're looking for buyers, not sellers. Here you should roughly estimate what the average rent costs and direct your appeal accordingly. For example, "After taxes, your monthly house payment would probably be only about $200 more than what you're paying in rent." Since many agents overlook renters in their farms, you may be able to tap into something big.

As for absentee owners, one Orange County, California Realtor® told me that his farm had only 10% absentee owners, but they made up 50% of his farm business.

Like renters, absentee owners are often ignored by other agents. But unlike renters, these people do have listings to give — and often more than one. Also significant is the fact that real estate investors buy and sell properties far more frequently than owner-occupants. This is especially true when tax laws relating to real estate investments change.

FOR SALE BY OWNER KIT

Type of farm: geographic

 GREENBRIER REAL ESTATE
Barbara Kozlowski, Realtor-Associate®
90067 Carbondale Road * Campbell, NC 60056
(w) 704/555-8900 (h) 704/555-8897
(fax) 704/555-8901 (pager) 704/555-7703

**Here's how to get your FREE
For Sale By Owner Kit**

March, 1997

Dear Mr. Hill,

    I drove by your home this weekend and noticed your "For Sale By Owner" sign in the front yard. Seeing it made me wonder if you'd be interested in a special free kit that I've prepared for owners trying to sell homes on their own.

    Your <u>For Sale By Owner Kit</u> includes:

* classified advertising rates and contact numbers for all local newspapers and throwaways,

* tips on showing your home and hosting an open house,

* complete directory of local lenders, appraisers and escrow firms,

* blank <u>sample documents including "Property Condition Addendum," "Earnest Money Contract" and "Pre-qualification Worksheet."</u>

    Why am I offering you this kit? Because I'm hoping that you'll let me help you find a new home. Or — if you change your mind and get tired of trying to sell your home yourself — you'll think of me.

    After more than six years of marketing Castle Pines homes, I know how difficult a sale can be. From setting the right price to finding a qualified buyer to the legalities of title insurance, tax transfers, and closing details, the <u>entire process can be frustrating and time-consuming</u>.

    I'd like to think that I've learned a thing or two over the years and that you'll find the information in this kit valuable. It will save you time and probably money.

(over, please)

Offer

Details of offer

Rationale

Benefit

You take the initiative

Your For Sale By Owner Kit is free. You have no obligation. I'll call you next week to see if you're interested. Or you can call me at 555-8900 (office), 555-8897 (home) or 555-7703 (pager). Call anytime. If you prefer, you can just drop the enclosed postage-paid reply card in the mail.

If you have any questions, I'll be happy to help however I can.

Good luck.

Sincerely yours,

Barbara Kozlowski
Realtor-Associate®

Adds urgency

P.S. I have seven buyers I'm working with right now. If you're interested in broker cooperation, I can bring them by after I preview your home. Call me today!

KEY POINTS

1. Soft sell

2. Offers valuable information

3. Deliver FSBO kit in person

4. Use cross directory to get name.

OUTER ENVELOPE

Greenbrier Real Estate
90067 Carbondale Road
Campbell, NC 60056

Bulk Rate
US Postage
P A I D
Campbell, NC
Permit No 1234

HOW TO GET YOUR <u>FREE</u>
FOR SALE BY OWNER KIT

Mr. Joe Hill
458 Center St.
Castle Pines, NC 60057

REPLY CARD

Photo

YES, BARBARA, I WANT THIS VALUABLE
INFORMATION

( ) PLEASE RUSH MY FREE FOR SALE BY OWNER
KIT TODAY.

Your Name _____

Your Address_____

_____

Your telephone number

(w)_____ (h)_____

Best time to call _____

BRE REPLY ENVELOPE

NO POSTAGE
NECESSARY
IF MAILED
IN THE
UNITED STATES

BUSINESS REPLY MAIL
First Class PERMIT NO.000 Campbell, NC
Postage will be paid by Addressee

Greenbrier Real Estate
90067 Carbondale Road
Campbell, NC 56

ATTN: Barbara Kozlowski

FOR SALE BY OWNER SHORT LETTER

GREENBRIER REAL ESTATE
Barbara Kozlowski, Realtor-Associate®
90067 Carbondale Road * Campbell, NC 60056
(w) 704/555-8900 (h) 704/555-8897
(fax) 704/555-8901 (pager) 704/555-7703

December 5, 1996

Mr. Joe Hill
458 Center St.
Castle Pines, NC 60057

Dear Mr. Hill,

While I was showing property to prospective buyers in your neighborhood, I noticed your "For Sale" sign.

Give specific details

As a specialist in Castle Pines real estate, I'm always on the look-out for new properties. Your home looks very attractive and is in an excellent location.

Offer

Because I have a number of eager buyers for Castle Pines, I was wondering if you'd be willing to allow me to show them your home. If so, I would appreciate a preview at your convenience.

I'll call in the next few days to see if you're interested. In the meantime, good luck.

Sincerely,

Barbara Kozlowski
Realtor-Associate®

Added benefit of offer

P.S. If you like, I can bring along sample real estate forms to help you sort through the waist-high paperwork involved in selling a home. Just let me know!

KEY POINTS

1. Short and to-the-point

2. Strong logic — saw with buyers

3. Added enticement of sample forms

OUTER ENVELOPE

Greenbrier Real Estate
90067 Carbondale Road
Campbell, NC 60056

FIRST
CLASS
STAMP

Mr. Joe Hill
458 Center St.
Castle Pines, NC 60057

FOR SALE BY OWNER /
FOUR WEEKS AFTER HOME GOES ON MARKET

GREENBRIER REAL ESTATE
Barbara Kozlowski, Realtor-Associate®
90067 Carbondale Road * Campbell, NC 60056
(w) 704/555-8900 (h) 704/555-8897
(fax) 704/555-8901 (pager) 704/555-7703

January 9, 1997

Dear Mr. Hill,

I drove by your house this weekend and noticed your "For Sale By Owner" sign is still up. As you may have discovered by now, selling a home is not as simple as it may appear. The time-consuming process can create considerable inconvenience and unfortunately, frustration. Even for those of us who have spent years doing it.

Offer

If you've reached the point where you would consider a Realtor's® help, I'd appreciate it if you'd keep me in mind. You may have noticed the many "Greenbrier Real Estate" signs in your neighborhood. Last month I sold the Ramirez home at 556 Lone Pine Road for $176,500. I also recently sold homes at 667 Trail Star Drive and 435 Rocky Road. Right now, I have a number of prospective buyers interested in Castle Pines and I'm looking for more homes to show them. If you're looking for a new home in the area, I have some very good listings that you may want to see.

Secondary offer

Even if you haven't decided to use a Realtor's® services, by now you probably have some questions. I'd be happy to help however I can. There's no obligation, of course. I'll call you next week. We can talk over the phone or meet in person, whichever you prefer. Or you can call me at 555-8900 (office), 555-8897 (home) or 555-7703 (pager).

In the meantime, the best of luck selling your home.

Sincerely yours,

Barbara Kozlowski
Realtor-Associate®

P.S. If you need help with escrow or loan financing...I can put you in touch with the best firms in town. Just give me a call.

KEY POINTS

1. Gives specific home sales to demonstrate expertise.

2. Offers to help on phone or in person.

3. No premium.

4. Use regular outer envelope.

TWO-STEP APPROACH
LETTER 1

GREENBRIER REAL ESTATE
Barbara Kozlowski, Realtor-Associate®
90067 Carbondale Road * Campbell, NC 60056
(w) 704/555-8900 (h) 704/555-8897
(fax) 704/555-8901 (pager) 704/555-7703

April, 1997

Dear Mr. Hill,

Grab attention

I see from your ad that you've decided to try to sell your home yourself. If you're like 90% of the homeowners who attempt this, it's because you want to save the broker's commission.

While this may seem like a good reason, in actuality <u>it's the buyer, not the seller, who truly pays the commission</u>.

Offer

<u>By trying to sell the home yourself, you lose a number of benefits</u> provided by listing with a real estate broker. These include:

1. We will enter your home in the <u>Multiple Listing Service</u> (MLS). This service produces a majority of local home sales.

2. We can help you set a <u>reasonable selling price</u> by providing market comparisons of the sales of similar homes in your neighborhood. Many owners have emotional attachments that lead to unrealistic assessments of their homes' value. These folks often wind up not being able to sell for a long, long time.

3. We can protect you by <u>screening genuine buyers</u> from the flood of "looky-loos" knocking at your door. This is important, as the number 1 reason that for-sale-by-owner deals fall through is buyer financing problems.

4. We can <u>more effectively advertise and promote</u> your home. When we list a home, we pay for the advertising — you don't. Because of our advertising volume, we get better rates than individuals like you.

5. Once you accept an offer, we take care of all the details. We qualify buyers, arrange loans, get loan approvals, set up appraisals, supervise the escrow, check the title, order a home inspection, etc. Overall we provide a level of expertise that you won't find

(over, please)

with many other real estate firms. In the long run, this will save you time and money.

Once you decide to sell through a broker, you have a choice. There are a number of qualified brokers in this area. Many, I'm sure, could quite competently handle the sale of your home. But not many specialize in the Castle Pines neighborhood. And not many have the in-house resources that you'll find at Greenbrier Real Estate.

What's most important, however, is that you feel comfortable with your real estate agent. And that you're convinced your agent has the level of expertise and follow-through you need. Part of that expertise involves the willingness to prepare a complete proposal for marketing your home. A proposal that you review and approve, then supervise the execution.

Right now, if you're thinking at all about using an agent, it's a good idea to interview several. <u>Let them tell you what they can do for you</u>. Even if you decide not to use an agent, you'll probably pick up a few tips on how to better market your own home.

Let the owner keep control

I have been an agent in this community for more than six years. My firm, Greenbrier Real Estate, is one of the largest and most respected real estate companies in this area.

If you do choose to work with a real estate agent, I hope you will give me a chance to be <u>one of the agents</u> whom you invite to present a proposal on how I would market your home. I'll call you next week to see if you're interested.

Secondary offer

In the meantime, the best of luck.

Sincerely yours,

Barbara Kozlowski
Realtor-Associate®

P.S. If you have any questions, I can be reached 24 hours a day. Call me at 555-8900 during the day or at 555-8897 (home) or 555-7703 (pager) any other time. Good luck!

KEY POINTS

1. Advantages of going with broker couched in "you" terms. (protect you, help you...)
2. Soft sell — let me be one of several agents...
3. Highlights owner involvement and supervision of sale.
4. Get owner's name from cross-directory.

TWO-STEP APPROACH
LETTER 2

Remind of previous offer

GREENBRIER REAL ESTATE
Barbara Kozlowski, Realtor-Associate®
90067 Carbondale Road * Campbell, NC 60056
(w) 704/555-8900 (h) 704/555-8897
(fax) 704/555-8901 (pager) 704/555-7703

May, 1997

Dear Mr. Hill,

About a month ago, I first noticed your "For Sale" ad. By now, you may have discovered that selling your home is not as easy as it looks.

You may remember my letter several weeks ago that explained how I and my firm, Greenbrier Real Estate, could help you sell your home. Briefly, the letter said:

1. We will enter your home in the <u>Multiple Listing Service</u> (MLS), which produces the majority of local home sales.

2. We can help you set a <u>reasonable selling price</u> by providing market comparisons of the sales of similar homes in your neighborhood. This will help avoid your home being on the market a long, long time.

3. We can protect you by <u>screening for genuine buyers</u>. This is important, as the number 1 reason that for-sale-by-owner deals fall through is buyer financing problems.

4. We can <u>more effectively advertise and promote</u> your home. When we list a home, we pay for the advertising — you don't.

5. Once you accept an offer, we <u>take care of all the details</u>. We'll qualify buyers, arrange loans, get loan approvals, set up appraisals, supervise the escrow, check the title, order a home inspection, etc. This will save you time and money.

Greenbrier Real Estate, a 22-year-old firm, is one of the largest and most respected companies in this area. We have contacts with major industries and access to out-of-town as well as local buyers. I have been a leading Greenbrier agent for more than six years, working almost exclusively with homes in your neighborhood.

(over, please)

If you can give me 30 minutes, I can give you a detailed proposal of how I would market your home. Backed by my company's extensive resources, this plan will include an aggressive advertising campaign, showings to real estate agents, open houses, and direct mail.

Details of offer

Just think — you'll no longer have to bother with taking telephone calls, placing classified ads, holding your own open houses, or asking friends if they know anyone who'd like to buy your home.

Benefits

I also could refer you to several other agents who can make similar proposals. You can decide for yourself who would put the most effort into selling your home and with whom you'd feel most comfortable.

Secondary offer

Of course, you'd have no obligation with any of these presentations. I'll call you next week to see if you're interested.

You take the initiative

Thank you for your time.

Sincerely yours,

Barbara Kozlowski
Realtor-Associate®

P.S. If you have any questions, I can be reached 24 hours a day. Call me at 555-8900 during the day or at 555-8897 (home) or 555-7703 (pager) any other time. Good luck!

KEY POINTS

1. Repeats benefits of using Realtor® — good reminder.

2. Emphasizes how much effort required to sell home.

3. Pitches presentation — but asks to consider several agents.

EXPIRED LISTING LETTER

GREENBRIER REAL ESTATE
Barbara Kozlowski, Realtor-Associate®
90067 Carbondale Road * Campbell, NC 60056
(w) 704/555-8900 (h) 704/555-8897
(fax) 704/555-8901 (pager) 704/555-7703

July 26, 1996

Dear Mr. Hill,

Offer

I recently drove by your house and noticed that the "For Sale" sign from Broadmoor Realty has disappeared. Yet I haven't heard that your home sold.

If you're no longer listed with Broadmoor Realty or any other real estate office and still interested in selling your home, I'd like to talk to you.

Details of offer

My specialty is marketing Castle Pines homes. Last month I sold the Ramirez home at 556 Lone Pine Road for $176,500. I also recently sold homes at 667 Trail Star Drive and 435 Rocky Road. I am a leading agent at Greenbrier Real Estate, a 22-year-old firm that is one of the most respected real estate companies in the area.

More details

If you can give me 30 minutes, I can give you a detailed proposal of how I would market your home. Backed by the extensive resources of my company, this would include an aggressive advertising campaign, Realtor® showings, open houses, direct mail, and lots of personal attention. I would work hard to sell your home quickly — my last Castle Pines listing sold within three weeks.

Owner keeps control

Hearing my proposal will put you under no obligation. I tell you what I can do for you, answer your questions, and say good-bye. Then you decide what you want to do.

You take the initiative

I'll call you next week to see if you're interested. Or you can call me at 555-8900 during the day or at 555-8897 (home) or 555-7703 (pager) any other time. If you've already re-signed with your previous agent or another agent, please disregard this letter and good luck with your sale. Thank you.

Sincerely yours,

Barbara Kozlowski
Realtor-Associate®

P.S. If you call me today, I have some qualified prospects ready and eager to buy!

KEY POINTS
1. Get name from MLS expired listing section.
2. Use plain outer envelope

RENTERS TO BUYERS
PERSONAL STORY LETTER

 Photo

GREENBRIER REAL ESTATE
Barbara Kozlowski, Realtor-Associate®
90067 Carbondale Road * Campbell, NC 60056
(w) 704/555-8900 (h) 704/555-8897
(fax) 704/555-8901 (pager) 704/555-7703

TAKE A BIG STEP...
...TO FINANCIAL FREEDOM

Dear Castle Pines Neighbor,

Four years ago, Rajiv and Helen Rimal walked into my office and announced they wanted to buy a home and end their years as renters.

Both had steady, well-paying jobs, but little cash. More than anything, they wanted the <u>freedom of owning their own home</u>.

We searched for months. We looked at small homes, run-down homes, new homes. Finally, we found it. A small 2-bedroom home with a white picket fence, bay window in the living room, and breakfast nook overlooking a big back yard.

Negotiating the deal took some work. But the <u>seller decided to help and the Rimals got the home they longed for</u>.

Outside of a few holiday greeting cards and an occasional phone call, I didn't hear from the Rimals until last month. Because of a few additions to the family — and one more on the way — they had outgrown their small home and needed another.

I sold their home in less than a month. In a little over four years, it had appreciated more than 40% in value.

With the profit, the Rimals were able to put more than 30% down on an exclusive, 4-bedroom Northern Ridge home. And they're delighted.

<u>In four short years, they went from renting an apartment to owning an estate property</u>.

What about you?

<u>Isn't it time you started thinking about owning a home?</u> Wouldn't you enjoy being free of hearing neighbors through the walls...shoveling quarters into laundry

(over, please)

*Story open
(Use one of your client's stories.)*

Benefits of offer

machines...and always conforming to somebody else's rules?

While I can't guarantee that you'll enjoy the same good fortune as the Rimals, it is true that hundreds of people every day move towards financial and psychological freedom by purchasing their own homes.

<u>Owning a home not only provides you with a significant tax deduction, it also makes home equity lines of credit and other financial advantages available to you</u>.

Offer
Qualify

If you're thinking about finally moving up to your own home, I'd like to meet with you. We could work out the specifics of how much you would benefit from home ownership compared to what you're now paying in rent. While I'm not an accountant or a financial adviser, I can also discuss the many options available if you, like the Rimals, lack sufficient cash for a down payment.

You take the initiative

I'll call you next week to see if you're interested. If you prefer, you can call me at 555-8900 (office) during the day or at 555-8897 (home) or 555-7703 (pager) any other time. Or you can drop the enclosed postage-paid card in the mail.

Start looking forward to a more secure and happy financial future.

Sincerely yours,

Barbara Kozlowski
Realtor-Associate®

P.S. If you'd like to talk to the Rimals, let me know. I'd be glad to set it up.

KEY POINTS

1. Personal story adds interest.

2. Gives very specific facts on home ownership.

3. Offers to work out personal finances.

4. Emphasizes it's OK if you lack sufficient down payment.

OUTER ENVELOPE

Greenbrier Real Estate
90067 Carbondale Road
Campbell, NC 60056

Bulk Rate
US Postage
P A I D
Campbell, NC
Permit No 1234

TAKE A BIG STEP...
...TO FINANCIAL FREEDOM

Mr. Joe Hill
458 Center St.
Castle Pines, NC 60057

REPLY CARD

Photo

YES, BARBARA, I WANT TO FIND OUT MORE
ABOUT HOW I CAN OWN A HOME.

( ) PLEASE CALL ME TODAY.

Your Name _____

Your Address_____

_____

Your telephone number

(w)_____ (h)_____

Best time to call _____

BRE REPLY ENVELOPE

NO POSTAGE
NECESSARY
IF MAILED
IN THE
UNITED STATES

BUSINESS REPLY MAIL
First Class PERMIT NO.000 Campbell, NC
Postage will be paid by Addressee

Greenbrier Real Estate
90067 Carbondale Road
Campbell, NC 60056

ATTN: Barbara Kozlowski

RENTERS TO BUYERS

FIGHT RENT INCREASES

Photo

GREENBRIER REAL ESTATE

Barbara Kozlowski, Realtor-Associate®

90067 Carbondale Road * Campbell, NC 60056

(w) 704/555-8900 (h) 704/555-8897

(fax) 704/555-8901 (pager) 704/555-7703

STOP WORRYING ABOUT RENT INCREASES...

Dear Castle Pines neighbor,

WHAM!!

Attention-getting open

That's the sound of another renter being slammed right between the eyes with an increased rent notice.

If you've gotten such a notice — or expect it any day — now might be just the time to fight back!

Tight fast-paced copy

And build for the future by discovering the financial freedom that comes from owning your own home.

If you currently rent, it's possible that you could actually pay less each month and own your home.

That's right. I said less.

Statistics add credibility

If you're in the 25% tax bracket, $800 a month rent may actually cost you more (after taxes) than a $1,110 monthly mortgage. And with current interest rates, $1,100 a month can put you in a much nicer home than most rental properties.

What's more, your hard-earned money will no longer be lining your landlord's and Uncle Sam's pockets. Instead you'll be investing in your own future by building equity and benefiting from your home's appreciation. You'll also have access to home equity credit lines and enjoy other financial perks.

Like to know more?

Offer

I'd be glad to meet with you, lay out the numbers, and figure out how you can start enjoying the many advantages of home ownership. If you're interested, I'll call you next week.

Or you can call me at 555-8900 (office) during the day or at 555-8897 (home) or 555-7703 (pager) any other time.

Urgency

Please don't put this off. Right now, the market for first-time home buyers is excellent. I know about a number of starter homes on the market and I can help

(over, please)

you arrange favorable financing specifically for first-time buyers.

Get ready to <u>start looking forward to a more secure and happy financial future</u>.

Sincerely yours,

Barbara Kozlowski
Realtor-Associate®

P.S. If you're not convinced, please read the enclosed note.

KEY POINTS

1. To the point.

2. Supports arguments with facts.

3. Gives specific numerical examples.

LIFT NOTE

Lift notes add credibility. They should be from someone with authority. In this case, a client whom you helped move from being a renter to a homeowner. Replace the story below with your client's story. Draft a version, then show it to the person you'd like to sign it. Let them make minor changes. This could be printed to look like a handwritten note or it could be typed. If folded over, the outside should read "If You're Still Not Convinced...read this"

Use your client's story—get permission

Dear Friend,

Four years ago, I was living in a $900-a-month apartment. My landlord had increased the rent three years in a row. When I received the third notice, I knew I had to do something. I called Barbara Kozlowski.

Barbara went to work right away. The first day, she lined up five homes for me to look at. The second day, she had six more. The next week, I found the perfect place.

Barbara handled everything. From negotiating the offer to finding exactly the right financing. When problems arose, she stepped in and looked out for me. Because of Barbara, today I'm living in a home I love.

Buying a home was the smartest financial move I ever made. The second smartest was asking Barbara to help me.

Sincerely,
George Stephanos
Owner
Independent Auto Shop

OUTER ENVELOPE

Greenbrier Real Estate
90067 Carbondale Road
Campbell, NC 60056

> Bulk Rate
> US Postage
> P A I D
> Campbell, NC
> Permit No 1234

EXPECTING A RENT INCREASE???

Mr. Joe Hill
458 Center St.
Castle Pines, NC 60057

REPLY CARD

Photo

YES, BARBARA, I WANT TO FIND OUT MORE
ABOUT HOW I CAN OWN A HOME.

( ) PLEASE CALL ME TODAY.

Your Name _____

Your Address_____

_____

Your telephone number

(w)_____ (h)_____

Best time to call _____

BRE REPLY ENVELOPE

> NO POSTAGE
> NECESSARY
> IF MAILED
> IN THE
> UNITED STATES

BUSINESS REPLY MAIL

First Class PERMIT NO.000 Campbell, NC
Postage will be paid by Addressee

Greenbrier Real Estate
90067 Carbondale Road
Campbell, NC 56056

ATTN: Barbara Kozlowski

RELOCATION LETTER
INDIVIDUAL

Offer

Details of offer

Free info

More free info

<u>You</u> *take the initiative*

GREENBRIER REAL ESTATE
Barbara Kozlowski, Realtor-Associate®
90067 Carbondale Road * Campbell, NC 60056
(w) 704/555-8900 (h) 704/555-8897
(fax) 704/555-8901 (pager) 704/555-7703

October 15, 1997

Dear Mr. Hill,

I'm writing because I heard about your planned relocation to Castle Pines. I'd like to welcome you to this area and offer my services. As a real estate agent, I've handled a number of relocations.

Let me start by assuring you that Castle Pines offers an excellent real estate market. Our average residential property has appreciated 30% over the past five years. Our neighborhoods are filled with lovely homes, excellent schools and an abundance of natural beauty.

Personally, I've specialized in Castle Pines real estate for more than six years. I'm affiliated with Greenbrier Real Estate, which is one of the largest and most respected firms in town.

To give you an idea of the market, on the Multiple Listing Service today, you'd find more than 3,000 homes to choose from. About 10% of these listings are handled by Greenbrier. I personally know of a number of attractive homes for sale; some are bargains listed below their market value. I've enclosed MLS descriptions of a handful of properties, just to help familiarize you with what's available.

I'm also including general information on Castle Pines — a map, local school statistics and a Chamber of Commerce booklet.

I'll plan to call you next week. In the meantime, if you have any questions, please call me at 704/555-8900 (office) during the day or at 704/555-8897 (home) or 704/555-7703 (pager) evenings and weekends. Call any time. Or you can drop the postage paid reply card in the mail.

(over, please)

I look forward to talking to you. Thank you.

Sincerely yours,

Barbara Kozlowski
Realtor-Associate®

P.S. If you need a good moving company, I know the best! Call me.

Final hook

KEY POINTS

1. Prepare a relocation packet that contains your card, a map, overview of the area, school stats, and other relevant information.

2. Emphasize number of homes available and size and competency of your brokerage.

3. Use plain outer envelope.

4. Make sure you have the phone number before sending the letter.

OUTER ENVELOPE

Greenbrier Real Estate
90067 Carbondale Road
Campbell, NC 60056

FIRST
CLASS
STAMP

Mr. Joe Hill
458 Center St.
Castle Pines, NC 60057

REPLY CARD

Photo	YES, BARBARA, I WANT TO TALK TO YOU ABOUT YOUR RELOCATION SERVICES. ( ) PLEASE CALL ME TODAY.

Your Name _____

Your Address_____

_____

Your telephone number

(w)_____ (h)_____

Best time to call _____

BRE REPLY ENVELOPE

NO POSTAGE
NECESSARY
IF MAILED
IN THE
UNITED STATES

BUSINESS REPLY MAIL
First Class PERMIT NO.000 Campbell, NC
Postage will be paid by Addressee

Greenbrier Real Estate
90067 Carbondale Road
Campbell, NC 60056

ATTN: Barbara Kozlowski

RELOCATION LETTER
CORPORATE

GREENBRIER REAL ESTATE
Barbara Kozlowski, Realtor-Associate®
90067 Carbondale Road * Campbell, NC 60056
(w) 704/555-8900 (h) 704/555-8897
(fax) 704/555-8901 (pager) 704/555-7703

October 15, 1997

Mr. Joe Hill
General Manager
ABC Manufacturing
1234 Main St.
Hometown, NC 33333

Dear Mr. Hill,

I'm writing because I heard about your company's planned relocation to Castle Pines. We welcome new businesses for the growth they bring — and the possibility of new neighbors to enjoy!

Offer

As a real estate agent, I've handled a number of relocations. I provide quick, efficient service, with an emphasis on responsiveness. That means fewer headaches for you, as I'll take care of your employees during every step of the relocation process — from sending them home buying information kits before they arrive to helping them find repair services, schools, and even restaurant referrals after they move in.

Benefits of offer

I've specialized in Castle Pines real estate for more than six years. I'm affiliated with Greenbrier Real Estate, which is one of the largest and most respected firms in town.

I'm sure that you're aware that Castle Pines is an excellent real estate market. Our average residential property has appreciated 30% over the past five years. Our neighborhoods are filled with lovely homes, excellent schools and an abundance of natural beauty.

To give you an idea of the market, on the Multiple Listing Service today, you'll find more than 3,000 homes. About 10% of these listings are handled by Greenbrier. I personally know of a number of attractive homes for sale; the average price ranges from $100,000 to $250,000. I've enclosed MLS descriptions

(over, please)

Free gifts

of a handful of properties to familiarize you with what's available.

I've also prepared a number of Relocation Kits which I would be happy to send you. These include sample MLS listings, a map of Castle Pines, local school statistics, a Chamber of Commerce booklet, and other brochures.

They're great for distributing to employees planning to move with you. Just let me know how many you'd like.

Offer to visit

Better yet, tell me in person. I'd like the opportunity to visit your office and describe in detail the many relocation services which I offer. I'll call you next week to see what we can arrange.

You take the initiative

In the meantime, if you'd like the Relocation Kits right away or have any questions, call me at 704/555-8900 (office) during the day. Or at 704/555-8897 (home) or 704/555-7703 (pager) evenings and weekends. Call any time. Or drop the postage paid reply card in the mail.

Good luck with the planning. I'll talk to you next week.

Sincerely yours,

Barbara Kozlowski
Realtor-Associate®

Always use a P.S.

P.S. If you're looking for a good moving company, I know the best! Call me.

KEY POINTS

1. Prepare a relocation packet that contains your card, a map, overview of the area, school stats, and other relevant information.

2. Emphasize number of homes available and size and competency of your brokerage.

3. Use plain outer envelope.

4. Make sure you have the phone number before sending the letter.

OUTER ENVELOPE

Greenbrier Real Estate
90067 Carbondale Road
Campbell, NC 60056

FIRST
CLASS
STAMP

Mr. Joe Hill
General Manager
ABC Manufacturing
1234 Main St.
Hometown, NC 33333

REPLY CARD

Photo

YES, BARBARA, I WANT TO TALK TO YOU ABOUT
YOUR RELOCATION SERVICES.

( ) PLEASE CALL ME TODAY.

Your Name _____

Your Address_____

_____

Your telephone number

(w)_____ (h)_____

Best time to call _____

BRE REPLY ENVELOPE

NO POSTAGE
NECESSARY
IF MAILED
IN THE
UNITED STATES

BUSINESS REPLY MAIL
First Class PERMIT NO.000 Campbell, NC
Postage will be paid by Addressee

Greenbrier Real Estate
90067 Carbondale Road
Campbell, NC 60056

ATTN: Barbara Kozlowski

ABSENTEE OWNER LETTER

GREENBRIER REAL ESTATE
Barbara Kozlowski, Realtor-Associate®
90067 Carbondale Road * Campbell, NC 60056
(w) 704/555-8900 (h) 704/555-8897
(fax) 704/555-8901 (pager) 704/555-7703

CASTLE PINES REAL ESTATE UPDATE

May, 1997

Dear Mr. Hill,

Grab attention

I'm writing you today because I see from the county records that you own a house at 887 Brookside St. in Castle Pines.

Lately home sales in this area have been brisk as interest rates continue to remain attractive. We're also benefiting from higher housing demand as more and more industries relocate here.

Benefits of offer

Because you own investment property, I assume that your goal is to maximize your return. If this is true, I urge you to seriously consider selling your property and taking your profit now. Today's market is the best we've had in years. Homes comparable to yours have been selling for $160,000 to $185,000. From what I know of yours, I believe it would sell around the upper end of this scale.

And it probably wouldn't take very long. In the past few months, I've sold homes at 556 Lone Pine Road, 667 Trail Star Drive and 435 Rocky Road — all in Castle Pines. My company, Greenbrier Real Estate, has been marketing Castle Pines homes for 10 years. We know the market and we think you have a highly desirable property.

Offer

If you're at all interested in selling, I'd be happy to discuss it with you. I could give you an evaluation of your property's value based on recent sales of comparable homes, describe an intensive marketing plan, and perhaps introduce you to other investment properties in the area. If you're open to it, this is a good time to trade up.

You take the initiative

I'll call next week to see what you think. In the meantime, if you have any questions, you can reach me at 704/555-8900 (office) during the day or at

(over, please)

704/555-8897 (home) or 704/555-7703 (pager) evenings and weekends. Please call any time. Or drop the postage-paid reply card in a convenient mail box.

The enclosed newspaper article about the flood of new businesses in this area explains why today's market is so good for owners like you.

I look forward to talking to you.

Sincerely yours,

Barbara Kozlowski
Realtor-Associate®

P.S. If managing your property is difficult, I can help. Just give me a call.

Free info

KEY POINTS

1. Use owner's name.

2. Give details on your recent sales.

3. If possible, add details about the owner's property.

4. If no new businesses are moving into the area, use article about boom in local real estate market or excellence of local schools — anything to support your position that it's a good time to sell.

5. Be specific on why this is a good time to sell.

6. Make sure you have the owner's phone number before promising to call the next week.

OUTER ENVELOPE

Greenbrier Real Estate
90067 Carbondale Road
Campbell, NC 60056

| Bulk Rate |
| US Postage |
| P A I D |
| Campbell, NC |
| Permit No 1234 |

CASTLE PINES REAL ESTATE UPDATE

Mr. Joe Hill
458 Center St.
Castle Pines, NC 60057

REPLY CARD

Photo

YES, BARBARA, I WANT TO TALK TO YOU ABOUT CURRENT REAL ESTATE OPPORTUNITIES.

( ) PLEASE CALL ME TODAY.

Your Name _____

Your Address_____

_____

Your telephone number
(w)_____ (h)_____
Best time to call _____

BRE REPLY ENVELOPE

| NO POSTAGE |
| NECESSARY |
| IF MAILED |
| IN THE |
| UNITED STATES |

BUSINESS REPLY MAIL
First Class PERMIT NO.000 Campbell, NC
Postage will be paid by Addressee

Greenbrier Real Estate
90067 Carbondale Road
Campbell, NC 60056

ATTN: Barbara Kozlowski

ABSENTEE OWNER
UNDEVELOPED LAND

GREENBRIER REAL ESTATE
Barbara Kozlowski, Realtor-Associate®
90067 Carbondale Road * Campbell, NC 60056
(w) 704/555-8900 (h) 704/555-8897
(fax) 704/555-8901 (pager) 704/555-7703

CASTLE PINES REAL ESTATE UPDATE

October 3, 1997

Dear Mr. Hill,

I'm writing because I work with Greenbrier Real Estate and frankly, we're in a tight spot. Over the last few months, just about all the marketable homes in the area have sold. Yet we still have buyers coming in every day looking for homes. Right now, their best alternative is developable land such as your property at 776 Lakeview Road. I'm contacting all Castle Pines property owners to see who would consider selling.

Tight, crisp copy

I've taken the liberty of including an agreement that allows me to market your property. Look it over and see what you think. My marketing your property won't cost you a penny. And with today's low house inventory fueling a high land demand, you're in a great position. When I find a buyer, you'll probably enjoy a nice profit.

Offer

I'll call you next week. If you have any questions, you can reach me at 704/555-8900 (office) during the day or at 704/555-8897 (home) or 704/555-7703 (pager) evenings and weekends. Call any time. If you're definitely interested, please sign the enclosed agreement and return it in the postage paid envelope.

Thank you for your time. And remember — now is a terrific time to sell.

Sincerely,

Barbara Kozlowski
Realtor-Associate®

Enc.: Exclusive right of sale contract

Businesslike

KEY POINTS

1. Include right of sale contract with owner's name & property description filled in.

2. If you're recently sold similar properties in the area, mention them in second paragraph.

3. If property has appreciated significantly since owner bought it, give percentage.

OUTER ENVELOPE

Greenbrier Real Estate
90067 Carbondale Road
Campbell, NC 60056

FIRST
CLASS
STAMP

CASTLE PINES REAL ESTATE UPDATE

Mr. Joe Hill
458 Center St.
Castle Pines, NC 60057

BRE REPLY ENVELOPE

NO POSTAGE
NECESSARY
IF MAILED
IN THE
UNITED STATES

BUSINESS REPLY MAIL
First Class PERMIT NO.000 Campbell, NC
Postage will be paid by Addressee

Greenbrier Real Estate
90067 Carbondale Road
Campbell, NC 60056

ATTN: Barbara Kozlowski

Follow-up Referrals

One of the strongest openings in a direct mail farm letter is a referral. By linking you to the reader through someone they know, a referral immediately gives you credibility and provides an incentive for the prospect to continue reading.

A referral from a prospect's friend is better than from another real estate professional, but both are far better than nothing.

Whenever you can reference someone familiar to a prospect in a mailing, do it.

CLIENT REFERRAL

GREENBRIER REAL ESTATE
Barbara Kozlowski, Realtor-Associate®
90067 Carbondale Road * Campbell, NC 60056
(w) 704/555-8900 (h) 704/555-8897
(fax) 704/555-8901 (pager) 704/555-7703

March 1, 1996

Dear Mr. Hill,

Referral at beginning

  Elizabeth Routledge suggested that I get in touch with you, as she thought you might be interested in moving to the Castle Pines area.

  Several years ago, I helped Elizabeth and Sam buy a lovely home on Windy Point Drive. We've stayed in contact over time, as I've referred them to insurance agents, repair services and even found their house-cleaner.

Offer

  At Elizabeth's suggestion, I wanted to let you know about several extremely attractive listings in north Castle Pines.

Details of offer

  One, also on Windy Point Drive, just came on the market this week. It's a contemporary 4-bedroom, 3-bath with stunning views. The owners are in the middle of a sticky divorce and have to sell in a hurry. So

Urgency

they'll accept any reasonable offer. Needless to say, this home won't be on the market for long. I'd really like for you to see it.

  I also could show you a smaller, exquisitely deco-rated home on a large lot just a half mile from the Routledge's as well as a half dozen other interesting properties.

Benefit

  By looking at these properties, you'd get a good idea of the types of homes available in Castle Pines and maybe a better sense of if you'd like living here. I'd gladly set aside several hours to show them to you and answer any questions.

Act!

  I'll call you next week to see what we can arrange. In the meantime, you can reach me at 704/555-8900 (office) during the day or at 704/555-8897 (home) or 704/555-7703 (pager) evenings and weekends.

  Thank you for your time.

       Sincerely yours,

       Barbara Kozlowski
       Realtor-Associate®

Personal P.S.

P.S. By the way, Sam asked me to say hello.

KEY POINTS

1. Consider first calling the referral, then sending the letter as a follow-up. If you do, change the first sentence to something like, "It was good to talk to you on the phone the other day..."

2. Keep mentioning clients who made referral.

3. Describe specific available properties.

4. Could include brochure on company or on specific homes or on Castle Pines area.

5. Push tour of homes.

6. Use plain outer envelope — make this letter very businesslike.

BROKER REFERRAL

GREENBRIER REAL ESTATE
Barbara Kozlowski, Realtor-Associate®
90067 Carbondale Road * Campbell, NC 60056
(w) 704/555-8900 (h) 704/555-8897
(fax) 704/555-8901 (pager) 704/555-7703

August 17, 1997

Dear Mr. Hill,

Victoria Chen, your real estate broker in Syracuse, asked me to get in touch with you since you're being transferred to the Castle Pines area.   *Referral*

First, let me welcome you to the neighborhood. Second, allow me to offer my services in helping you find your new home here.   *Offer*

I want to start by assuring you that Castle Pines is an excellent real estate market. Over the past five years, the average property has appreciated 30%. We also have a number of lovely homes, excellent schools, and natural beauty.   *Benefits of offer*

Personally, I've specialized in Castle Pines real estate for more than six years. I'm affiliated with Greenbrier Real Estate, which is one of the largest and most respected firms in town. I've handled a number

(over, please)

Urgency

You take the initiative

Free gift

of relocations and can help you with everything from statistics on the schools to moving company referrals.

Right now, we have a number of attractive homes on the market. Some are bargains listed below their market value.

Since finding the right home takes time, I'd like to begin as soon as possible by talking to you at length and then pulling together a list of homes for you to look at.

I could send or fax you descriptions and pictures of the properties in advance so we can maximize your time here.

I'd also be happy to provide you with information on the schools, health clubs, hospitals, public transportation and other aspects of Castle Pines life — just let me know what interests you.

I'll call you next week. In the meantime, if you have any questions, you can reach me at 704/555-8900 (office) during the day or at 704/555-8897 (home) or 704/555-7703 (pager) evenings and weekends.

Thank you for your time.

Sincerely yours,

Barbara Kozlowski
Realtor-Associate®

P.S. I've enclosed a map so you can begin to get familiar with the Castle Pines area.

KEY POINTS

1. Consider telephoning the referral first and then sending this letter. If you do, change the first sentence to something like, "It was good to speak to you on the telephone yesterday." Make other changes as necessary.

2. Start with broker referral.

3. Emphasize variety of services.

4. Give brief description of local real estate market.

5. Include a free gift — such as the map.

6. You call them — don't wait for them to call you. Call when you say you will.

7. Use plain outer envelope.

Thank You Letters

HOME ANALYSIS

GREENBRIER REAL ESTATE
Barbara Kozlowski, Realtor-Associate®
90067 Carbondale Road * Campbell, NC 60056
(w) 704/555-8900 (h) 704/555-8897
(fax) 704/555-8901 (pager) 704/555-7703

THANK YOU!

May 15, 1996

Dear Mr. Hill,

Thank you for meeting with me yesterday and taking me through your lovely home. I've been to dozens of homes in the Castle Pines neighborhood and yours is one of the nicest. I particularly liked the large screened porch on the back and the bay window in the living room.

Right now, I'm working on your Market Comparison. I should have it done in a day or two. Then I'll give you a call and we can meet at your convenience.

In meantime, if any questions came to mind after I left, please call me. Thanks again.

Sincerely yours,

Barbara Kozlowski
Realtor-Associate®

Make them feel special

Refer to unique details

Thank you's are always good.

KEY POINTS

1. Personalize the letter by mentioning two specific features of the home in the third sentence.

2. Mail this letter right after the meeting to make sure it arrives before you call.

3. If something special strikes you (such as a new kitchen or landscaping) that will increase the home's selling value, mention it in a handwritten P.S.

4. Keep your promise and call when you said you would.

5. Use plain outer envelope.

REFERRAL

GREENBRIER REAL ESTATE
Barbara Kozlowski, Realtor-Associate®
90067 Carbondale Road * Campbell, NC 60056
(w) 704/555-8900 (h) 704/555-8897
(fax) 704/555-8901 (pager) 704/555-7703

THANK YOU!

May 5, 1997

Dear Mr. Hill,

Thank you for introducing me to Victoria Chen.

We met last week and made plans to actively look for a home here in Castle Pines.

One of the perks of my job is getting to work with people as nice as yourself.

If I can ever return the favor, please give me a call.

Sincerely yours,

Barbara Kozlowski
Realtor-Associate®

P.S. Victoria Chen asked me to say hello to you.

Sincere compliments work wonders

Client Farm

HOME SOLD

Photo

GREENBRIER REAL ESTATE
Barbara Kozlowski, Realtor-Associate®
90067 Carbondale Road * Campbell, NC 60056
(w) 704/555-8900 (h) 704/555-8897
(fax) 704/555-8901 (pager) 704/555-7703

November 15, 1996

Dear Mr. Hill,

Now that your home has been sold and the papers signed, I want to let you know how much I appreciate the opportunity to have worked with you. The good will of people like yourself is the basis of my business and I hope that I've merited your long-term trust and confidence.

Although your home has sold, I want you to call upon me whenever you have questions about refinancing, insurance, even gardeners or repair services. I have extensive contacts and will be more than happy to help you. If any of your friends or relatives need real estate services, I hope that you'll pass along my name and number. I'm enclosing a few extra business cards just in case.

Thank you for inviting me to participate in this important transaction and for your unfailing graciousness.

Sincerely yours,

Barbara Kozlowski
Realtor-Associate®

Keep in touch

Pick the word that describes the client's nicest trait

KEY POINTS

1. Language in paragraph 2 should be adjusted for specific situation. If owners are moving out of area, you might just want them to call you if they have any questions about real estate in general or invite them to drop by whenever they're in the area.

2. Keep this warm and personal. If you can add a sentence that refers specifically to your feelings about this particular sale, do it. For example, you may want to add a sentence such as "Even though we had to make a few unexpected adjustments, they paid off."

3. Include extra business cards.

BIRTHDAY LETTER

Free Birthday gifts

Offer

GREENBRIER REAL ESTATE
Barbara Kozlowski, Realtor-Associate®
90067 Carbondale Road * Campbell, NC 60056
(w) 704/555-8900 (h) 704/555-8897
(fax) 704/555-8901 (pager) 704/555-7703

**HAPPY BIRTHDAY!!!HAPPY BIRTHDAY!!!
HAPPY BIRTHDAY!!!HAPPY BIRTHDAY!!!
HAPPY BIRTHDAY!!!**

January 11, 1997

Dear Mr. Hill,

I want to wish you a very happy and prosperous birthday, with many more to come.

In this letter, you'll find a number of coupons from local businesses. Jack's Burger Box, Lisa's Treat Shop, The Pizza Connection, and Castle Pines Dry Cleaners have contributed "Happy Birthday Bargains" to you. Please use and enjoy them.

In the past, I've really appreciated the opportunity to handle your real estate needs. I hope that if anything comes up in the future (if you think about selling or develop an interest in investment properties, for example), you'll call me. Of course, I'll always available to help however I can.

Once again, a very happy birthday.

Sincerely yours,

Barbara Kozlowski
Realtor-Associate®

P.S. Be sure to check your driver's license for possible renewal.

KEY POINTS

1. This is a great direct mail package. Take the time to solicit 5 coupons from popular local businesses, especially fast food places. Design your own "Happy Birthday Bargains" based on the sample.

2. After you sell a house, remember to ask about the sellers' birthdays (or get off documents).

SAMPLE "HAPPY BIRTHDAY BARGAINS"

HAPPY BIRTHDAY TO YOU!
Your Birthday Bargain
FROM

BUY ONE HAMBURGER & GET A FREE FRIES

PHOTO

JACK'S BURGER BARN
448 CENTRAL AVE.
CHERRY HILL, NC

BARBARA KOZLOWSKI
GREENBRIER REAL ESTATE
704/555-8900 (WORK) / 704/555-8897 (HOME)

OUTER ENVELOPE

Greenbrier Real Estate
90067 Carbondale Road
Campbell, NC 60056

FIRST
CLASS
STAMP

HAPPY BIRTHDAY TO YOU!

Mr. Joe Hill
458 Center St.
Castle Pines, NC 60057

HOLIDAY GREETING

GREENBRIER REAL ESTATE
Barbara Kozlowski, Realtor-Associate®
90067 Carbondale Road * Campbell, NC 60056
(w) 704/555-8900 (h) 704/555-8897
(fax) 704/555-8901 (pager) 704/555-7703

December 15, 1997

Dear Mr. Hill,

Warm and sincere

During the holiday season, it's traditional to pause and reflect upon all the good fortune we've enjoyed over the past year.

One of the things I'm most thankful for are friends and associates like you.

Offer

I'm very grateful that in the past, you've chosen me to assist you with your real estate concerns. I hope that you'll do the same in the future.

In the spirit of the season, best wishes for your health and happiness throughout the coming year.

Happy Holidays,

Barbara Kozlowski
Realtor-Associate®

KEY POINTS

1. If you can add a handwritten, personal P.S., do it.

2. Use plain outer envelope.

3. Use holiday stationery, but make sure your name, address, phone & photo are on it.

SECTION FOUR

How to Create a Farm Newsletter

CHAPTER 14

ALL ABOUT NEWSLETTERS

You've been thinking. It's great to send out all these farm letters. But wouldn't it be nice to do something a little different? Something that maybe doesn't push quite as hard? Something that people in your farm could use — and that won't cost you very much?

Try a newsletter. They come in all shapes and sizes. If you have a lot of time (and you don't!), you can write it yourself. For most of us, however, buying a pre-produced newsletter and customizing it works best. You can do this inexpensively or pay a premium. Either way, you'll have more time for farming.

Read on to find out more about what newsletters do and how they can work for you.

In *Do-It-Yourself Direct Marketing*, Mark Bacon lists four potential benefits of a newsletter. It can:

1. build rapport between you and your prospects,

2. improve your image,

3. give prospects opportunities to call about your services or provide feedback,

4. communicate important news about your services.

While newsletters should be timely and full of information, they also are promotional vehicles. The key is to balance "news" and "sales" copy. But don't expect many leads from them. Newsletters primarily enhance your relationship with your farm community.

According to Dr. Michael Abelson in *Real Estate Today*®, newsletters are popular among top-performing agents. Most spend about 2% of their annual earnings on newsletter expenses. Although that percentage rate doesn't change as performance levels rise, the amount of money salespeople spend on personal promotion does increase with earnings.

Real Estate Today® reports that salespeople distribute newsletters with the following frequency:

Annual income	Newsletter frequency
$15,000-25,000	2-3 times/year
$35,000-70,000	3-4 times/year
$90,000 or more	4-5 times/year

Realtor® Donald J. Gerberg of Sparta, New Jersey, has been publishing a local newsletter since 1991. In *The Real Estate Professional*, he writes that he receives at least one favorable comment a week from the newsletter and averages four to five current market appraisals a year. After less than two years, he can point to $6,000 in commissions that resulted directly from it. He adds that agents should make a commitment to publishing newsletters for at least five years. Within that time span, he estimates that 20 to 40 percent of the readers will consider real estate transactions.

To reduce expenses, most newsletters are sent as self-mailers, or single pieces with no envelopes. Newsletters can be mailed monthly, bimonthly, quarterly or every six months. Mailing frequency should be coordinated with other aspects of your marketing program, particularly your farm letters.

Castle Pines

Home Newsletter

Are our property taxes going up?

Jill Jones, GRI

Newsletters will generate few leads for you — but they can help improve your image and increase your visibility in your farm.

The goal of the newsletter, similar to farm letters, is to motivate prospects to read it in a few minutes as they open the mail. Above all, you don't want them to set it aside for "later."

TYPES OF NEWSLETTERS

When starting a newsletter, you first must decide whether to produce your own or purchase one of the many pre-produced newsletters.

Pre-produced Newsletters

Currently, about a dozen firms sell pre-produced real estate newsletters. These newsletter publishers offer you a range of options:

(1) your name, photo, and, if you pay extra, own logo on finished, printed newsletters ready to mail,

(2) all of the above and a panel of personalized copy on finished, printed newsletters ready to mail,

(3) a finished newsletter with a custom heading made from your business card and photo,

(4) a camera-ready newsletter that you can change by covering its stories with your own and by creating a personalized heading. You take everything to your local printer for reproduction.

In considering which to purchase, look at your farm's demographics. Ask yourself these questions:

- **Would people in my farm prefer a newsletter oriented towards real estate information or a more "home-oriented" approach?**

- **Would they prefer a slick, full color look or a simpler one?**

    Don't assume that expensive is always better. In direct mail, less expensive packages often pull a higher number of responses.

- **Does the newsletter have a reply card?**

    Even if you can't expect your newsletter to generate a large number of leads, it doesn't make sense to send <u>any</u> mailing without describing your services and giving prospects a way to take advantage of them.

- **What charges are tacked onto the newsletter price?**

  These can include folding, shipping, set-up fees and ZIP code exclusivity. Exclusivity means that you pay a fee and the publisher promises not to sell the newsletter to any other real estate agent mailing to that ZIP code area. Some publishers also offer mailing and list maintenance services for additional fees.

  In terms of format, newsletters come in a variety of shapes, sizes and colors. Some are four 8-1/2" by 11" pages. Others have "digest" size pages of 4-1/4" by 5-1/2". Some are two pages. One is only one side of a page. "Mini-newsletters" are printed on oversized and fold-out postcards.

  In the table on the following page, we describe products offered by some of the larger newsletter companies. The prices, which are provided solely for purposes of comparison, are from 1995.

  When you buy one of these newsletters, it will probably arrive in the middle of the month. Your bulk indicia will already be printed on it so you won't have to worry about that. Just sticking on the labels will take enough of your time.

  The main disadvantage of preproduced newsletters is their lack of flexibility. The articles are pre-written. You have no say in what stories appear or how they're slanted. Also, they have no local angles. Having a local angle is often more important than layout or appearance!

  But you can get around that. Some allow you to write your own copy on a strip that folds out of the third page. Although space is limited, you can describe your current listings, special offers and general information about your services. If a newsletter doesn't give you that option, consider preparing a special one-page insert to slip inside. You can totally personalize this — check with the publishing company to see how or if the insert will affect the folding.

  When you buy camera-ready newsletters, you have slightly more flexibility. As long as it conforms to the size of existing copy, you can easily add material. For example, one publisher showed how to change a large recipe inside a bulletin board graphic by just gluing a picture and description of a listing over it. You then take the revised copy, together with your letterhead, logo, and photograph, to your local printer.

  The cost for either preproduced or camera-ready newsletters is not exorbitant. The finished newsletter firms make their money on low per-unit costs achieved through large print runs. And camera-ready publishers profit from selling their artwork to you.

Cypress Publishing
12715 Telge Rd.
Cypress, TX 77429
1-800-34-EAGLE / 1-800-532-1560

Newsletter	Color	Size	Customized	Price	Reply Card	Paper	Style	Exclusivity	Folding	Shipping	Minimum	Set-Up
Home Wise Briefing	Two	4p, 4¼ x 5½	Name/Photo Personalized Panel	9¢	Yes	Medium	Informal RE & non RE topics	No	$6/ shipment	$5 1st 200 $2.50 ea. addtl 100	200	$38.50
Home Wise Calendar	Four	2p, 10½ x 17	Name/Photo	200, .30 500, .28 1000, .27	Yes	Card Stock	Calendar w/non-RE topics	No	$6/ shipment	$5 1st 200 $2.50 ea. addtl 100	200	$38.50
Home Wise Newsletter & Cornerstone Newsletter (ReMax Only)	Full	Up to 8½ x 11	Name/Photo	200, .185 500, .175 1000, .17	Yes	Heavy	Informal RE & non RE topics	No	$6/ shipment	$5 1st 200 $2.50 ea addtl 100	200	$38.50

The Gooder Group
2724 Dorr Ave.
Fairfax, VA 22031-4901
(703) 698-7750

Newsletter	Color	Size	Customized	Price	Reply Card	Paper	Style	Exclusivity	Folding	Shipping	Minimum	Set-Up
Pre-Printed Homeletter Newsletter	Two	4p, 8½ x 11	Nameplate, name/photo	.17 - .23 ea.	Yes	Heavy	Professional RE topics	Yes (Monthly subs. only, $50/zipcode)	nc	nc	200	$55-100
Ready-to-Print Homeletter	Two	4p, 8½ x 11	You can change & print locally	$25-35 per issue per agent or $60-90 per issue per office	Yes	n/a	Professional RE topics	Yes (Monthly subs. only, $50/zipcode)	n/a	n/a	n/a	n/a
Color Impact Newscard	Full-both sides	Overside Postcard 8½ x 5½	Name/photo	.16 - .22 ea.	No	Heavy, glossy	Ad-like, RE topics	Yes (Monthly subs only, $50/zipcode)	n/a	nc	200	n/a
Double Newscards	Two	2 panel postcard 5½ x 4¼ folded	Name/photo	.09 - .15 ea.	Yes	Heavy	Professional RE topics	Yes (Montly subs only, $50/zipcode)	nc	nc	200	n/a
Triple Newscards	Two	3 panels 5-2/3 x 3-2/3 folded	Name/photo	.10 - .16 ea.	Yes	Heavy	Professional RE topics	Yes (Monthly subs only, $50/zipcode)	nc	nc	200	n/a

Newsletter Services, Inc.
Box 3433
Englewood, CO 80055
1-800-231-1579, 1-303-771-4008

Newsletter	Color	Size	Customized	Price	Reply Card	Paper	Style	Exclusivity	Folding	Shipping	Minimum	Set-Up
Home News Digest	Cream Stock	4p, 8½ x 5½ + 3" panel	3 areas: heading, mailing area, panel	300, .19 500, .17 1000, .14	Can add on panel	Medium, linen finish	Professional RE & consumer topics	No	nc	nc (office) $3.00 (home)	200	$20 +$5/ photo
Ready-to Print Happy Home	Your choice	2p, 8½ x 11	You can change & print locally	300, $18 $23 per issue	Can add	n/a	Professional RE & consumer topics	Yes free	n/a	nc	3 mo. subscription	n/a

Professional Newsletters
33082 Sea Bright Dr.
Dana Point, CA 92629
(800) 854-8282, (714) 496-8425

Newsletter	Color	Size	Customized	Price			Reply Card	Paper	Style	Exclusivity	Folding	Shipping	Minimum	Set-Up
					1p	2p								
You name	Cream stock	1p, 8½ x 11 2p, 8½ x 11	Name/photo 2p-camera- ready 2nd side	300 500 1000	$39 $59 $109	$59 $83 $143	No	Medium	Professional RE topics	No	nc	nc	300	$20
Tomorrow's Insights on Real Estate	Yellow Stock	4p, 4¼ x 7	Name/photo	300, $59 500, $83 1000, $143			No	Medium	Professional RE topics	No	nc	nc	300	$20

Your Marketing Assistant
10777 Northwest Freeway, Suite 325
Houston, TX 77092
800-997-4771

Newsletter	Color	Size	Customized	Price				Reply Card	Paper	Style	Exclusivity	Folding	Shipping	Minimum	Set-Up
					2p	4p	tp								
Your Home	Full	2p, 8½ x 11 4p, 8½ x 11 Triple postcard	Name/bio 3 photos	100 250 500 1000	.146 .135 .125 .100	.185 .175 .170 .160	.176 .165 .160 .140	Yes	Heavy	Formal look RE & non-RE topics	No	nc	$5-1st 200 $2.50 ea. addtl 100	100	$29.95

With either type of newsletter, you can save a considerable amount of time over writing and producing your own. If you can add local copy, a pretty good package results. Unfortunately, the average farm size of around 400 homes will only qualify you for minimal discounts from newsletter publishing companies.

Your Own Newsletter

Starting your own newsletter is no simple task. Before beginning, you must decide whether you'll type it on a typewriter or invest in a computer set-up.

If you decide to use a computer, Joe Grossman in *Newsletters from the Desktop*, recommends that you get the following:

- any Apple Macintosh or Microsoft Windows system with 8 megabytes of RAM.

- 160 megabyte hard disk.

- full-featured word processor such as Microsoft Word, Ami Pro or WordPerfect or page layout program such as Aldus PageMaker, QuarkXPress, FrameMaker or Microsoft Publisher.

- basic library of high quality typefaces.

- laser printer, preferably with PostScript.

Now you must decide three critical issues. They are:

1. Your logotype or heading.

2. Page, column and graphic format.

3. How to use color.

Your Logotype

The logotype heading is the single most important design element. Not only will it be seen first by your readers, but they'll remember you (and your newsletter) by it.

Generally, the logo appears on top of page one and rarely changes from issue to issue.

More than anything else, you want your logotype to stand out. At the same time, you want to make sure it doesn't dominate. Your goal is to call attention to the newsletter (and its publisher), not the logotype.

Naming Your Newsletter — Within your logotype you will include your newsletter's name. The name should briefly describe the newsletter and make a connection to you.

Too many newsletters have bland and meaningless titles such as "Homeowner's Outlook," "Real Estate Tidings," or "Home Watch."

The main value of creating your own name is the ability to localize it. Look at these examples:

Sierra Madre Homeowners Times
Rialto Real Estate Report
La Jolla Home Digest
Real Estate News for Singles

Often Realtors® write a small descriptive line under the name that specifies the newsletter's purpose or audience. For example, "...an exclusive report on the Sierra Madre real estate market"...or "the latest in real estate information for the La Jolla area"...or "a quarterly report on real estate activity in Rialto."

<u>Putting Your Name in the Logotype</u> — You'll also want to include your name in the logotype. Usually you can add your name in the upper left-hand corner, above the newsletter name and in smaller size type. This not only makes a logical up-front reference, but also gives you a valid reason for including your photograph in or very near the heading. Include your photo whenever possible.

<u>Designing Your Newsletter Logo</u> — Since you'll use your newsletter logo over and over, it makes sense to spend a few dollars on it.

Most graphic artists or typesetters can design an adequate logo for a very reasonable fee. Your best approach is to comb through several newsletters (not just real estate ones) and see which you like best. Then take samples to your typesetter or graphic artist and tell him or her that you want something like it.

One popular, simple logo can be created by printing a color strip across the top of the page and having the type show through in white against it. It's also nice to put a graphic element in the background.

This easy-to-make logo features a simple graphic, white type showing through a color background and a local reference.

Graphics for Your Newsletter

Before deciding on graphics, you must determine the size of your newsletter. The most popular two formats are the 8-1/2" by 11" page (the same as a standard sheet) and the 11" by 17" page. Both are simple and inexpensive, since your printer most often prints with these paper sizes. Usually the 11" by 17" page is folded in half (across the 11" side) to produce four 8-1/2" by 11" pages (front and back). This allows for more room and gives you a truer newsletter-looking format.

Typed or Typeset — After determining the page size, you need to decide whether you want to type your newsletter with a conventional typewriter or word processor or typeset it at a printer's with traditional typesetting equipment.

Typed newsletters are less expensive. You also have more flexibility since you can easily add, delete, or change material. And by typing it yourself or hiring someone, you'll speed up the production process.

But typesetting looks more professional. Books, newspapers, and magazines are almost always typeset. Professional correspondence, like a letter, is typewritten.

The Best Way — You also can desktop publish your newsletter. Desktop publishing uses personal computers and high-quality laser printers to create "near typeset quality" graphics. These systems are ideal for newsletter publishing, but they take time to learn. However, a number of people provide freelance desktop publishing services.

Laying Out the Page — Whether you have your newsletter typed or typeset, you need to decide how many columns to have on each page. Most newsletters have either one, two, or three columns.

For a typed newsletter, we recommend a single column format. Three columns narrow the column width so much that it will be hard to fit in typewritten text. This is especially true if you try to justify text — that is, even up both left- and right-hand margins on each column.

In general, we prefer the one-column with scholar's margin format. These are easier to work with than three-column formats and look more newsletter-like.

For a graphic look, put lines or borders either on the page's edges or between columns. It's best to have your graphic artist make "dummy" pages so you can see what the lines will look like. You can

The two-column newsletter format shown here is good for either typed or typeset newsletters since the columns are wide enough to fit most text.

then have these reproduced and apply your typed or typeset copy directly.

If you're desktop publishing, you can use pre-printed newsletter forms available at your local office supply store or through mail order companies such as Queblo (1-800-523-9080). These provide full-color sheets with printed guide templates, meaning that the columns and graphics are already on the paper. You just fill in your logotype, paste in the copy and take it to a local print shop.

The three-column newsletter format shown here can work if you have your newsletter typeset, but fitting typewritten text into such narrow columns is difficult.

Color In Your Newsletter

Color appears in newsletters in a variety of ways. Less expensive versions sneak in color by using colored paper stock. Others have full color picture spreads.

Before deciding about color, take a few facts into consideration. First — the more colors of ink you use, the more costly the printing. Second — colored paper almost always costs more than white paper.

This doesn't mean you need to stay with black ink on white paper. Just realize that anything else will cost you more.

Interest Rates
Are Down

Neighborhood
Listings and
Sales

Doing Your
Own
Home Repairs

The one-column format with a scholar's margin for headlines, graphics and quotes is especially good for typewritten newsletters.

Most real estate agents use two colors, black plus one other. This provides the greatest flexibility at the least additional cost. Often it makes sense to add the second color in your nameplate and run a sufficient number of blanks for several issues. Since printing prices are based on quantity, this will save you money.

As for the paper color, in *Fundamentals of Successful Newsletters,* Thomas Bivins says that shades of white from pure white to ivory hues give a business-like appearance or a clean, organized feel. Light grays on heavyweight stock also create a business look. Light browns are natural looking and less formal. Never use extremely dark paper or colored paper without texture, he adds. And avoid light blue unless it has black in it, as slate blue does.

Typing Your Own Newsletter

If you type your own newsletter, start with a sheet of legal-sized paper. As Joyce Caughman recommends in *Real Estate Prospecting*, type a line across the top, paste a screened picture of yourself in the left hand corner, and create a catchy title. Add the company logo, with your name and telephone number under it. Start typing short paragraphs on a variety of subjects separated by headlines.

Desktop publishing, however, is a much easier way to go. If your software program doesn't have extensive graphic capabilities, you can at least type your copy and do a dummy lay-out. Don't forget to sketch in your logotype and leave room for margins. Half-inch margins are fine.

At this point, you can add clip art. Clip art is art available in books at your local office supply store. Buy the book and you have the right to use the art. Your office supply store will also have graphic letters for your newsletter's name. Both are inexpensive ways to improve your newsletter's appearance.

If you want to use photographs, leave spaces for them. Black and white photographs usually reproduce better than color ones. Your printer will have to screen your photos, but this is inexpensive.

When you're done, it's a good idea to get written bids from several printers before awarding the job.

Lay-out sheet for camera-ready newsletter.

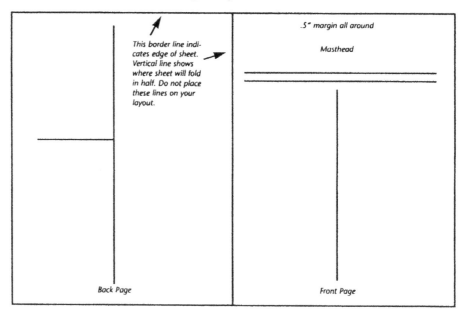

This border line indicates edge of sheet. Vertical line shows where sheet will fold in half. Do not place these lines on your layout.

.5" margin all around

Masthead

Back Page

Front Page

What to Say

The most often asked question is what to write in a newsletter. After all, the local newspaper reports stories that affect your farm.

But that's just it. Newspapers cover <u>all</u> the local news — you're only concerned with news that relates to real estate and home ownership.

Editorial Viewpoint

Before you begin writing, take a minute to jot down everything you'd like to see in your newsletter — things that affect homeowners in your farm. You might include:

- Property taxes
- New businesses in the area
- Zoning and rezoning issues
- School issues
- State of the local economy
- Home improvement ideas
- Gardening ideas
- Home protection ideas
- New home sales or listings (YES!!!)
- Anything that relates to real estate or owning a home

Now start looking for information on these stories.

Information Sources

<u>The Media</u> — Your primary information source is your local newspaper. Sure, people in your farm may read the same paper, but they won't select and analyze relevant information the way you will. If a new school or factory is opening in your town, how many of your readers will be able to speculate on its impact on property values?

In addition to your local paper, there are thousands of general and special-interest publications with information appropriate for your newsletter. But always remember to look for a local angle. For example, if you read in a national real estate publication about increased use of adjusted rate mortgages, call a local mortgage broker and ask whether ARM's popularity is increasing in your area. If mortgage interest rates are going up nationwide, find out what local lenders are doing. Then tell your readers.

The media and your prospects are great information sources. But don't overlook other sources such as your local chamber of commerce.

You also can scan real estate trade publications, such as *Real Estate Today®* which feature articles that people in your farm will not have read. While many of these may be "trade oriented," they could provide statistical information or background for a piece you write.

Popular magazines (such as *Money*) have relevant articles, especially those related to home improvements or home finance. These stories, coupled with a local angle, tend to generate high reader interest.

Don't be afraid to tell your readers the source of your information — such as "I recently read in *The Wall Street Journal*" or "I saw on the 'CBS Evening News' the other night . . " Your readers don't expect you to be an editorial genius, just a real estate expert.

A caution about copyrights: Almost all publications — whether magazines, newspapers, or books — are copyrighted. Copyright laws are not crystal clear, but extensive, verbatim reproduction of copyrighted material is illegal unless you have the copyright owner's permission.

This doesn't mean that you can't extract bits and pieces. But in most cases, it's better to use another's work only as inspiration for your own.

Use Your Prospects As Sources — Don't limit yourself to newspapers and magazines for information. Within your farm, you have a whole wealth of expertise waiting to be tapped.

For example, if you're writing a story about a new tax law, call up an accountant who lives in your farm to get his or her viewpoint. Not only will this add local credibility to your story, it gives you a reason to personally contact a prospect.

Always be sure to credit your source — i.e., "Ted Jones of Ted Jones & Associates, Certified Public Accountants" — and double-check what you're quoting for accuracy. You can do this by providing them with a written copy of the quote before you print it. There's nothing worse than incorrectly quoting someone in a newsletter.

You can also feature columns or tips from people who live in your farm, such as "Gardening Tips from Sue's Nursery" or "Recipe of the Month from Joe's Little Italy Diner."

Other Sources — Many local associations and organizations will be more than happy to provide you with items for your newsletter. Your local real estate board, chamber of commerce, and visitors and convention bureau are all good sources. Just call up their offices and get on their mailing lists. Of course, this is a great way to build up your network of local contacts.

Your Newsletter's Editorial Style

Like your farm letters, your newsletter needs to sound warm and personal. Often people think that a newsletter should sound like a newspaper, objective and impartial.

But that's wrong. As one of many ways you communicate with your farm, a newsletter should reflect your caring and warmth. If your newsletter sounds stodgy and impersonal, people in your farm will think that you're stodgy and impersonal. However, you do want them to think that you're professional. So, as with most things in life, you have to strike a balance.

Integrated Sales Pitch

One final word about what to include: remember that each newsletter is a chance to communicate one-on-one with a prospect in your farm. Somewhere within your newsletter, you should have an offer or advertisement for your services.

Many agents include a traditional sales pitch on the final page which goes something like this:

"Thank you for taking the time to read this issue of Lionel Hampton's Real Estate Tidings. Remember if you have any real estate needs or questions, give me a call at 555-8888. I'm here to help."

Don't forget to pitch yourself in your newsletter. Try to devote at least a single column to a promotion.

While better than nothing, such a sales pitch is rather unimaginative. A good alternative is to devote a single column or article to a special offer or promotion — such as a Free Home Market Comparison, Home Safety Kit, or an offer to compare renting versus buying.

In addition to copy describing your offer, you should include a tear-out response coupon. While only a small percentage of your readers will respond, you'll have a chance to meet those who do.

Printing Your Newsletter

To print your newsletter, you have two choices: (1) photocopying or (2) offset printing.

Photocopying — Most of us are familiar with photocopying — almost all of us have copiers right in our offices. However, you should think twice about using the office machine for your newsletter. While it may be cheap, the quality is likely to be poor.

What's more, if your newsletter is 11" by 17" (which typically folds down to 8-1/2" by 11"), then your office copier probably won't handle it anyway. And, in almost all cases, you'd be limited to black ink.

Offset Printing — If you print more than 250 newsletters, opt for offset printing. In this quantity, offset printing costs roughly equal those of photocopying.

Not only do you receive better quality printing, but with offset you have a choice of ink colors. It pays, however, to shop around at several local "quick printers" and get prices. In selecting a vendor, remember to:

- review samples of their work,
- look for hardware and software compatibility if you're using a computer,
- request price quotes and turnaround times,
- set a deadline,
- agree in writing to a fee for the job.

You also should pay the printer to fold your letters. Manually folding several hundred newsletters, especially if they're more than one page, is a lot of work and not much fun.

Mailing Frequency

There is no set rule for how often you should mail your newsletter. But remember that producing a newsletter steals away time from more productive pursuits, such as prospecting.

In general, we recommend mailing newsletters no more than every other month. Six times a year is plenty. Four times a year is even better.

The first year that you farm, concentrate on your farm letters. But begin "idea files" for your newsletter. Set up two files: one for story ideas and the other for graphics and formats you find appealing. Start the newsletter your second year, especially if you plan to produce your own. By then, the mechanics of its production should be easier for you.

Combining newsletters and farm letters in an overall marketing strategy works well for many agents, as it both increases your visibility in your farm and generates direct lead inquiries.

How to Mail Your Newsletter

For mailing your newsletter, you have two choices: (1) mail it in an envelope or (2) mail it as a self-mailer without an envelope.

Unlike sales letters, which should be mailed in envelopes, there's nothing wrong with mailing newsletters without envelopes. Not only will people immediately see what it is — as well as your name and possibly a photograph — self-mailers are easier to work with. If your printer strips in a postal indicia (either First Class or Bulk Rate) when he or she prints the newsletters, all you have to do is apply the labels and take them to the post office.

On the other hand, if you have the time or the resources for using envelopes, why not give them a try? If you choose to use coupon offers, such as a free-gift premium, you can even test the two methods by sending half your farm a newsletter in an envelope and the other half as a self-mailer. To test the results, simply have your printer put two different codes on the coupons — such as "Env" and "No Env" — and compare the return rates.

Finally, depending on whether you have dated material such as open house announcements, you can either send your newsletters by first-class mail (for faster service) or bulk-rate mail. If you use bulk-rate, you'll save money but spend more time getting everything ready. If you plan to deliver your newsletter in person, don't make the mistake of leaving it in residents' mailboxes. If you do and the U.S. Postal Service catches you, you may have to pay first class postage to the entire carrier route to which you delivered them.

Introducing Your Newsletter

You can introduce your newsletter to your farm in a number of ways. If you're using a preproduced newsletter and adding only a small slip of personalized copy, you might just want to add a P.S. to one of your farm letters that reads something like, "Watch for something new in your mailbox in the next three weeks! Let me know how you like it."

If you're preparing a full-page slip insert to a prepared newsletter or writing your own, you might want to send a letter like this:

Notice the use of "you's" throughout the letter.

Get your farm involved.

GREENBRIER REAL ESTATE
Barbara Kozlowski, Realtor-Associate®
90067 Carbondale Road * Campbell, NC 60056
(w) 704/555-8900 (h) 704/555-8897
(fax) 704/555-8901 (pager) 704/555-7703

[Photo]

Look for something new in your mailbox!

July, 1997

Dear Castle Pines Neighbor,

Within a few weeks, you'll find something new in your mailbox. I'm pleased to announce the debut of the Castle Pines Home Newsletter, which is designed especially for Castle Pines residents like yourself.

I really think that Castle Pines is a terrific place to live and full of wonderful people. This newsletter is just for us and I hope that it strengthens our already existing sense of community.

In it, you'll find all the latest news about the local real estate market, which will give you a good idea about how much your own home is worth. I'll also have reports about the mortgage market in case you're considering refinancing, special property taxes and assessments that affect you, development issues that concern all of us, and other useful information.

You may be interested, for example, in how much neighborhood homes are listing and selling for and what's on the market right now.

If you have something you'd like to put in the newsletter, let me know. I'm always on the look-out for stories or story ideas. You can reach me at the office (555-8900) during the day or at home (555-8897) or on my pager (555-7703) evenings and weekends. Call anytime. I'd love to hear from you.

Sincerely yours,

Barbara Kozlowski
Realtor-Associate®

P.S. Let me know what you think of the newsletter. Since it's for you, it's important to me that you like it!

SUMMARY

Whether you produce your own newsletter or go with a pre-produced newsletter it is important that it meet the needs of your farm.

If you produce your own newsletter, make sure that you use a attractive format. But don't get too elaborate or the cost might be prohibitive. Keep the newsletter at a manageable size. It is far better to produce a short, simple newsletter four times a year than a long, elaborate one only once a year.

If you choose to use a pre-produced newsletter, you should ask yourself the following questions:

- Is the information timely and easy to use?
- Does the newsletter promote my services? Does it motivate people to use my services?
- Are the articles brief and to the point? Is the newsletter length too long?
- Is the newsletter helpful and useful to the people in my farm?

How to Produce a Successful Mailing

CHAPTER 13

PRODUCING
YOUR MAILING

It's late afternoon. The sun is streaming through the bare tree branches at a low angle. It directly strikes the piece of paper in front of you. You look down, slightly amazed. You've just created your first farm letter. It looks neat and clean, with your photo staring out from the top.

You slowly read out loud the first sentence. You notice the "you's" and "I's." Sounds good. Will people keep reading? You hope so. You think so. You know that they'll benefit if they do.

Until now, you've done it all alone. Now it's time to bring in some help. People who can take your creation and finish it off.

You notice a spelling error and correct it.

What happens next?

It's time to get on the phone. Then get out of your chair. Head over to your local printers and talk about what you need.

If you're proud of your letter now, just think how you'll feel when you see it folded and ready to go...

Pretty good, we'd say.

WORD PROCESSING

There's no reason why you can't type your own letters, especially if you have a word processor or computer. However, if you have neither the time nor the desire, many outside services can do this for you at a very reasonable cost.

But since most services probably handle primarily business letters, you may need to show them exactly what you want. Take a sample direct-mail letter to illustrate what you're looking for.

TYPESETTING

For letterhead, outer envelopes with teasers, reply cards and business reply envelopes, you will want to consider typesetting.

Good typesetting makes reading easier. And you want to make it as easy as possible for your prospects.

In terms of typeface, literally thousands of styles exist. Most are very similar.

Some stylish typefaces, such as *Cascade Script* (this one), are difficult to read. Limit them to special situations.

Overall, styles can be broken into two groups — serif and sanserif.

Serif letters have light lines and curls in them. This book, for example, is set in a serif face, as are most magazines and newspapers. Serif provides "hooks" for the eye, which makes it easier to read. Here are some examples of serif type:

> Goudy
> New Century Schoolbook
> Times Roman

Sanserif does not have "hooks." For large blocks of copy, this style is hard to read. But it's fine for short copy blocks, such as picture captions.

Here are examples of sanserif type:

> Helvetica
> Futura
> Tekton

It's a good idea to stick with one style, but use many variations. One way to vary it is through using *italic*, **bold** or ***bold italic*** type. These are hard to read in large copy blocks but great for emphasizing headlines, important points and subheads.

Type size also can be varied. Keep most of your copy between 10- and 14-point. This book, for example, is set in 12-point type. But other sizes can add visual interest.

Headlines, for example, should be at least 18-point type.

This is 9-point type.

This is 10-point type.

This is 12-point type.

This is 14-point type.

This is 18-point type.

This is 24-point type.

One final note on type size — not all typefaces are exactly the same size, but they're pretty close.

AVOID USING ALL CAPITALS. These tend to hinder reading. You can use all capitals for headlines.

Finally, avoid large blocks of reverse copy (white type on a dark background). While this is often a favorite "gimmick," it, too, is difficult to read.

What your words say — not how they look — will entice prospects into accepting your offer. But the harder your words are to read, the less likely your prospect is to find out what you have to say.

DESKTOP PUBLISHING

Desktop publishing systems enable you to produce near-typeset-quality documents using your personal computer and a laser printer.

They're ideal for small businesses such as real estate firms, which produce a lot of printed materials. You can reduce artwork costs to a fraction of traditional typesetting fees and save hours of time.

The first step is choosing the right software. For about $500, you can buy a word processing software package such as Microsoft Word for Windows, AmiPro, or WordPerfect for Windows. You can find both PC (IBM compatible) and Macintosh programs.

You'll also need a high-end desktop publishing package. They cost $500 to $900. According to Elaine Floyd in *Newsletter News & Resources*, the most popular software products with her readers are:

Program	% of readers who use
Aldus PageMaker	44%
Ventura Publisher	15%
QuarkXPress	14%
Word Perfect	12%
MS Word	5%
Publish It	2%
MS Publisher	2%

Good laser jet printer prices keep dropping. Right now, they're between $800 and $3,000. Get one with color capability.

PHOTOS AND ART

As with a newsletter, you may want a designer to create your letterhead. Otherwise, your art needs are fairly simple. If you want to include an additional photo, perhaps on the reply card, find a friend with a good eye and ask him or her to help. A professional photographer can eat up your marketing budget in no time.

Black-and-white photos must be converted to screened halftones. Your printer should be able to do this at a nominal charge.

Color photos are different. They must be "separated," or broken down into primary colors before printing. This is extremely expensive and, frankly, unnecessary in direct mail farming packages.

You also can use clip art, which we described in the newsletter chapter. Available at your local office supply store, this is pre-done, mass-produced art work sold in volumes. With it, you can dress up your letters very inexpensively.

PRINTERS

For the average farm mailing, your local "quick" printer is best. Check out franchise operators such as Kinko's, Postal Instant Press (PIP), Sir Speedy, and The Big Red Q. Sometimes small independent printers offer comparable prices.

When you first start farming by mail, visit several printers. This is important, since you need to find a printer whom you can work with over a long period of time.

Get price quotes for your specific job — namely, your first mailing — and let the printer know that you're planning regular, consistent printings of roughly the same size.

Sit down and talk about how much lead time the printer requires and the types of services that the shop offers. Ask to see work samples. Don't assume that the lowest-priced printer is best. If you can find someone whom you like, who tolerates a lot of questions, and who is reasonably priced, pay the difference. In the long-run, it'll be worth it.

Ways to Save Money on Your Printing

It's possible to save substantial sums on printing. Here are some ideas:

Stick to Conventional Paper Sizes and Formats

Most quick printers use standard paper sizes — letter size (8-1/2" by 11"), legal size (8-1/2" by 14") and double letter size (11" by 17"). If you deviate from these sizes, it will cost you.

But you can use other sizes. For example, a reply card is usually one-third of an 8-1/2" by 11" sheet. Just have the printer print three on a page and cut it up.

Use Black and a Second Color Ink

The more colors you use, the higher your printing cost. Two colors, such as red and blue, cost more than black and a second color (i.e., red). And if you print two colors on both sides, it will cost more than printing two colors on one side and black-only on the other.

In most instances, stay with black as your main color and use a second color as an accent.

Sometimes printers "run" a color other than black on a specified day — i.e., blue on Monday, red on Tuesday, green on Wednesday. Often they'll cut the price if you run your second color that day.

Use Standard Paper Stock

Paper color and weight also affect your printing costs. Most small print shops stock 24-pound bond, 50-pound offset (or book), and 60-pound offset (or book). However, they'll also offer a wide variety of other paper types, including glossy, textured and colored paper. These all cost more.

If you are printing two sides of the sheet, stick with the slightly heavier 60-pound paper. It has a better feel and won't show through as much.

If you just print one side, consider 24-pound bond or 50-pound offset. But compare their costs first.

Textured stocks look rich, but get expensive in a hurry. That's why almost all the letters sent by large mail order firms are on 60-pound offset or similar stock. Yet for a small quantity, textured stock might be worth it.

Black type on white paper is the easiest to read and the least expensive to print. If you want colored stock for your letter, keep it subtle, such as light gray, buff, or ivory.

Also avoid harsh colors in other elements of the direct mail package, such as the reply card or lift note, as they cheapen your "look."

Get Bids on Folding

If you've ever actually folded a mass mailing, you'll understand why we recommend having your printer fold your letters. It's a lot of work to fold 300 to 500 letters — and a lot more if you add two or three pieces to the envelope.

If you're using a mail service, ask them for a quote to fold the letters. Compare their bid with your printer's before you have the printer run the letters through the folding machine.

Also — if you're using a mail service, ask about their fold requirements. If they use inserting machines (instead of manual inserting) they'll most likely need a fold-only edge — that is, an edge which does not have an unfolded flap. If this is the case, you need a "letter-fold" (copy out and headline up) versus a "Z-fold" (folded in the shape of the letter "Z").

Avoid Rush Jobs

Ninety percent of a printer's (and other vendors') customers need their jobs yesterday.

Some rightly charge a premium for faster service. But in most cases the customer drops off the job and says, "Well, see what you can do."

Your printer will appreciate a little leeway. When he or she asks when you need a job done, try replying, "What's your schedule like?" or "I'm not in a big hurry. A couple of days is fine."

The printer will remember your cooperativeness. This will pay off when it comes time to return the favor — namely, when you really do need a job ASAP.

HOW TO HANDLE THE ACTUAL MAILING

Once you have your list done and mail pieces printed, it's time to prepare your letters for the post office. You can either do this yourself or pay someone to do it.

Doing It Yourself

Inserting, sealing and organizing a mailing is a lot of work. This is especially true if you mail by third-class bulk-rates where you have to sort it a particular way and fill out a form or two.

Considering that your time is money, spending hours stuffing envelopes doesn't make much sense. But if you wish to, carefully read Chapter 14 on U.S. Postal Service requirements.

Getting Someone Else to Do It

Most real estate offices have limited support staff, which means you'll probably need outside help.

Large commercial mailing houses usually have minimums of 5,000 to 10,000 pieces and are prohibitively expensive for smaller mailings.

In the Yellow Pages, you can find some mailing houses which cater to small mailers; often, however, they are rather costly.

A good alternative is community service groups, particularly those serving the disabled. They generally do a very good job and may entitle you to special tax credits.

When you use an outside service to prepare your mailing, give them a "dummy" sample of the pieces in the exact order and position you want them. It's a good idea to number the pieces in case they fall out along the way.

When you work with any outside service, you should prepare a "dummy" mail piece. This is a sample of the finished mailing in the exact order and direction in which you want the elements inserted. It's also a good idea to number the pieces so if they fall out, they'll be put back correctly.

RECOMMENDED READING:

The Copy-To-Press Handbook
Judy E. Pickens
John Wiley & Sons
New York, New York

Fundamentals of Copy & Layout
Albert C. Book and C. Dennis Schick
National Text Book Co.
Lincolnwood, Illinois

Graphic Arts Manual
Arno Press/Musarts Publishing Corp.
New York, New York

CHAPTER 14

THE UNITED STATES POSTAL SERVICE

Whew!

It's finally almost over. You wrote the letter, had it printed and took it to a shop for folding and inserting.

One step at a time, you kept telling yourself throughout the process.

Looking back, you realize that it was more complicated than you expected. But now that you know the ropes, you think it'll get easier.

Your letters look so neat and clean lined up in straight rows in the boxes.

Don't get too comfortable yet. You have one last battle with bureaucracy as you muddle your way through the maze at the Post Office.

Get ready to read fine print.

To get started, it's a good idea to contact your local post office and find out who works with small business bulk mailers. The U.S. Postal Service has set up more than 100 Postal Centers to serve small businesses. Anyone who spends less than $200,000 a year on postage and fees is considered small.

HOW TO SAVE UP TO 41% ON YOUR POSTAGE

The U.S. Postal Service offers four classes of domestic mail: first, second, third, and fourth. Your farming letters won't qualify for either second or fourth class: second is used by newspapers and magazines that mail at least four times a year. Fourth, "parcel post," is reserved for books and packages weighing more than a pound.

First-Class Mail

First-class mail is the most prompt service available without paying additional fees for special delivery, priority or Express Mail. There are certain weights and limits, but the cost for a single parcel weighing 1 ounce or less is 32 cents (as of January, 1995). However, several discounts are available.

Presorted First Class — If you mail a minimum of 500 pieces and sort them by 5-digit ZIP Code, you receive a discount of 4.6 cents per piece on letters (2.1 cents per piece on postcards). In addition, there is an annual fee of $85.

Carrier Route Presorted First Class — If you mail at least 500 pieces and sort them by individual carrier routes, you can receive a discount of 6.6 cents per piece on letters and 4.6 cents per piece on postcards. As with presorted first class, there is an annual fee of $85.

You also can receive a 5.3 per-piece discount for ZIP +4, if you presort it and pay an annual fee of $85. ZIP +4 non presorted, requires no annual fee but costs 30.5 cents per piece.

Third-Class or "Bulk" Mail

Referred to as "bulk mail" or "advertising mail," this class costs less and moves more slowly than first-class mail. It can include circulars, booklets, advertisements, and other printed matter, as well as parcels weighing less than a pound. As of January 1995, the basic bulk rate mail price was 22.6 cents for a letter.

To qualify for this rate, you must mail at least 200 identical pieces or 50 pounds. These must be sorted by ZIP code and packages according to postal regulations

In mailing third class, you have three options:

1. meter from a standard postage-metering machine — you pay a $85 annual bulk rate fee,

2. use pre-canceled third class stamps. This option also requires the annual bulk rate fee.

3. use a third class permit by printing "Bulk Rate U.S. Postage Paid" in place of a stamp. This printed notice, which also contains your permit number, is called the indicia. In addition to the bulk rate fee, a permit to use indicia requires a one-time $85 fee.

Metered bulk-mail postage can look much like first-class mail. And it's easier to do than apply stamps. Pre-canceled stamps are effective but have more of a personal than a business look.

The preprinted imprint looks something like this:

> BULK RATE
> U.S. POSTAGE
> **PAID**
> POMONA, CA
> PERMIT No. 1

Indicia permits vary and the wording changes depending on the service you're using (i.e., carrier route). Some indicias look very much like metered imprints.

Beyond the basic bulk mail rate, you can get further discounts.

- 3/5 presort — you sort and bundle mail according to either the first 3 or 5 digits of the ZIP code. An additional discount of 3.8 cents per piece (for a standard letter) is given if 200 or more pieces go to the same ZIP Code. This is common in real estate geographic farms.

- carrier routes — if 200 or more pieces go to the same carrier route, you can receive an additional discount of 3.8¢ per piece. This is quite possible in a geographic farm.

- saturations — if you mail to at least 75% of the residences in an area and sort the mail for the carrier's route in sequence according to street addresses, you receive a discount of up to

17.8¢ per piece. That is approximately 14¢ postage for a standard letter.

Letter size also affects cost. For standard rates, the envelope should be no larger than 6-1/8" by 11-1/2" and weigh less than 3.3 ounces. This is a substantial advantage over first class mail, which requires additional postage for anything more than one ounce.

With letters to a geographic farm, you'll probably qualify for most if not all of the above discounts. If, however, you have a social farm, you can at least qualify for the 3/5 presort discount.

There are additional bulk mail discounts available such as ZIP + 4. However, your mail must be certified for automation to qualify for this discount. As a service to small businesses, the Post Office will add the ZIP + 4 to all the names on your list if you give them a diskette. They'll also standardize your addresses and validate or correct your 5-digit ZIP code. Post Office business centers provide this service free one time and afterwards at a modest charge.

Sorting your letters in ZIP code order works like this: you take batches of 10 or more going to the same 5-digit ZIP code and tie a rubber band around them, address side up. On the top envelope at the lower left of the address, you put a colored label with a letter on it. Or you could make up packages of letters with the same first 3 ZIP code digits. These would get a different colored sticker with a "3" on it. If all your letters go to the same ZIP code, you put them in a mail bag and write the ZIP code and other data on its tag. Each mail sack contains 125 pieces or 15 pounds.

Once you've sorted, stamped and bagged the letters, you have to fill out a postal form describing the mailing, its total number of pieces and other information. These are usually Postal Form 3602R (Statement of Mailing Matter with Permit Imprint) or Form 3602-PC/Meter (Bulk-Rate Mailing Statement). You then take the form, together with your letters, to the bulk mail clerk at the Post Office.

Approximately 5 to 10% of the average third class mailing is not delivered. This is cut in half with the ZIP + 4 service.

Address-Correction Services — Bulk Mail

For address corrections, you include the endorsement "Address Correction Requested" on bulk mail; it will normally be returned to you with the new address or reason for non-delivery. A single-piece rate is charged for each returned letter.

You also can use the more complete endorsement, "Do Not Forward, Address Correction Requested, Return Postage Guaranteed," which some post offices prefer.

Your post office's bulk-mail department can provide you with more information about this.

Business Reply Mail (BRM)

Business Reply Mail lets you supply prospects with postage-paid return envelopes. You only pay for the ones mailed back. To qualify for BRM, keep the size of your reply card or envelope to 4.25" by 6" or less.

To use business reply mail, you have to get a permit and permit number. You print this number on your return envelope. The Post Office has regulations about the location of the address, bar code, indicia, and other elements on the envelope.

Using BRM requires that you pay an $85 annual fee. When you receive a return envelope, you're charged first class postage plus 44¢ per piece. You pay 10¢ (plus first class postage) a piece if you establish a BRM advance deposit account. However, there is an additional annual accounting fee of $205 for this service. That means you have to receive over 600 pieces back to break-even on the accounting fee. If you qualify for a BRMAS, you only pay 2¢ in addition to the first class postage. Contact the bulk-rate mail clerk at your Post Ofiice for more information.

Sample Business Reply Envelope

WHAT THIS ALL MEANS

For direct-mail farming, you have two choices of service: first-class or third-class bulk-rate mail.

Even if you had a farm of 500 homes and could get a first-class presort discount, you would still pay 27.4¢ per piece versus 18.8¢ per piece for 3/5 presort bulk mail — a savings of 31%!

Without presorting, you'll pay 32¢ for first class versus 22.6¢ for basic bulk mail — a savings of 29%.

Furthermore, because the bulk-rate presort minimum is only 200 pieces (versus 500 for first class presort), you are more likely to qualify for the bulk-rate discount.

By mailing bulk rate, you are likely to save 13.2¢ (32¢ regular first class versus 18.8¢ 3/5 presort bulk rate) per piece — a savings of 41%!

Just think — you can save 41% on the single most expensive part of your mailing!

Look at the numbers — and use third-class mail as often as possible.

Doesn't Bulk Rate Mail Lower the Response?

Many people wonder: "Doesn't bulk mail hurt response?"

In *Successful Direct Marketing Methods,* direct mail expert Bob Stone reports, "Third-class mail ordinarily pulls as well as first-class mail."

That's why almost all major direct mailers use third-class bulk-rates. In short, first class does not pay — at least not enough to pass up savings of up to 41%!

Look in the appendix for complete USPS regulations.

CHAPTER 15

WRAPPING THINGS UP

Now you can relax.

Take a long walk.

Read a good book.

Head over to your favorite stream for a little fishing.

You've set your bait...

thrown out your line...

*you can take a little break
before you start reeling them in.*

Just relax.

*Soon enough it'll be time to start thinking about your
next mailing.*

This book has covered everything from sizing your farm to writing farm sales letters to knowing postal requirements.

Once again, remember that your farm efforts — personal contact, phone calls and direct mail — must work together.

CO-OP MAILINGS

In addition to letters and newsletters, you can use other formats in mailing to your farm.

In many areas, commercial advertising companies put together "co-op" mailings. Usually sent on a weekly or monthly basis, these include coupons from local restaurants and shops as well as offers from service-related businesses such as insurance agencies and eye-care centers.

These mailings can cost very little since all the participants share postage, printing and production costs.

As an individual agent it's probably best to avoid these mailings. But for your brokerage office, it could work well. Still — be careful: some mailers who claim to send 10,000 packets really only mail 2,000 and include "pass-along" readership in their counts.

To prevent this type of fraud: (1) never pre-pay for a mailing and (2) require that the firm attach the USPS Form 3602 (Bulk-Mailing Statement) to your invoice. If they won't, forget it.

TRACKING YOUR MAILINGS

As we mentioned earlier, one of the biggest advantages of direct mail is your ability to track both costs and returns. You should create a master mailing file which contains several samples of each mailing, as well as charts that break down your costs and returns. That way, you can compare mailings and see which ones work best.

Figuring out what "works" doesn't necessarily mean that the mailing generates a high response. If you send out an expensive mailing, the cost per piece will greatly reduce your net return, even with a high response rate. On the other hand, fewer responses with a less expensive package could pay off well. The point is that you need to calculate in real dollars how much your marketing costs and what your return is.

Start by preparing a budget worksheet for each mailing. Here's a sample:

MAILING BUDGET WORKSHEET

Mailing Name:
Date:
Number:
Offer:
Premium:
Notes:

Printing/Graphics

	GRAPHICS	PRINTING
Cover letter	_____	_____
Insert piece	_____	_____
(e.g. lift note)		
Reply card	_____	_____
Outer envelope	_____	_____
BRM envelope	_____	_____
TOTAL	_____	_____
PRINTING/GRAPHICS TOTAL		_____

Mailing

Folding	_____	
Inserting/Prep	_____	
Postage	_____	
MAILING TOTAL		_____

Premiums

Front-end	_____	
Back-end	_____	
PREMIUMS TOTAL		_____

Misc.   _____

TOTAL MAILING COST   _____

Now you need to figure your return. To check who responds to your mailing, use what direct mail firms call "key coding."

Key coding simply involves typing or printing a small code somewhere on the reply card. A sample key might be, "FM-6/97."

> ❏ Yes! I'd like to find out how much my home is worth today. Please set me up for a Home Market Review!
> The best time to reach me is _____
>
> | Preprinted label with respondent's name, etc. | **This offer expires soon, so don't delay in returning this card.** |
>
> FM-6/97

Tracking responses to compare costs with return is the heart of direct mail. A key code on the reply card tells you which offers are working.

You also should ask people who call where they heard about your offer. If it was from a mailing, note it and add it to your records.

If you're using a software contact management or farming program on your computer, it should have the capability of keeping these records. If not, they're simple enough to do by hand. On the following page is a sample response record.

LOW RESPONSE

When you farm by mail, don't expect scores of reply cards to flood your desk. Depending on your offer, a 1% response is good — 2% is outstanding.

Two percent of 500 homes is only 10 reply cards.

But remember, just a handful of leads will make your whole farm mailing program work. Additionally, it has the PR benefit of familiarizing prospects with your name — even if you never hear from them. They'll know who you are. And at some point, someplace, they may just pass along your name to a friend.

TESTING

Testing is the backbone of the direct mail industry.

Because you're sending so few letters, it's hard to run accurate tests. One or two random responses will totally throw off the results. But don't be afraid to experiment on a small-scale. As we suggested earlier, try testing newsletters sent with and without envelopes. Or

MAILING RESPONSE RECORD

Mailing Name:
Date:
Number:
Offer:
Premium:
Notes:

DATES

Name & Address & Telephone	Reply Card	Tele-phone	Visit	List

mail one offer to half your farm and another to the other half. Change the time at which you drop a mailing. Maybe the tax records Kit would work better in April than in December.

And if an offer works for you, don't be afraid to repeat it more than once a year. Remember — in direct mail, repetition leads to familiarity — not boredom. Boredom only kicks in when a prospect has seen the same letter five or six times in a short time span.

FOLLOWING UP YOUR LEADS

Direct-mail leads are "hot." If someone took the time to read your offer and call or return your reply card, get back to him or her quickly. Above all, you don't want a "hot" prospect losing interest because you procrastinated.

FINAL COMMENTS

Farming takes time. Just like the crop farmer who plants in the spring and harvests in the fall, you, too, have to be patient and hardworking. Don't expect results for at least six months. But be assured that if you persist and keep up with regular mailings, you will benefit.

It's not easy. But as thousands of real estate professionals nationwide have demonstrated, the long-term rewards are well worth it.

References

Real Estate Selling

Berger, Warren. *Specializing: An Outlet for Bigger Profits?,* Real Estate Today®, October 1993. Reprinted by permission of the National Associaton of Realtors®. Copyright 1993. All rights reserved.

Bleasdale, Julie A. *Think Globally, Sell Locally,* Real Estate Today®, June 1992. Reprinted by permission of the National Association of Realtors®. Copyright 1992. All rights reserved.

Real Estate Farming

Huckfeldt, Klaus D. (1983). *Seeding Right Through Impact Farming.* Palm Springs, CA: Real Estate Edition.

Caughman, Joyce L. (1994). *Real Estate Prospecting: Strategies for Farming Your Markets* (2nd Edition). Real Estate Education Company.

Thompson, P.J. (1989) *Real Estate Farming: Campaign For Success* (2nd Edition). Kricket Publications.

Direct Mail

Bacon, Mark S. (1994). *Do-It-Yourself Direct Marketing: Secrets For Small Business.* NY: John Wiley & Sons, Inc.

Bayan, Richard. (1984). *Words That Sell.* Westbury, NY: Caddylak Publishing.

Gosden, Freeman, F., Jr. (1985). *Direct Marketing Success: What Works And Why.* NY: John Wiley & Sons, Inc.

Hahn, Fred E. (1993). *Do-It-Yourself Advertising: How To Produce Great Ads, Brochures, Catalogs, Direct Mail And Much More.* NY: John Wiley & Sons, Inc.

Hatch, Denison. (1992). *Million Dollar Mailing$.* Washington, D.C.: Libey Publishing, Inc.

Hoge, Cecil C., Sr. (1976). *Mail Order Moonlighting.* Berkeley: Ten Speed Press.

Kennedy, Daniel S. (1990). *The Ultimate Sales Letter*. Holbrook, MA: Bob Adams, Inc.

Lewis, Herschell Gordon. (1983). *More Than You Ever Wanted To Know About Mail Order Advertising*. Englewood Cliffs, NJ: Prentice-Hall.

Lewis, Herschell Gordon. (1988). *On The Art Of Writing Copy*. Englewood Cliffs, NJ: Prentice-Hall.

Moroney, Mary H. (1985). *Creative Sales Letters: 4 Ready-To-Use Methods*. Westbury, NY: Caddylak Publishing.

Paper Corporation of America. (1986). *Dictionary Of Graphic Arts Terms*. Wayne, PA: Paper Corporation of America.

Shurter, Robert L. & Leonard, Donald J. (1984). *Effective Letters In Business*. NY: McGraw-Hill.

Westenberg, Bob. (1994). *Sure You Can Write Great Sales Letters*. Roanoke, VA: The Windsor Group.

Wilbur, L. Perry. (1985). *Money In Your Mailbox: How To Start And Operate A Mail-Order Business*. NY: The Wiley Press.

Newsletters

Bivins, Thomas. (1993). *Fundamentals Of Successful Newsletters: Everything You Need To Write, Design And Publish More Effective Newsletters*. Lincolnwood, IL: NYC Business Books.

Floyd, Elaine. (1994). *Quick & Easy Newsletters On A Shoestring Budget*. St. Louis, MO: Newsletter Resources.

Floyd, Elaine. (1994). *Copy-Ready Forms For Newsletters: A Do-It-Yourself Kit*. St. Louis, MO: Newsletter Resources.

Floyd, Elaine. (1992). *Marketing With Newsletters*. St. Louis, MO: EF Communications.

Grossman, Joe with Doty, David. (1994). *Newsletters From The Desktop* (2nd Edition). Chapel Hill, NC: Ventana Press.

Hudson, Howard Penn. (1982). *Publishing Newsletters: A Complete Guide To Markets, Editorial Content, Design, Printing, Subscriptions, Management And Much More...* NY: Charles Scribner's Sons.

Advertising

Caples, John. (1974). *Tested Advertising Methods* (4th Edition). Englewood Cliffs, NJ: Prentice-Hall.

Estes, Sherrill Y. (1993). *Sell Like A Pro: A Buyer-Friendly Approach To Sales And Success*. New York: Berkeley.

Levinson, Jay Conrad. (1993). *Guerrilla Marketing: Secrets For Making Big Profits From Your Small Business*. Boston: Houghton Mifflin.

Appendices

Appendix A – Farm Worksheet

Sizing Up Your Farm

Prospective Farm #1	***Prospective Farm #2***

Prospective Farm #1

Your Annual Commission Goal $ _____

1. **Average Gross Comm. Percentage**
   - #___Co-Op Listings   x___%   = _____
   - #___Solo Listings   x___%   = _____
   Sum_____   Total%   = _____
   Divide Total % by # of listings   + _____
   Average Gross Commission % = _____%

2. **Average Sales Price**
   - Add up all sales prices for farm area
     and divide by the # of homes sold= $ _____

3. **Average Gross Comm. Dollars**
   - Multiply Avg. Sale Price (#2)   _____
     by Avg. Gross Comm. % (#1)   x _____
     Avg. Gross Comm. Dollars $ _____

4. **Number of Listings Needed**
   - Divide Annual Comm. Goal   _____
     by Avg. Comm. Dollars (#3)   ÷ _____
     Number of Listings Needed   = _____

5. **Annual Turnover Rate**
   - Divide number of sales for year   _____
     by total number of homes in pro-
     spective farm (or MLS) area   ÷ _____
     Annual Turnover Rate   _____%

6. **Farm Size if You Got 100% of Listings**
   - Divide Number of Listing (#4)   _____
     by Ann. Turnover Rate (#5)   ÷ _____
     Farm Size at 100% of Listings = _____

7. **Farm Penetration**
   - Est. percentage of homes in the farm
     on which you'll get the listing = _____%

8. **Final Size of Farm Needed for Goal**
   - Divide Farm Size at 100% (#6)   _____
     by Farm Penetration (#7)   ÷ _____
     Actual Size of Farm Needed   = _____

Prospective Farm #2

Your Annual Commission Goal $ _____

1. **Average Gross Comm. Percentage**
   - #___Co-Op Listings   x___%   = _____
   - #___Solo Listings   x___%   = _____
   Sum_____   Total%   = _____
   Divide Total % by # of listings   + _____
   Average Gross Commission % = _____%

2. **Average Sales Price**
   - Add up all sales prices for farm area
     and divide by the # of homes sold= $ _____

3. **Average Gross Comm. Dollars**
   - Multiply Avg. Sale Price (#2)   _____
     by Avg. Gross Comm. % (#1)   x _____
     Avg. Gross Comm. Dollars $ _____

4. **Number of Listings Needed**
   - Divide Annual Comm. Goal   _____
     by Avg. Comm. Dollars (#3)   ÷ _____
     Number of Listings Needed   = _____

5. **Annual Turnover Rate**
   - Divide number of sales for year   _____
     by total number of homes in pro-
     spective farm (or MLS) area   ÷ _____
     Annual Turnover Rate   _____%

6. **Farm Size if You Got 100% of Listings**
   - Divide Number of Listing (#4)   _____
     by Ann. Turnover Rate (#5)   ÷ _____
     Farm Size at 100% of Listings = _____

7. **Farm Penetration**
   - Est. percentage of homes in the farm
     on which you'll get the listing = _____%

8. **Final Size of Farm Needed for Goal**
   - Divide Farm Size at 100% (#6)   _____
     by Farm Penetration (#7)   ÷ _____
     Actual Size of Farm Needed   = _____

*This form is designed to help you determine the size of your farm or to compare a couple
of prospective farms.*

Appendix B
USPS Postal Regulations

On March 24, 1995, the United States Postal Service filed a mail classification reform with the Independent Postal Rate Commission. The classification reform proposals, if adopted, will reform and restructure portions of First-, second-, and third-class mail.

In brief, the proposal suggests the following changes:

- Convert First Class letter and card subclasses into two new automation and retail subclasses.
- Restructure third-class bulk regular mail into three new subclasses (Standard Mail-automation rated, enhanced carrier route, and regular).
- Add a new subclass to existing second-class mail to be known as Publication Service.

If adopted, these changes would take place sometime in 1996.

The following regulations are current as of the time of publication of this book.

FIRST-CLASS MAIL

First-class is the most prompt service available without the payment of additional fees for special delivery or Express Mail.

Any mailable matter may be mailed at the First-Class letter rate. The following materials are considered First-Class matter and must carry postage at First-Class or Priority Mail rates.

1. Matter wholly or partially handwritten or typewritten (including identical copies prepared by automatic typewriter), originals or carbons, invoices (except when accompanying the matter to which they relate), postal cards, post cards.

   Exception: Authorized additions to second-, third-, or fourth-class mail.

2. Matter sealed or closed against postal inspection (except as explained under Sealing Third- and Fourth-Class Matter).

3. Bills and statement of accounts, regardless of method of preparation or quantity of identical pieces mailed, except authorized additions to second-, third-, or fourth-class mail.

4. Price lists with written-in figures changing items or prices.

5. Any business reply mail.

6. Blank printed forms filled out in writing, including cancelled or uncancelled checks.

7. The product of a computer may or may not be First-Class matter. It depends on the content. Contact your post office mail classification section for additional information.

Weight and Size Limits

Minimum Sizes

All mailing pieces must be a least .007 of an inch thick. They must be at least 3 1/2 inches high and at least 5 inches long, unless they exceed 1/4 inch in thickness.

All pieces must be rectangular in shape, unless they exceed 1/4 inch in thickness. Mailing pieces that do not meet the above criteria will be prohibited from the mail.

Maximum Sizes

The maximum size is 108 inches, length and girth combined. The maximum weight is 70 lbs. Nonstandard First-Class Mail is all First-Class Mail weighing one ounce or less and that

1. exceeds 11 1/2 inches in length, or

2. exceeds 6 1/8 inches in height, or

3. exceeds 1/4 inch in thickness, or

4. that has a height to length ratio that does not fall between 1 to 1.3 and 1 to 2.5, inclusive.

Mailing pieces in the above category will be subject to a surcharge.

Sealing

Pieces which are not sealed or secured on all four edges so that they may be handled by machines are not recommended.

Postage Rates

Obtain current Rates and Fees schedule from Postmaster.

First-Class Mail Discount Rates

There are three categories of presorted First-Class Mail that offer substantial discounts from the single piece rate.

The three categories are presort First-Class, carrier route First-Class, and barcoded First-Class. These mailings must consist of a minimum of 500 pieces, presorted according to postal specifications to 3 or 5 digit ZIP Code areas, to individual carrier routes, or must meet the barcoding requirements, respectively. Payment of an annual mailing fee allows a mailer to enter mail materials in all three categories.

Complete information and assistance with your mailing lists can be obtained from your post office. Bundle labels, rubber bands, sack labels, sacks and mail trays are available at no cost to the mailer.

Post Card Size and Shape Specifications

Post cards must be:

1. At least .007 of an inch thick.

2. Not larger than 4 1/4 inches by 6 inches, nor smaller than 3 1/2 by 5 inches. (Minimum dimension for international post cards is 3 1/2 by 5 1/2 inches).

3. Rectangular in shape. A ratio of width (height) to length between 1 to 1.3 and 1 to 2.5 is recommended.

Note: The regulations regarding nonstandard First-Class Mail apply to post cards mailed at the First-Class rates. See nonstandard regulations.

Payment of First-Class Postage

Postage for First-Class Mail may be supplied by:
1. Affixing stamps of proper denomination.

2. Postage meter machine (license required).

3. Printed permit imprints (permit required).

4. Precancelled stamps (permit required).

Note: Check with your postal representative for proper use of precancelled stamps on First-Class Mail (for example, their use on presorted First-Class Mail).

In order that First-Class pieces, larger than letter size, may be readily identified, it is recommended that a green diamond border be printed around the edges. Matter mailed with a green diamond border must carry First-Class postage.

Incidental First-Class Matter

Incidental First-Class matter may be enclosed in or attached to second-class matter, third-class merchandise (including books but excluding merchandise samples) and fourth-class matter. The attached or enclosed incidental matter may be mailed at the applicable postage rate of the host piece with which it is attached or enclosed.

Eligibility Requirements

An incidental attachment or enclosure must be closely associated with or related to the piece to which it is attached or in which it is enclosed; it must be secondary to that piece; and it must not encumber postal processing.

An incidental attachment or enclosure includes, but is not limited to, one or more of the following items:
a. A bill for the product or publication;

b. A statement of account for past products or publications;

c. A personal message or greeting included with a product, publication or parcel.

Payment of Postage

Incidental First-Class attachments or enclosures may be mailed with second-class matter, third-class merchandise (including books but excluding merchandise samples) and fourth-class mail. Postage is based on the combined weight of the incidental attachment or enclosure and the host piece with which it is attached or enclosed, and is to be paid at the rate applicable to the host piece.

Note: For incidental attachments or enclosures with second-class matter, if the second-class piece consists entirely of non-advertising matter, the attachment or enclosure is also considered non-advertising matter; in all other instances the attachment or enclosure is considered part of the advertising portion of the second-class piece.

Markings

There are no marking requirements for incidental First-Class attachments or enclosures.

Forwarding, Return and Address Correction Service for First-Class Mail

Note: The following regulations apply to First-Class Mail including postal and post cards and Priority Mail. They also apply to Express Mail.

All First-Class Mail (including Priority Mail and postal and post cards) and all Express Mail, covered by a change of address order, will be forwarded at no charge for a total of twelve months from the effective date of the request.

Endorsement Dictates Service Desired

The endorsement placed on a First-Class mailing piece by the sender dictates the service desired. There are seven authorized endorsements, each providing a different service.

If there is no endorsement on the mailing piece, it will be forwarded at no charge. If the piece is undeliverable, it will be returned to the sender with the reason for nondelivery, also at no charge.

Following is a list of authorized endorsements and the services each provides:

- Address Correction Requested — The mailing piece will not be forwarded. Mailer will be provided with an address correction or the reason for nondelivery and will receive the mailing piece back at no charge. First-Class Mail endorsed, "Do Not Forward" will be treated in the same manner.
- Forwarding and Address Correction Requested — Mail will be forwarded at no charge and a separate address correction will be sent to the mailer for a fee. See Rates and Fees schedule for the fee for this service. If the mail is undeliverable, it will be returned to the sender with the reason for nondelivery at no charge.
- Return Postage Guaranteed — Mail will be forwarded at no charge for 60 days. If mail is undeliverable, it will be returned to the sender with the reason for nondelivery, at no charge.
- Do Not Forward/Address Correction Requested/Return Postage Guaranteed — Mail will not be forwarded. It will be returned to the sender with address correction or reason for nondelivery attached, at no charge.

- Forwarding and Return Postage Guaranteed — Mail will be forwarded at no charge. If the mail is undeliverable, it will be returned to the sender with reason for nondelivery, at no charge.
- Forwarding and Return Postage Guaranteed Address Correction Requested — Mail will be forwarded at no charge. A separate address correction notice will be sent to the sender for a fee. See Rates and Fees schedule for the fee for this service. If the mail is undeliverable, it will be returned to the sender with the reason for nondelivery, at no charge.
- Insured Mail — Mail will be forwarded at no charge. If mail is undeliverable, it will be returned to the sender with reason for nondelivery.

BUSINESS REPLY MAIL (BRM)

Persons who wish to distribute and receive business reply mail must apply to the post office for a permit. An annual fee is required. The fee is for a 12-month period. See Rates and Fees schedule for fee. Any user of the business reply service may establish a business reply account. When business reply postage and fees are paid from a business reply account, a lower business reply piece charge is applicable. An annual accounting fee is required to establish a business reply account. See Rates and Fees schedule for fee. Once a business reply account has been established, a customer may apply for BRMAS. Under BRMAS, a lower reply piece is charged. Pre-barcoded BRM envelopes must be used. The postal service will provide artwork for these envelopes on request.

Business reply mail pieces may be distributed in any quantity desired. The permit holder guarantees payment on delivery of postage and fees on returned business reply mail.

Envelopes, cards and labels prepared for business reply may be enclosed with other matter. However, labels can only be used on nonstandard size mail.

Business reply mail pieces will be accepted for return mailing at all post offices in the United States and its possessions including military post offices overseas, except the Canal Zone. They should not be sent to any foreign countries, including Canada, Cuba, Mexico, Philippine Islands and the Republic of Panama, as they cannot be returned from any foreign country without prepayment of postage.

Note: Special services such as registered mail, insured mail, C.O.D., certified mail, return receipts, special delivery, etc., may not be used in conjunction with business reply mail.

Printing Regulations

All forms of printing are permissible provided they are legible to the satisfaction of the Postal Service.

However, handwriting, typewriting, or hand-stamping cannot be used to prepare the address side of business reply mail.

Printed borders are not authorized on business reply letters and cards. However, they are allowed on business reply labels and cartons and envelopes larger than 6 1/8 inches high or 11 1/2 inches long or 1/4 inch thick.

All colors of ink are acceptable provided there is at least a 30 percent reflectance difference throughout the red spectral range of 550 to 775 nanometers (nm) between the paper and the ink.

For additional help in determining mail design and printing regulations, call the mailpiece design analyst at your local post office. There is no charge for this service.

Illustration of Business Reply Mail

The bottom line of the address must be no lower than 3/4" from the bottom edge of the mail piece.

Horizontal identification bars, above right, must be at least 1 inch in length and must not extend vertically below the delivery address line.

Required Format Elements

All of the pre-printed endorsements and markings shown above are required. They include:

1. The endorsement, No Postage Necessary if Mailed in The United States, which must be printed in the upper right hand corner of the piece, no further than 1 3/4 inches from the right edge.
2. The appropriate Business Reply legend must appear above the address in capital letters at least 3/16" in height. Authorized legends are: Business Reply Mail - All business reply mail except for business reply labels. Business Reply Labels - The legend "Business Reply Label" means that the permit holder guarantees payment of First-Class postage upon the return of mailable matter with the permit holder's business reply label. Items printed with the legend, "Business Reply Mail" are not acceptable as labels.
3. "First Class Permit No." must be shown in capital letters immediately below the business reply legend followed by the permit number and the name of the issuing post office (city and state).
4. The legend, "Postage Will Be Paid By Addressee" must appear below the First-Class permit no.
5. The complete address, including the name of the permit holder, street address and/or post office box number, city, state and ZIP Code must be printed directly on the mail piece.
   Exception: Preprinted labels with only delivery address information are permitted for addressing BRM. However, the permit holder's name must still be printed on the BRM. The bottom line of the address must be no lower than 5/8" from the bottom edge of the mail piece. The space 5/8" from the bottom edge and 4 1/2" from the right edge of the mail piece is reserved for bar codes. A clear margin void of any extraneous matter (except for horizontal bars) of at least 1" is required between the left and right edges of the mail piece and the address.

6. A company logo is permitted if it is located no lower than the top of the street address or the post office box line. The logo must not interfere with any of the required business reply endorsements.

7. To facilitate rapid recognition of BRM, a series of horizontal bars parallel to the length of the mail piece must be printed immediately below the endorsement "No Postage Necessary if Mailed in The United States". These bars must be uniform in length, at least 1" long and 1/16" to 3/16" thick and evenly spaced. The vertical column of horizontal bars must not extend below the delivery address line, which is the line above the line containing the ZIP Code.

8. Facing Identification Mark (FIM) is a vertical bar code pattern printed at the top right portion of the address side of the BRM piece. FIM functions as an orientation mark for automatic facing and cancelling equipment.

A FIM must be printed on all BRM except business reply labels, or BRM larger than 6 1/8" high or 11 1/2" long or 1/4" thick.

For additional BRM specifications and for FIM negatives which are free of charge, please see your post office customer service representative or mailpiece design analyst.

SECOND-CLASS MAIL

Second-Class matter includes newspapers and periodicals regularly issued from a known office at stated intervals of at least 4 times a year and bearing notice of entry as second-class matter. Make application for entry through local postmaster.

Postage for Re-Mailing of Second-Class Matter

Postage at the third- or fourth-class rate must be paid on all copies mailed by the general public.

THIRD-CLASS MAIL

Third-class mail consists of mailable matter which is:
1. Not mailed or required to be mailed as First-Class Mail;

2. Not entered as second-class mail; and

3. Which weighs less than 16 ounces.

Note: Incidental First-Class enclosures and attachments are allowed with third-class merchandise (including books but excluding merchandise samples).

Third-class matter includes: circulars, booklets, proof sheets, corrected proof sheets with manuscript copy accompanying same, house organs, printed by letterpress or lithography. Also merchandise, farm and factory products, seeds, bulbs, cuttings, roots, scions, and plants, photographs, keys and drawings. Copies of drawings are also third-class matter, but they may not be hand lettered. If a drawing is hand lettered, it is subject to First-Class postage.

See your postmaster for mail classification of products produced by data processing or computers.

All impressions obtained upon paper or cardboard by means of printing by letterpress or lithograph, engraving, or any other mechanical process easily recognized - except the typewriter, or manifold copy - are matter which can be mailed third-class when not in the nature of actual or personal correspondence.

Circulars, including printed letters which, according to internal evidence, are being sent in identical terms to more than one person, are third-class mail. A circular does not lose its character as such when a date and the name of the addressee and of the sender are written therein, nor by the correction in writing of typographical errors.

Printed matter weighing less than 16 ounces may be sent as third-class mail. For the purpose of this section, printed matter means paper on which words, letters, characters, figures, or images, or any combination of them not having the character of a bill or statement of account, or of actual or personal correspondence, have been reproduced by any process other than handwriting or typewriting. Computer prepared material is considered to be printed matter and is not considered to have the character of actual or personal correspondence merely because it contains:

   a. Specific information about a product offered for sale or lease such as size, color or price.
   b. Specific information about a service being offered such as the name, address, and telephone number of a company representative to contact to obtain the service.
   c. Information relating the addressee directly to an advertised product or service.
   d. Information such as the amount paid for a previous purchase, pledge, or donation, when associated with a sales promotion or solicitation for donations.

Hand-stamped imprints on third-class matter do not affect its classification except when the added matter in itself is personal or converts the original matter into a personal communication.

Postage Rates

See Rates and Fees schedule for regular single piece rates and for bulk rates.

Weight and Size Limits

Third-class mail must weigh less than 16 ounces, per piece. All pieces up to 1/4 inch in thickness must be rectangular in shape.

Also, all mailing pieces must be at least .007 of an inch thick and at least 3 1/2 inches high and at least 5 inches in length, unless exceeding 1/4 inch in thickness.

Note: Keys and identification devices are exempt from the above criteria. Mailing pieces that do not meet the above standards will be prohibited from the mails.

Nonstandard Third-Class Mail

Nonstandard third-class mail is all single piece third-class mail weighing one ounce or less and that -
1. exceeds 11 1/2 inches in length, or
2. exceeds 6 1/8 inches in height, or
3. exceeds 1/4 inch in thickness, or
4. that has a height to length ratio that does not fall between 1 to 1.3 and 1 to 2.5, inclusive.

Mailing pieces in the above category will be subject to a surcharge. See Rates and Fees schedule for surcharge amount.

Maximum Size

There is no maximum size limitation for third-class mail except for carrier route presorted mail, which must not be more than 3/4 inch thick, 11 1/2 inches high, or 13 1/2 inches long.

Payment of Third-Class Postage

Postage for third-class mail may be supplied by:
1. Affixing stamps of proper denomination (provided they are not used in an irregular location as stickers or closures).
2. Precancelled stamps. Permit required.
3. Postage meter stamp.
4. Permit imprint. Permit required.

Forwarding, Return and Address Correction Service

No forwarding or return service is provided on bulk business mail (third-class bulk mail) without an endorsement. Unendorsed single piece third-class mail will be returned if undeliverable.

Insured third-class mail will be treated as though endorsed Forwarding and Return Postage Guaranteed.

Undeliverable third-class mail bearing the endorsement Forwarding and Return Postage Guaranteed will be forwarded for 12 months when the new address is known. No forwarding fee will be charged to the recipient. During months 13 through 18, the piece will not be forwarded but will be returned with the correct forwarding address or the reason for nondelivery attached.

If the endorsement Forwarding and Return Postage Guaranteed, and Address Correction Requested is used, the mail will be forwarded for the first 12 months if the forwarding address is known. A separate address correction notice (Form 3547) will be sent to the mailer, and the appropriate address correction fee will be charged. No forwarding fee will be charged the recipient. If the piece is not forwardable, it will be returned. During months 13 through 18, the piece will be returned with the correct forwarding address or the reason for nondelivery attached.

Whenever the mail piece is returned to sender the mailer will pay the appropriate single piece rate multiplied by a factor of 2.733. This factor is derived from the ratio of the number of third-class pieces nationwide that are successfully forwarded to the number of these pieces that cannot be forwarded and are returned. There is no charge for the "on piece" address correction provided.

Return

Bulk business mail that cannot be delivered as addressed and bears the endorsement Do Not Forward, Address Correction Request, Return Postage Guaranteed will not be forwarded but will be returned at the appropriate single piece rate with an address correction or the reason for nondelivery attached at no charge. Unendorsed bulk business mail will not be returned. Unendorsed single piece third-class mail that cannot be delivered as addressed will be returned to the sender at the appropriate single piece rate with the reason for nondelivery attached at no charge. Mail that qualifies for a single piece fourth-class rate will be returned at that rate if the mailer's endorsement includes the name of the fourth-class rate.

Address Correction

The recipient's new (forwarding) address, or the reason for nondelivery if the new address is not known, may be obtained by the sender either independently of, or in combination with, the return and forwarding services.

To obtain these services, the mailing piece must bear the endorsement: Address Correction Requested, Forwarding and Return Postage Guaranteed or Address Correction Requested. Temporary changes of address are not provided. Forwarding address information will not be provided for mail bearing the exceptional address format.

The following conditions govern this service:

a. Pieces generally weighing 1 ounce and bearing only the endorsement Address Correction Requested will be used to notify the sender with the new address or the reason for nondelivery endorsed on the piece. Only the appropriate single piece rate will be charged.

b. For pieces generally weighing more than 1 ounce and bearing only the endorsement Address Correction Requested, Form 3579, Undeliverable 2nd, 3rd, 4th Class Matter, or a markup label will be used to notify the sender.

    Exception: When address labels are affixed to plastic wrappers, or a window address format is used on a mailing piece, or it is more expeditious for the Postal Service, then Form 3547, Notice to Mailer of Correction in Address, may be used to provide the requested information.

c. Mail that qualifies for a single piece fourth-class rate will be returned at that rate if the mailer's address correction service endorsement includes the name of the applicable fourth-class rate. For example, if a third-class piece qualified for mailing at the special fourth-class rate for books, the endorsement would be Special fourth-class rate: Forwarding and Return Postage Guaranteed.

No Service Requested

If the services as described above are not requested by the mailer, and the piece is undeliverable as addressed, and the period for forwarding has expired, then the Postal Service will treat the piece as dead mail.

Sealing of All Third-Class Mail

Third-class mail must be prepared by the mailer so that it can be easily examined. Third-class mail which is not sealed or secured so that it may be handled by machines is not recommended. Mailing of sealed articles at the third-class rates of postage is deemed to be with the consent of the mailer to postal inspection of the contents.

All sealed pieces mailed at the single piece third-class postage rate must be legibly marked on the address side, preferably below the postage and above the name of the addressee, with the two words Third Class. The marking may be included as a part of a permit imprint, and it may be printed adjacent to the meter stamp by postage meter.

The marking will not be considered adequate if it is included as a part of a decorative design or advertisement.

It is not necessary to use the endorsement "third-class" on sealed matter mailed at bulk third-class rates. The bulk rate endorsement will suffice.

Enclosures in Bulk Rate Third-Class Matter

The following may be enclosed with articles mailed at third-class:

1. An invoice, same as for fourth-class mail.
2. Manuscripts accompanying related proof sheets.

Note: Under certain conditions, attachments can be made to third-class books and catalogs. See your post office for details.

How to Mail Third-Class Matter

All third-class matter (except bulk rate mail and mail bearing precancelled stamps) may be deposited singly in any collection box. However, volume mailings of regular third-class mail should be taken to a post office for deposit.

All third-class bulk rate mailings must be presented at a post office or substation as designated by the postmaster.

THIRD-CLASS BULK MAIL

There are four categories of third-class bulk mail that offer substantial discounts from the single piece rates. They are:

1. Basic bulk rate presort.
2. 3/5-digit ZIP Code presort.
3. Carrier route presort.
4. Barcoded presort.

These mailings must be presorted to specific postal requirements. All four categories require the prepayment of annual mailing fees. Bundle labels, rubber bands, sack labels, sacks and mail trays are available from the post office at no cost to the mailer.

Complete information and assistance may be obtained from the post office.

Basic Bulk Rate Presort

Mailings must consist of at least 200 pieces or 50 pounds, presorted by ZIP Codes in packages and sacks to the finest extent possible.

3/5-Digit ZIP Code Presort

Each mailing must consist of at least 200 pieces or 50 pounds of mail presorted to 5-digit destinations. Each piece must be part of a package of 10 or more pieces to the same 5-digit ZIP Code and the package must be sacked to the same 5-digit ZIP Code. Each sack must contain a minimum of 50 pieces or 10 pounds of mail to the same 5-digit ZIP Code in order to be eligible for the 5-digit presort level rate.

Exception: Mailers may commingle different 5-digit packages of 10-49 pieces in sacks for the unique 3-digit multi-ZIP Code cities, providing:
1. Each sack contains at least 50 pieces or 10 pounds of mail, and
2. No 3-digit city packages are included in the sack, and
3. 50 pieces or 10 pounds of mail for a single 5-digit ZIP Code (within the unique 3-digit city) must be sacked separately.

Residual pieces (those not part of a group of 10 or more pieces to a particular 5-digit ZIP Code) may be included in a 5-digit presort level rate mailing subject to the following provisions:
1. Residual pieces do not count toward the minimum quantity requirements for the 5-digit presort level rate.
2. Residual pieces are not eligible for the 5-digit presort level rate and must have postage paid at the appropriate third-class "basic" level bulk rate.
3. Residual pieces must be prepared in accordance with the applicable sortation requirements.

Listing Required

When a third-class 3/5-digit presort level rate mailing consists of pieces to be mailed at the basic rate, the mailer is required to provide the post office with a list of the number of qualifying pieces to each ZIP Code destination except as noted below:

A list of the number of qualifying pieces being mailed to each ZIP Code destination is not required when all sacks containing identical weight third-class 5-digit presort level rate pieces are physically separated at the time of mailing from all sacks containing identical weight pieces to be mailed at the basic rate.

Carrier Route Presort

Each mailing must consist of at least 200 pieces or 50 pounds of mail presorted to carrier routes. Each piece must be part of a group of 10 or more pieces sorted to the same carrier route, rural route, highway contract route, post office box section, or general delivery unit, in order to be eligible for the carrier route presort level rate.

Residual pieces (those not part of a group of 10 or more pieces to a particular carrier route) may be included in a carrier route presort rate mailing and may bear the Carrier Route Presort endorsement subject to the following provisions:

1. Residual pieces do not count towards the minimum quantity requirements for the carrier route presort level rate.
2. The number of residual pieces to any single 5-digit ZIP Code area may not exceed 5% of the total qualifying presorted carrier route pieces addressed to that 5-digit area.
3. Residual pieces are not eligible for the carrier route presort level rate and must have postage paid at the appropriate third-class "all other" level bulk rate.
4. Residual pieces must be prepared in accordance with sortation requirements.

Pieces may be identical or nonidentical in size and weight, provided they are all within the same processing category (i.e. letter-size, flats, machinable parcels, or irregular parcels). Pieces must not exceed 11 1/2 inches in width, 13 1/2 inches in length, or 3/4 of an inch in thickness. Merchandise samples with detached labels may exceed these dimensions if the detached labels meet postal requirements.

Listing Required

Mailers must at the start of each mailing, provide the post office a listing indicating the number of qualifying and residual pieces mailed to each five-digit ZIP Code area. After the first mailing, the postmaster may authorize the mailer to retain the records and submit them upon request by the postmaster. These records must be kept for a period of 90 days following the date of the mailing, or until any pending action regarding the recalculation of postage is resolved to the satisfaction of the Postal Service.

Barcoded Presort

Obtain information at the Business Mail Entry Unit at your local post office. You may also contact the Postal Business Center.

POSTAL REGULATIONS GOVERNING BULK RATE MAILINGS

Bulk Rate Mailings Consisting of Identical Pieces

All pieces must be identical in weight. Textual matter need not be identical. Mailing pieces printed on different weight stock are not considered identical.

Method of Paying Postage on Bulk Rate Mailings Consisting of Identical Pieces

Postage for the entire mailing must be prepaid by precancelled stamps, permit imprint, meter stamps or in precancelled government-stamped envelopes. You may not mix methods of paying postage.

Bulk Rate Mailings Consisting of Non-Identical Pieces

Bulk rate mailings consisting of non-identical pieces may be accepted only under the following conditions:

1. Bulk rate mailings on non-identical weight pieces are to be of only one characteristic type. For example, letter-sized pieces, flats, regular parcels or irregular parcels.
2. All pieces in a permit imprint mailing must be subject to the same rates. For example, pieces subject to the minimum per piece rate shall not be included on the same permit mailing with pieces subject to the pound rate.
3. Regular bulk rate mailings may include pieces subject to the minimum per piece and pound rate, when postage is paid by postage meter imprint.

Payment of Postage on Non-Identical Weight Pieces

Pound Rates

Permit Imprint - When pieces in a non-identical mailing are subject to a pound rate and the pieces qualify for mailing at the basic or 5-digit rate, postage may be paid by permit imprint provided the mailer has been specifically authorized by the Director, Office of Mail Classification, Rates and Classification Department, U.S. Postal Service Headquarters. Pieces which are subject to the pound rate and are mailed at the basic or 5-digit rate are also subject to a per piece rate.

Meter Stamps - Postage may be paid by meter stamps on mailings subject to the pound rate. Each piece must have full metered postage affixed. For pieces qualifying for the carrier route rate, postage for each piece will be computed by multiplying the weight (in pounds) of the piece by the pound rate. The postage must be rounded up to the nearest tenth of a cent or whole cent, depending upon what type of postage meter is used.

Precancelled Stamps - Postage may be paid by precancelled stamps on mailings subject to the pound rate. Each piece must have full precancelled stamp postage affixed. For pieces qualifying for the carrier route rate, postage for each piece will be computed by multiplying the weight (in pounds) of the piece by the pound rate. For pieces that qualify for the basic or 5-digit rate, postage for each piece will be computed by multiplying the weight (in pounds) of the piece by the pound rate and adding to it the applicable per piece rate.

Alternative Available

As an alternative, mailers may affix the applicable per piece rate (5-digit or basic) to each piece and pay the pound rate for the mailing through a permit imprint advance deposit account. The mailer is then required to submit both Form 3602, Statement of Mailing with Permit Imprints, and Form 3602-PC, Statement of Mailing - Bulk Rates. (When the alternative method of paying postage is used, the endorsement: "Pound Rate Pd via Permit _____" must appear on each mail piece). Markings made by postage meter, special slug, ad plate, or other suitable means ensure a legible endorsement.

Minimum Per Piece Rates

Postage may only be paid by postage meter stamps, precancelled stamps or precancelled envelopes for mailings of non-identical weight pieces subject to the minimum rate.

Mailing Statement Required

The weight of a single piece must be entered on Form 3602 or Form 3602-PC as "non-identical" when mailing consists of pieces of different weight. The mailer must also enter the number of pieces mailed and the total postage paid on Form 3602-PC. Enter the total postage paid on the space which reads, "Postage Chargeable Per Piece."

Bulk Rate Mailings Cannot Be Registered, Insured or Sent C.O.D.

Matter mailed in bulk mailings will not be postmarked. It shall be accepted only as ordinary mail and cannot be registered or sent as insured or C.O.D. mail, since the pieces are not accepted and handled individually at the mailing office, but only in bulk.

Bulk Rate Mailing Fee Required

A fee must be paid each calendar year by or for any person who mails at the bulk third-class rates. Any person who engages a business concern or another individual to mail for him must pay this fee. If postage is to be applied by a permit imprint, then an additional fee is charged. This latter fee is paid only once and lasts indefinitely, providing that at least one mailing a year is made under this permit. See Rates and Fees schedule for annual fee and for permit imprint fee.

Note:

1. All bulk rate mailings must be mailed at the post office from which the permit was issued.
2. Each separately addressed piece must bear, adjacent to the postage stamp or imprint, the printed endorsement "Bulk Rate" or "Blk. Rt."
3. For carrier route presorted bulk rate mailings, the words "Carrier Route Presort" or "Car-rt-sort" must be included in the permit imprint or imprinted on the mailing piece within 2 lines directly above the address.

Each bulk mailing must be accompanied by a Statement of Mailing on Form 3602 or 3602-PC which are obtainable from your postmaster.

Boxholder, Customer or Householder Mailings

When general distribution of mail is desired for each boxholder on a rural or star route, or for each family on a rural route at any post office or for all boxholders at a post office that does not have city or village carrier service, mailers may use this simplified address: Postal Customer. A more specific address such as Rural Route Boxholder followed by the name of the post office and state may be used. The use of the word "Local" is optional.

Upon request, the postmaster will furnish mailers with the number of boxes served by rural and star route carriers. This information is also contained in the combined national ZIP Code and Directory of Post Offices available at all post offices. Postage on such mail should be fully prepaid by means of permit imprint, meter stamp, or precancelled stamps, and all pieces for the same post office must be put up by the mailer, so far as may be practicable, in packages or units of 50 and properly labeled according to the distribution. If pieces are made up in quantities other than 50 for each separation, the number in a package shall be shown on the label.

Simplified Addresses for Post Offices with City Delivery Service

Occupant
123 West Front Street
Lincoln, Nebraska ZIP Code

Complete street address, city, state and ZIP Code must be shown. In the case of apartment houses, etc., the address must show the apartment or unit number. Presorting regulations for bulk rate mailings are required.

Alternate Address Form for Bulk Third-Class Mail

Name of Addressee, or Current Occupant, or Name of Addressee, or Current Resident.

Both of the above examples are to be followed by the complete address. The purpose of the above addressing forms is to assure that mailing pieces will be delivered to the current occupant in the event that the addressee has moved.

Note: The exceptional address format cannot be used on mail which is registered, certified, insured or has C.O.D. service.

Material mailed with the exceptional forms of address may receive address correction service, but will not be returned or forwarded. Exception: First-Class Mail which is undeliverable as addressed will be returned to sender. Note: The alternate address form applies to all classes of mail except Express Mail.

ZIP Code and Presorting Regulations for Third-Class Bulk Rate Mailers

In order to qualify for third-class bulk rates, you must ZIP Code and presort your mailings in ZIP Code sequence, or to the individual carrier route, if the carrier route presort rate is desired.

At the time the permits are issued, the post office will supply complete sorting regulations, bundle labels, rubber bands, sack labels, sacks, mail trays, etc. The above items are supplied to the mailer at no cost.

Also, most post offices will supply personal assistance to new bulk mailers. Note: Special services such as registry, insurance, certified and C.O.D., may not be used for third-class bulk rate matter.

How To Prepare Bulk Rate Third-Class Mail

Due to the various regulations based on the discounts taken it is recommended you contact your local post office. Request publication 49 "Preparation of Third-Class Mail".

Package Labels

Pressure sensitive package labels must be applied to the lower left corner of the address side of the top piece on letter size packages and next to the address on larger packages. Facing slips must be placed on the address side of the top piece in mixed states and foreign packages. Pressure sensitive labels and facing slips are available from the post offices.

The total weight of third-class mail placed in one sack must not exceed 70 pounds.

Labels Furnished by the Mailer

Labels, other than those prepared by the post office, must show the name of the mailer on the back.

Distribution Points

A list of the proper distribution points for papers, mixed circulars, and direct circulars from each postal region is available from your local postmaster.

Special Services

The registry, insurance, special delivery, certified, and C.O.D. services may not be used for third-class bulk matter.

Methods of Paying Postage

There are four different ways of prepaying postage:
1. Affixing stamps.
2. Affixing of precancelled stamps. (Permit required).
3. Use of postage meter machine. (Permit required).
4. Use of printed permit imprints. (Permit required).

Use of Stamps

Stamps of the proper denomination should be affixed to the envelope or package in the upper right-hand corner of the address area. Stamps must be precancelled for use in bulk rate mailings. (Parcels which bear address labels shall have the regular or postage meter stamps overlap the upper right-hand corner of the label. This eliminates over-labeling and possible loss of the parcel).

Use of Precancelled Stamps

Precancelled stamps may be used without further cancellations or defacement of First-Class presorted mail, third- and fourth-class mail and also on remailed second-class matter.

Precancelled stamps may be used on any quantity of pieces - for single mailing or large bulk mailings.

A permit is required to purchase and use precancelled stamps. The permit is free. Make application at your post office.

Precancelled postage stamps may be purchased and used only by the persons or concerns who have been issued permits and matter may be mailed only at the office where precancelled postage was purchased. Persons holding permits to use precancelled stamps do not need to obtain an additional permit to use them on third-class matter mailed at bulk rates. (A bulk mailing fee, however, must be paid).

If precancelled postage on a single piece is over $1.00, the precancelled stamps must be over-printed in black ink by the mailer, with the mailer's initials and the numerical abbreviations of the month and year. These stamps are only acceptable during the month shown and through the 10th of the following month. These stamps may not be used on articles such as boxes, bags, cases or other containers specially designed to be reused for mailing purposes.

Mail bearing precancelled postage must be presented to authorized postal employees at weigh units, window units, or detached mail units of the post office where the permit is held. Deposit of mail bearing precancelled postage in street collection boxes is not permitted.

Use of Postage Meter Machine

Meter stamps may be used on all classes of mail. Persons or firms desiring a license for mailing metered matter should apply to the local postmaster.

Metered mail (with the exception of mailings made at bulk rate) may be presented in any quantity and need not be identical in size and weight. Metered mail must be mailed the same date as metered, except in the following cases:

1. When using the meter directly on second-, third-, or fourth-class mail, the month, day and year may be dropped from the meter. This enables the sender to run the envelopes through the postage meter machine at any time prior to actual mailing. The month and year must be shown on tapes on second-, third-, and fourth-class mail, but the day may be omitted.

2. If the sender is including a postage metered courtesy reply envelope as an enclosure and has the printed words, "No postage stamp necessary - postage has been prepaid by" and his name and address in the center of the envelope, the month, day and year must be omitted from the meter impression and it may be mailed at any future date from any part of the United States. When you use such a postage metered envelope, the rate is the same as if you used a stamp - there's no added postal service charge, since the post office doesn't have to collect postage from you upon delivery. The amount of postage on the envelope must be sufficient to prepay the postage in full.

Print Metered Postage as Follows (on Envelopes and Labels)

All Classes - Always show month, day and year, (except on second-, third-, and fourth-class, day may be omitted). If gummed address labels are used on mailing piece, be sure meter tape overlaps labels.

Print Metered Postage as Follows (on Envelopes)

First-Class - Always show month, day and year, except on pre-paid courtesy reply envelopes omit month, day and year.

Second-, Third-Class and Ordinary Fourth-Class - Omit month, day and year when impression is applied directly to mailing piece.

Bulk Rate Third-Class - Omit month, day and year. Show words "Bulk Rate." If non-profit organization, show "Non-Profit Org." in place of "Bulk Rate."

Use of a postage meter is the responsibility of the firm, or individuals licensed by a post office. Metering of mail of other firms or individuals should not be done unless the preparation and mailing regulations are complied with by the user, since the licensee may lose his meter license for infractions.

Metered mail, other than bulk mailings of third-class mail, may be deposited in collection boxes or at the post office or other designated depositories located in the city where the postage meter license is issued. All metered mail (5 or more pieces) must be faced in the same direction and tied in bundles.

Users of postage meters should make daily recordings of register readings in a book provided for the purpose (Form 3602-A). Each time additional postage is purchased and the meter set, the book must be presented. If the meter is not set within a period of 6 months, it must be presented with the book at the post office of setting for examinations and verification of register readings.

Under certain conditions, a meter may be set at one post office for use at another post office. Consult your local postmaster.

A computerized remote postage meter resetting system is available which permits the users of certain specially designed postage meters to have such meters reset at their places of business. Consult your local postmaster.

Use of Permit Imprints

A permit must be obtained from your local postmaster for use of permit imprint. See Rates and Fees schedule for permit imprint fee. This fee is nonrecurring, provided that at least one mailing is made under the permit during a period of 12 months. If at any time the time elapsed between mailings exceeds 365 days, the permit is subject to cancellation.

Content of Permit Imprints

First-Class Mail - Permit imprints must show City and State; First-Class Mail; U.S. Postage Paid; and permit number. They may also show the mailing date, amount of postage paid or the number of ounces for which postage is paid.

The ZIP Code of the permit holder may be shown immediately following the name of the state or in a separate inscription, when it is possible to include the ZIP Code without creating uncertainty as to permit holder's correct address or permit number.

Second-, Third- and Fourth-Class Mail - Permit imprints must show same information as First-Class, except date and words, First-Class Mail must be omitted.

Second-, Third-, and Fourth-Class Mail (Single Piece Rates) - When using the permit we suggest that the face of each mailing piece be endorsed with the appropriate class of mail.

Bulk Rate Third-Class - If the permit imprint is to be used on bulk rate third-class mailings, a special bulk rate mailing fee for the calendar year must also be paid. See Rates and Fees schedule for fee.

Carrier Route Presort Indicia - For carrier route presort bulk rate mailings the words, "carrier route presort" or "car-rt-sort" may be included in the permit imprint or imprinted on the mailing piece within two lines directly above the address.

If the permit imprint is to be used on bulk rate third-class mailings, a special bulk rate mailing fee for the calendar year must also be paid. See Rates and Fees schedule for fee.

Minimum Quantity - Bulk and Presort Rate Mailings

- First-Class presort 500 pieces
- First-Class carrier route presort 500 pieces
- Regular bulk rate third-class and non-profit bulk 200 pieces or 500 pounds
- Carrier route presort bulk rate third-class or non-profit rate 200 pieces
- Special fourth-class presort 500 pieces

Place of Mailing

Permit imprint matter is mailable only at the post office that issues the permit, the name of which appears in the permit imprint. The postmaster shall designate a point at the main office or station thereof where permit imprint mail may be deposited and such mail must not be accepted at any other point. In no case may it be deposited in street letter boxes.

Statement of Mailing Required

Each mailing must be accompanied with a statement on Form 3602, filled out in ink or typewritten and signed by the person or a listed member of the firm to whom the permit is issued, showing the permit number, the class of matter, the number of pieces presented, and the weight of a single piece. In the case of third-class matter mailed under the bulk rates, on which postage is paid at the pound rate, the mailer's statement shall show the number of pounds presented and such other information as may be provided for on the form.

Postage Payment Must Be Prepaid

Postage in full on the entire quantity must be paid at or before the time the matter is presented for mailing, either in money, or at the option of postmaster and, at his risk, by check drawn to his order. The postmaster may receive from the mailer a deposit of money in advance (for which a receipt shall be given) sufficient to pay for more than a single mailing. The deposit shall be charged with the proper amount of each mailing, but if the amount on hand is not sufficient at any time to cover the postage due on the entire mailing, an additional amount must be deposited before any part of the mailings is dispatched. Credit for postage will never be allowed. Postage may not be prepaid by two methods - that is, partly in money and partly by ordinary stamps affixed. Whenever the computation of postage results in a fraction of a cent in the total, the next higher even cent must be paid.

Improper Use of Permit Imprint

Matter bearing permit imprint should not be distributed otherwise than through the mails and may not be mailed at a post office other than the one shown in the imprint.

Company Permit Imprints For Any Class of Mail

A special company permit for firms that hold mailing permits at two or more post offices is available. The special permit imprint (see illustration examples below) allows bulk mailers to deposit large volume mailings at several post offices with the use of a single permit indicia. The purpose is to facilitate inventory problems for printed envelopes.

Bulk Rate
U.S. Postage Paid
John Doe Company

U.S. Postage
(rate goes here)
John Doe Company

The city, state and permit number may be omitted if the permit holder has permits at two or more post offices, provided the exact name of the company or individual holding the permits is shown in the permit imprint. When this style of company permit imprint is used, the mailing piece must bear a complete return address. The permit holder must maintain for a 1-year period and make available for inspection and audit upon request of post office officials, records showing the post office at which any particular mailing was made, date of mailing, total weight of the mailing, weight of a single piece, and the amount of postage paid. A sample piece from the mailing must also be available. Your local postmaster may grant permission to use a company permit format after submission of proof by applicant that they have mailing permits at more than one post office.

Optional Procedure for Accepting Permit Imprint Mail

An optional procedure (for large volume mailers) for accepting permit imprint mail is available. Its purpose is to use the minimum amount of space, time and manpower and utilize the latest developments in mechanization, facilities and transportation while maintaining adequate control of the collection of correct postage charges. For complete information, consult your local postmaster.

Index

CONTINUING REAL ESTATE FARMING EDUCATION FROM ARGYLE PRESS...

The Ultimate Companion to This Book
—*How To Farm Successfully–By Phone*

Continue your real estate farming education with the all-new *How To Farm Successfully–By Phone*. This new book is completely updated for the 90s!

Exclusively written for real estate professionals, authors Johnson and Kennedy teach you how to apply proven telemarketing techniques to your real estate farm.

Step by step, example after example, this invaluable reference will show you how to...

- ■ **Make the telephone work for you!**
- ■ **Create and maintain your farming directory**
- ■ **Know what to say in those first critical 15 seconds!**
- ■ **Write wining farm phone scripts**
- ■ **Overcome the 6 most common objections in real estate**
- ■ **Turn incoming callers into *your* clients**
- ■ **Keep in touch with your past—and future—clients by phone**

How To Farm Successfully–By Phone is the perfect companion to the book you already own, and is sure to increase your listings, sales—and commissions!

Continue your real estate farming education with the exciting new book *How To Farm Successfully–By Phone*. Order your copy today!

How To Farm Successfully–By Phone
8-1/2 x 11" • Approx. 300 pp. Softcover • $29.95

For the location of the real estate board store or bookstore nearest you, or to order direct, please contact:
ARGYLE PRESS, INC., 675 Fairview Drive, Ste. 246-231, Carson City, NV 89701 • 702/884-0600 • Fax: 702-883-6934.

OUR GUARANTEE TO YOU!
At Argyle Press, your satisfaction is our #1 concern. That's why we offer both a 15-day free trial examination as well as a 15-day Money Back Guarantee (should you pre-pay your order by check or charge card). If you ever have any questions or problems please call our Customer Service Department at 702/884-0600.

ARGYLE PRESS, INC.
675 Fairview Drive, Suite 246
Carson City, NV 89701
702/884-0600 • Fax 702/883-6934

ALSO AVAILABLE FROM ARGYLE PRESS...

Improve Your Advertising With *Real Estate Advertising That Works!*

Written specifically for real estate professionals, *Real Estate Advertising That Works!* is the ultimate guide to creative advertising.

Now, *Real Estate Advertising That Works!* shows you step-by-step how to use this powerful selling force to maximize your real estate sales effectiveness. In 11 fast, easy-to-read chapters, you'll learn . . .

- How to write eye-stopping ads for your listings
- How to maximize your advertising with simple brochures
- How you can create flyers that sell listings!
- How to get the most from your ad budget
- What buyers really want—from a national survey

Real Estate Advertising That Works! also gives you complete glossaries of both real estate adjectives and advertising, printing and newspaper terms that you can use in your own advertising and flyer production. Plus it's loaded with hundreds of examples and idea-starters for headlines, body copy and powerful closing phrases.

If you've ever advertised a listing, *Real Estate Advertising That Works!* is a must-read for you.

***R/E Advertising That Works!* • 5-1/2 x 8-1/2" • 298 pp. Softcover • $19.95**

2,001 Winning Ads for Real Estate —*Less Than 1.5¢ Each!*

Now you can own the most complete volume of real estate ads ever written. Cover-to-cover this easy-to-use reference is jam-packed with 2,001 winning real estate ads for just about any listing you'll ever have—*all for less than 1.5¢ per ad!*

- Low-Priced, Mid-Range, Prestige & Custom Homes
- Farms, Ranches & Horse Properties
- Condos, Town Homes & Mobile Homes
- Vacation Homes & Investments
- And much, much more!

Organized for quick reference and fully indexed, each chapter is broken down by location, size, terms, style and special features.

2,001 Winning Ads for Real Estate also includes dozens of ad tips and a list of hundreds of words and phrases to help you describe even the most difficult properties in just the right way.

In short, it's like having your own advertising copywriter on staff—*only cheaper!*

***2,001 Winning Ads for R/E* • 7-1/2 x 8-1/2" • 348 pp. Softcover • $29.95**

For the location of the real estate board store or bookstore nearest you, or to order direct, please contact:
ARGYLE PRESS, INC., 675 Fairview Drive, Ste. 246-231, Carson City, NV 89701 • 702/884-0600 • Fax: 702-883-6934.